D0984372

To President Jimmy Carter

THE KING
WHO CAME TO
EARTH

A Biography

by

RICHARD LAWRENCE

and

BRIAN KENEIPP

With Blessings,

Richard Lawrence

AETHERIUS PRESS

First Published
2019

Aetherius Press

ISBN: 978-1-941482-09-4

Library of Congress Control Number: 2019939144

Published by The Aetherius Society ®

European Headquarters: 757 Fulham Road, London, SW6 5UU, UK

American Headquarters: 6202 Afton Place, Hollywood, CA 90028, USA

www.aetherius.org

© The Aetherius Society 2019

Cover design by Noémi Bates

All rights reserved. No part of this book, *The King Who Came To Earth*, including all photographs, may be reproduced or utilized in any form or by any means, electronic or mechanical, including photocopying, recording or by any information storage and retrieval system, without written permission from The Aetherius Society.

OTHER BOOKS BY THE AUTHORS

RICHARD LAWRENCE

Unlock Your Psychic Powers

Contacts With The Gods From Space (co-author for George King)

Realize Your Inner Potential (co-author for George King)

The Magic Of Healing

Gods, Guides And Guardian Angels (with Mark Bennett)

Prayer Energy (with Mark Bennett)

UFOs And The Extraterrestrial Message

BRIAN KENEIPP

Operation Earth Light

CONTENTS

ILLUSTRATIONS

ILLUSTRATIONS (CONT.)

ACKNOWLEDGEMENTS

We deeply appreciate the contribution made in so many ways towards this book. In particular we wish to thank Nikki Perrott, Noémi Bates, Chrissie Blaze, Richard Medway, Pat Higginson, Ayub Malik, Elizabeth Trimble and Rodney Crosby.

All the costs of publishing this book were borne by personal donors and we would like to thank them for their generosity. There are too many to name them all, but we must express our appreciation to David Trimble and Dieter Scheid who ensured that it was fully funded.

We are most grateful to the International Directors of The Aetherius Society for wholeheartedly approving its publication and for the valuable input we received from individual members of the Board. Neither of us will receive royalties from this book and all profits will go to The Aetherius Society.

The Authors

PROLOGUE

I am so pleased that this biography of my dear husband and spiritual master, Dr. George King, has been published. He was and always will be a towering figure in the annals of true accomplishment who deserves, more than any other I know of, to have his outstanding life recorded for posterity.

The generations who will come after us will be deeply grateful to all who made this book possible. Think of it, what wouldn't we give to have had such a true record of the life of the Master Jesus directly from those who lived close to him when he was on Earth.

Since my very first meeting with George in Los Angeles in 1959, I recognized his unique stature and extraordinary compassion, and from that moment forth dedicated myself to his service as disciple, friend and, some eleven years later, his wife. No words can express the joy I feel at the privilege of having stood by his side for most of his world-transforming mission.

My husband was the hardest working man I have ever met or heard of. His commitment to the "work ethic" exceeded that of even the most assiduous of devotees to their vocational callings. But I will also always remember him for his kindness, generosity and infectious sense of humour. I have lost count of the number of times I was simply unable to speak for laughing at his wit and repartee.

It would be wrong to pretend that his life was a pleasant, comfortable, or always happy one. It was fraught with difficulties, problems and pressures of all kinds. You cannot save a planetary race and rest easy in your bed at the same time. I saw at first hand, more than any other, the agonies and tensions he endured as he wrestled with what would have been to anyone else, insurmountable trials of mental strength and endurance. It was as though, at times, he carried on the frail shoulders of a terrestrial human body the entire karma of humanity.

I fully endorse and welcome this biography co-authored by my dear friends and colleagues, Richard Lawrence and Brian

Keneipp, both of whom worked closely with my husband and knew him personally for many years. They have also drawn on the accounts and experiences of other people and sources to complete the picture of his life since his birth on our planet on January 23rd, 1919, until his passing on July 12th, 1997.

I invite you to study well the life of this spiritual giant of a man placed in our midst. I am in a position to know that he was everything he claimed to be and far, far more than that. If you take the pattern he left us deep into your consciousness and allow yourself to be changed by it, you will never look back. More importantly you will become more of a force for good than you have ever been before, and that is ultimately what his life was all about.

Read on, with my blessings, the true story of a cosmic avatar[1] who walked among us and saved our world.

Monique King

PREFACE

The King Who Came To Earth reveals the essence of a remarkable man; more human than any of us, and yet more godly than we can ever fully understand. It is about his love and sacrifice for all; his mission of transmuting light; his other-worldly origins; and a genius so rare that it will raise and inspire our world for centuries to come.

Dr. George King was a spiritual giant who in his lifetime undertook humanitarian feats of global proportions. He transformed the tenets of true spirituality on this planet. He laid foundations that will not crumble like the shaky infrastructure of materialism but will last for future generations. He was a lover of God in the true sense, revealing that love is energy, above emotion. His wisdom was elevated, stretching our minds and hearts inwards and upwards to the truth. He was a pioneer and, like all true spiritual pioneers, through his personal suffering and sacrifice, he laid vibrant pathways of change that we could follow to unlock our own spiritual potential.

Do not expect Dr. King to be like any person you have ever encountered – either in your lifetime or even recorded in history. Within these pages is the story of an exceptional superhuman being, and yet also very much a man.

If you study this book with an open mind and heart, I believe you will yourself become a more enlightened, more confident and more inspired person than you were before. However, do not close this new chapter of your life as you close this book. Dr. King's life represents a new era on this planet and, if we embrace this, an extraordinary, relevant and new era for every one of us.

You may fervently wish you could meet such a person. If only you could talk to him and look into his eyes to understand what truly motivates him. What moves him to sacrifice so very much for apparently so little recognition or reward? Why is he so very different from the people you meet; so unique; rare like a precious jewel and yet, like great avatars before him, remains – for the most part – misunderstood?

I believe this biography, written in the way it is, from a place of great inspiration and tempered with the love and devotion of two of his closest disciples, gives us the answers to these questions – and more. The authors take you on a journey through his life. It is a journey that he took from this beautiful planet Earth, up to the highest places in the cosmos and down to the darkest realms there to shine his healing light and power. To take this incredible journey with him requires courage and an open mind.

Very often biographers have the task of writing about a person they hardly knew and learn about him or her from their research. This is not the case in this biography. Both Richard Lawrence and Brian Keneipp worked by their master's side for over twenty years, and today they continue to work hard and tirelessly to support and promote his work and mission into the future.

I felt honoured to be asked by them to write this Preface. The offer came because I too, like Richard and Brian, am a published author. Inspired as I was by Dr. King, I wanted to help spread his teachings in a way I knew how – through writing metaphysical books based largely upon his profound yet practical teachings. Also, I had worked with Dr. King, together with a few dozen people like myself who volunteered all their spare time to help this amazing man and master at one of the headquarters or branches of the spiritual organization he founded in 1955, The Aetherius Society. It was a perpetual inspiration to work with him, for he created a constant atmosphere of dynamic and intense spirituality.

I first met Richard Lawrence, the lead writer of this biography and now an international bestselling author in his own right, in 1971. This was at the European Headquarters of this Society in London when Richard was only 18. I remember even then that he stood out as a dynamic personality and leader, albeit at his young age. By the age of 26, in September 1979, he was appointed as Executive Secretary of the European Headquarters of this international organization by Dr. King, which position he still holds today – 40 years later!

Richard has also taken on many other executive responsibilities and as well as this has promoted Dr. King and The Aetherius

Society relentlessly through teaching and through the media, in many different countries. In 1987, when Richard was still only 34, he was consecrated as one of the first two Bishops in The Aetherius Churches together with Dr. King's wife, Monique.

Richard would agree that his most precious experiences and achievements centred around his spiritual master. Dr. King trusted Richard to run the European Headquarters, which also included all the branches and groups in Africa and certain other parts of the world. Being the hands-on master and great communicator that he was, he was on the telephone with Richard almost daily for 20 years. Also, as well as this, they spent a great deal of time together working hard on many important projects and global missions. Richard became not only one of his closest disciples but also a true and trusted friend.

Another of Dr. King's many talents was his command of the written word. He loved to write and authored many books and Richard collaborated with him on two of these – *Contacts With The Gods From Space* and *Realize Your Inner Potential*.

Richard's own spiritual evolution and writing ability allowed him to draw upon a high level of inspiration so necessary to describe the life and works of his remarkable spiritual master. Because of this skill, Richard wrote the majority of this biography, but collaborated closely with his co-author Brian Keneipp with writing, ideas and research, as well as Brian's own experiences and realizations about Dr. King.

Brian spearheaded the website as a companion to this biography. From the pages of this book, you can then turn to the website and listen to Dr. King's profound words and hear some of the other-worldly teachings channelled through him. You can first read about his achievements and then hear and feel his extraordinary dynamism and a confidence borne of lifetimes of spiritual accomplishment in other places at other times.

Brian's contribution has been invaluable in helping to bring this biography to life and his own experience ran side-by-side with Richard's in another part of the world – Los Angeles, California, which had become Dr. King's primary residence. Brian, together with a dozen or so other disciples in LA worked closely with him just as those in England and other parts of the world did when he visited.

Brian first met Dr. King in 1978 and assisted him in personal ways and in many of the global healing missions you will learn about in this biography. However, it was from October 1987 that he played an extremely important role. From this point on, until Dr. King's demise in 1997, Brian was with his master as his aide 24 hours a day – either in the same building or complex, or driving him wherever he needed to go.

It was around that time that I first met Brian when I visited the American Headquarters, and later got to know him well when I moved there in 1994 to be closer to Dr. King as, for health reasons, he could no longer travel to England. I was struck by Brian's intelligence and the way he could turn his hand to anything – from complex technical aspects to creative writing or whatever was needed by his spiritual master. Brian became one of his closest confidants. He assisted Dr. King in preparing for the many mental transmissions[1], as well as numerous aspects of running The Aetherius Society worldwide.

In the last four years of Dr. King's life, due to his failing health, Brian and two other disciples moved with him to his home in Santa Barbara, California. Despite his health, Dr. King was still extremely active on many fronts, as you will learn.

It was seven years after Dr. King's demise that Brian became the Executive Secretary of the American Headquarters in 2004. In 2010 he was consecrated as a bishop in the American jurisdiction of The Aetherius Churches.

Since Dr. King's passing, Richard and Brian have not only worked closely in running the Society worldwide, together with other colleagues and disciples of Dr. King, they have also become close friends. This collaboration was a natural one between two people who knew and loved Dr. King and, at the same time, who respected each other's different talents and contributions to make this project successful. They also have provided deep, thought-provoking perceptions about not only what was happening in Dr. King's lifetime – but the deeper reasons for this.

When you read *The King Who Came To Earth*, you may realize that it is not only the story of Dr. George King but also of The Aetherius Society. This unique master is front and centre of this spiritual organization and, despite the fact that he passed away from this physical plane on July 12th, 1997, he always will be.

A great master, an avatar, sets a pattern for us to follow. Like other great ones before him, Dr. King's way of thinking was very different. He didn't start with preconceived ideas but created his own pioneering pathways in the ethers which changed and transformed existing thought patterns. The pattern Dr. King has set, as you will see from these vibrant pages, is as a man of action who embraces truth. He teaches us that the way to our spiritual evolution is through diligent practice; the way we can really make a difference on this planet is through sheer hard work motivated by an overriding desire to serve humanity.

If you are a seeker, searching for truth, you will find it here. If you wish to find a true master, you will find him here. You may never have met him but you can still follow him and support his vitally important mission to secure the future of this planet.

Chrissie Blaze
International Author and Radio Host

FOREWORD

The life of Dr. George King is as much a story of mystery as it is one of mastery. Even those who knew him best were never able to unravel the full depths of his kaleidoscopic personality. You never quite knew what he would say or do next. You thought you knew him, and then repeatedly he proved that he could not be predicted. And no one realized this more than his closest disciples and friends.

The co-authors of this biography were honoured to spend many years in his company as colleagues, disciples and friends. Like others, we saw different qualities expressed by this outstanding individual. It was like being exposed to the many-hued colours of light radiating from a multi-faceted diamond, so rich and varied was the personality of this extraordinary man and master.

He was far from the conventional image of an enlightened master of yoga, shunning the role of the peaceful, smiling guru for that of the practical man of action. He was interested in getting results in the everyday world, where they were most needed. He was down-to-earth, straightforward, and at times a strict disciplinarian, if he considered it necessary for the betterment of others. He rejected high-flown, complex phraseology, in favour of a simple, direct style of speaking and writing. He believed in saying what you mean whether it is popular or not, and meaning what you say by living your beliefs.

Although his life and everything he stood for was controversial to many, his personal taste was traditional and private. He did not enjoy publicity for its own sake, but only when it was necessary to spread his message to others. Even then, he was shy of public attention preferring the company of a few close confidants. He made many television and radio appearances and conducted lecture tours of America, the United Kingdom, Australia and New Zealand, sometimes to large audiences. But, considering his unique claims and the abundance of experience and evidence to support them, his public and media appearances over the 43 years of his mission were remarkably few. Instead, he chose to focus on working to accomplish the world-saving tasks which were entrusted to him by the cosmic masters.

Some of those who read this biography will not have heard of Dr. King before doing so. If you are one of those, then it is our privilege to introduce you to one of the most significant men in the history of this planet. By the time you have finished reading this book, you will either agree with that statement or dismiss it as being unbelievable. There is really no middle ground with Dr. King as you will soon discover.

Our purpose here is not to list his key accomplishments, many of which are well documented elsewhere; nor to give an exact timeline of where he went when; nor to provide a comprehensive summary of his teachings. If we were to do so it would consist of many volumes and probably millions of words in length. Even then it would not necessarily achieve our goal of revealing the man behind the master and, just as importantly, the master behind the man.

We are attempting something not found, at least in any depth, in biblical gospels and other spiritual texts. They tend to focus on key events and teachings in their subject's life without exploring what motivated them, what made them tick at a personal level. This is probably because those who wrote these scriptures simply did not know. In all likelihood they never met the spiritual figure they were writing about and there was nothing on the record for them to fill in the gaping holes, from a biographical point of view, in these writings – much better to leave these empty spaces than to invent something which could be wrong.

One thing which has become clear to us in undertaking this project is that it is as much a task of detective work as it is of research. This is because barriers were erected around him, usually by himself, to hide his true elevated being. His whole strategy was to appear to be as ordinary as he possibly could, and he would put up smokescreens so that people could not see what was, at times, right in front of them. On the whole this worked, but so extraordinary was he that it could not work entirely. Now the bushel must be removed so that his light can shine forth for all who are ready to see.

Our investigations have so far taken us on an exponential curve of enhanced appreciation. He was already our hero, guru and mentor, but we must admit that our perception of the master we were privileged to know fell far short of what he really was.

It is always difficult to describe someone to those who have never met him. In the case of Dr. King it is more difficult than usual since there really is no one in history to compare him with. He was the generous teacher of spiritual wisdom, who was willing to take responsibility for sharing formerly secret knowledge with the uninitiated. He was the military-style commander who gave directives to his devoted staff. He was the humorist who could entertain or be entertained by lengthy comic improvisations with his closest disciples.

The paradoxes in his character abound. He was the strict master who could be amazingly tolerant and forgiving of his students. He was distinguished and handsome and always perfectly, if somewhat conservatively, dressed for any formal occasion. At other times he was the most casual of dressers, preferring well-worn jackets and thoroughly-darned trousers in his relaxed moments. He seemed effortlessly psychic at times, but often favoured logical analysis over unsubstantiated impressions. He was completely detached when his work demanded it, but could be vulnerable in a world which was alien to him. He was a man's man, who enjoyed female company, and a celibate yogi who enjoyed a drink and a smoke for most of his life. There was not an ounce of prejudice or prudishness about him, but his personal moral code was uncompromising. He did not suffer fools gladly, but he was willing to accept anyone who was sincere and willing to work into his fold.

His mission was such that he had no option but to challenge the religious, political and scientific establishment of his day. In some ways this did not suit him personally. But he did it because the truth demanded it, not because he was by nature anti-establishment. Later in life when he did receive well-deserved recognition from some traditional chivalric, religious and even political sources, he welcomed it wholeheartedly. He was not a rebel so much by choice as by conviction.

Knowing he was in touch with beings from other worlds

he felt obligated to spread that news even though it flew in the face of governments, religious dogma and scientific beliefs. Since he started his mission in 1954, public opinion has become more inclined to accept the type of claims he was making then, and with it government attitudes have become more open. Science too has moved on and, to a lesser extent, so has religion. But Dr. King's original claims have not changed. What he said in 1950s Britain, much to the ridicule and condemnation of almost anyone in officialdom or the media who was prepared to comment, he was still saying up to his death in California in 1997 to a far more receptive world. But not nearly receptive enough to take him as seriously as he undoubtedly deserved.

He went out of his way to change accepted standards of spiritual behaviour. His priorities were to bring the greatest good to the world as a whole whatever it took, and he was willing to take anyone with him who accepted his very demanding standards. He could abide bad behaviour in others, though he did not approve of it, but he had a very low threshold for laziness. His yardstick was not so much the conventional spiritual values which are so often stressed in the context of personal relationships, such as kindness, patience, humility and forgiveness, though these things were important to him. His priority was service, service, service and more service to the world as a whole as his mission was centred on evolving the world as a whole rather than individuals. It was results that counted for him and it was results that he got.

If he was often an enigma, even to those around him, there was no enigma about what he believed, taught and stood for. One of his own aphorisms – **speak truth to find truth** – was a dictum he lived by. He was also characterized by his exceptional sense of urgency. Another of his aphorisms – **move and live, stand still and die** – encapsulates his passion for doing things NOW. He did not claim patience as one of his greatest virtues though, when you consider the conditions he was willing to tolerate by foregoing the peaceful lifestyle so many gurus opt for, he was patience personified. But no one can dispute his hands-on determination to see things through to their practical conclusion as speedily as humanly possible, and sometimes faster than that! **Go towards God now**, he said, remember – even a saint cannot reclaim a wasted minute[1].

Having lived and worked with Dr. George King for many years we know he was the real thing. We also know from experience that it can be difficult for those who did not meet him face-to-face to understand and believe how extraordinary he was. Fortunately for us all Dr. King left an amazing and rich legacy of teachings – written, audio and video. His teachings build upon the rich spiritual truths of our world and focus them on the necessities of today. The teachings he brought down to this Earth in these days of transition explain both the mysteries of the past as well as the essence of science – they are crucial for our future.

There is a tendency to believe that great beings do not come to Earth in our lifetime. These things happened long ago and we read about them in the Bible, the Hindu scripts or some other ancient religious text. They seem much more credible to us somehow if they took place at some distant time in history. But there is no logic to this. The latter part of the twentieth century was the most dangerous time for humanity in our recorded history because it was then that we gained the nuclear technology to bring destruction to our planet, as we had in the previous civilizations known as Lemuria and Atlantis[2]. If ever there was a time for divine intervention from above, this would surely have been it. This biography aims to show that it was indeed such a time, and that the main emissary for this intervention was this King who came to Earth.

Dr. King had the highest integrity and was completely honest in all his dealings; he had the finest mind you could hope to encounter; he was everything he claimed to be and even more than that. Our aim and ardent desire in this biography is to convey to you as much of the essence of Dr. King and his mission to Earth as possible.

At significant times in our history, towering spiritual beings have appeared in the world: Sri Krishna, the Lord Buddha, the Master Jesus, Sri Patanjali, Confucius, Lao Tzu, Sri Shankaracharya to name some of the most famous. The Hindu term for such great ones is 'avatar', which means 'divine incarnation'. The authors of this book believe that one of the greatest of all cosmic avatars to come to Earth was Dr. George King.

He came at a pivotal period which required the presence of a truly unique master among us – for this was to be the end of an old age and the dawning of a new one. In astrological terms, we are in the process of moving into the Age of Aquarius and it is not by chance that Dr. King's sun sign of the zodiac was Aquarius, being born on January 23rd, 1919.

This heralds a new age when science will come to the fore; when barriers between different religious beliefs and dogmas will be broken down; it will be a period of new philosophy mixed with ancient, mystical thought and its hallmark will be an open-minded pursuit of truth. It will also be a period when ecology will be of paramount importance to all the inhabitants of the planet, when racism and other forms of division among people will disappear and when technological solutions to the world's problems will cohabit with spiritual ones.

Looking at this list you might say "dream on". To this we would reply that all the great accomplishments in history started out as a dream. The New Age will be the 'heaven on earth' as prophesied in many different sources including Hindu and biblical writings. It is not all good news though, for just as many sources speak of a heavenly future, they also warn of danger and calamity in this period. Some have even prophesied the end of the world during the period before it. Dr. George King came to our world to prepare us for a bright new age, but also for the catastrophes which were due and which still darken our skies today. He came, above all, to help save us – and teach us to save ourselves – from the worst of them.

If ever the stage was set for a drama of unparalleled impact this was it: a recipe for untold destruction with the opportunity for limitless splendour just visible on the horizon. A divine appointment had been made to meet the challenges of this most exceptional karmic moment. And it was kept by the cosmic avatar known simply as Dr. George King.

Chapter One
GROWING INTO A MASTER

"My God, Mary, this child is not of this Earth!"

These were the words of Sarah Pritchard spoken to her daughter, Mary, at the birth of her grandson, George King, on January 23rd, 1919, in the small village of Donnington Wood near Wellington, Shropshire.

Forty-five years later, on October 27th, 1964, during a lecture at the American Headquarters of The Aetherius Society in Crenshaw Boulevard, Los Angeles, Dr. King gave a far more precise coordinate for his place of birth. Using the word Terra as the cosmic masters often did in reference to the Earth – this being a Latin name for this female Goddess – he said: I was born on Terra – position 009 neem 648218. That's it, that is true, that is so!

* * * *

The birth of an avatar upon Earth is a carefully planned move. It is the result of ancient beings of vast intelligence and god-like stature seeing, probably centuries beforehand, exactly what is required for the salvation and enlightenment of humanity. Throughout the centuries, avatars have been spoken of with boundless veneration and justly deserved praise by the faithful.

They came from other planets in this solar system such as Mars, Venus and Saturn. These worlds are inhabited by advanced intelligences, though not on this physical plane of existence – hence the inability of science to detect them. All life in the universe exists in multi-dimensional levels of frequency. Those occupied by these highly evolved beings vibrate at a higher rate than the dense physical realm on which we exist.

The coming of avatars to Earth is a story of wonder, triumph, compassion and divine brilliance. Yet it is also a story of overcoming limitation and suffering on a grand scale. When the

Master Jesus hung on the cross it was not the glorious passion as it is sometimes depicted – it was a horrendous crime perpetrated upon a living avatar. In their own ways, Sri Krishna, the Lord Buddha, Moses, Lao Tzu, Sri Patanjali and others, some hardly known, endured their own crucifixions. They did not need to be here for their own evolution but still they came to help mankind in our hour of need.

This does not mean that they led miserable lives – on the contrary, they experienced at times the most elevated and joyous states of consciousness which any human being could attain. But even that is way below their natural habitat: the cosmic realms of the gods where enlightenment, samadhi, cosmic consciousness, nirvana are normal fare. Selfishness, violence, greed, and war are all part of a primitive savagery which is completely alien to them. Yet still they came.

What is the love that motivates these gods to walk among us? Not for themselves, nor for those closest to them, nor even for the race to which they belong. The depth of their compassion is so foreign to us we have been unable to understand it properly. We have put these great ones upon pedestals and have been unable or unwilling to think of their great sacrifice and what they really endured to make it. Yet it is vital to realize not only that they were great gods, but also humans living in ordinary bodies like

Dr. King's mother, Mary King, seated in her living room.

us. Far from being easy for them to do what they did, it was more difficult than we could possibly imagine.

Now, at last a more complete story of a cosmic avatar can be told. For such a one has come and left and we can, at last, reveal such a life as it really was. Not just what he did for us, and how we can benefit – but what it was really like for him. We will never fully know or understand this, but at least we can try to look beyond the veneer and the shining beauty of the persona to the harsh reality of life on this planet for one who is not of this Earth. A god among mortals, a superman in the body of an ordinary person, yet expected to accomplish the extraordinary for the salvation of a whole race. It would be like us taking on the body of a pig and living in a sty among other pigs. That shocking image might give us some idea of the squalor these gods have chosen to endure in order to save our world.

Dr. George King was one of these. If you had known him and spent a lot of time in his company; if you had worked closely with him and helped him in his mission for many years, you would see it. Because he was experiencing it second by second, day in day out – and at night-time too. He lived, breathed, spoke, ate, laughed, scolded, cared, worked very hard indeed and just occasionally relaxed, as the avatar that he was and knew himself to be. The tell-tale signs were there – he just did not look at things as we terrestrials do. He succeeded brilliantly in assuming human characteristics, but they were only a fraction of him. There were times when this was clear to see – with hindsight it is glaringly obvious.

*   *   *   *

In 1870 a cosmic adept received a Diploma in Terrestrial Psychology. This interplanetary master had agreed to incarnate upon the planet Earth and it was necessary for him to take an educational course on the mindset of humanity before living among us. Courses such as this are carried out by specially-run computer imprints. The applicant is first closely scanned to see whether he can withstand the pressures to be exerted upon him. If he is willing and able to mentally absorb the high-speed information which will be transmitted to him by computer, the course proceeds.

Such knowledge would be valid beyond 1870 because this particular programme would have predicted and made allowances for advancements in terrestrial psychology into the future. One who had agreed to live in a terrestrial body, as a human being, in order to help mankind as a whole would need to understand the ways of a world that was completely alien to him.

It is because of our dire karmic pattern that great cosmic beings are asked to take karma upon themselves by suffering the limitation of being born through the womb of an earthwoman in an ordinary terrestrial physical body, in order to accomplish their tasks. In the case of Dr. King, the cosmic adept in question, this suffering was compounded by a very frail physique in his early years which meant that his childhood was a constant battle against ill health of one kind or another. This too must have been part of the karmic price he was willing to pay in order to perform his mission. As it turned out, it was also to be one of the keys to its success.

He was born just months after the conclusion of the First World War. His father, also called George King, had as a Quaker joined the Royal Army Medical Corps, leading non-combatant stretcher-bearers who were desperately trying to save lives in the blood and guts of this horrific conflict. His mother, Mary King, was a nurse at a local army hospital, and they met while George King Senior was on leave. Mary's mother, Sarah, was an accomplished medium, healer and psychic who was to later become the young child's most beloved relative, whom he would enthusiastically visit whenever he could.

It would soon become clear that young George was prone to severe breathing difficulties. George King Senior, together with his wife and son, moved to Middlesbrough, in North East England, with very little resources. Dr. King would later say that if there was a silver spoon in his mouth when he was born, he never found it. The family was enlarged when a daughter, Mary, was born. She became known as Mollie.

When George was five, the family moved to the small village in southern England of Littleham in Devon where his father gained employment as a schoolteacher. He was fascinated by the Sunday school classes he attended at the local Anglican church, part of the established religion in England. This was his first introduction to religion and, as well as the doctrine, he remembered being mesmerized by the stained glass windows. He loved the rural life, often helping out on local farms, as well as the small piece of land his parents had with a few chickens and pigs.

It was in Littleham that one of the key events of his life occurred at about the age of six. He told one of his close disciples, Ray Nielsen, that he had been affected with an illness from which he could have died and which impaired his health throughout the remainder of his childhood. This may have been caused by a devastating incident in which he was, at this young age, callously thrown into the River Torridge nearby and almost drowned. Years later, during a lecture on service in Los Angeles on May 19th, 1961, Dr. King revealed that: **According to my stars I should have been dead at eight.**

On June 19th, 1978, on Roseberry Topping in North Yorkshire, North East England, Dr. King had a highly enlightening contact with his own master. This was part of a mystical pilgri-

Dr. George King can be seen in the distance seated in deep reflection on top of Roseberry Topping in North Yorkshire during his mystical pilgrimage in 1978.

mage during the summer of 1978 in which he was accompanied by Ray Nielsen. He was inspired to undertake this pilgrimage to bring a certain understanding and, as he put it, magnetic polarization in the process. He re-kindled memories of his childhood and realized, as never before, the significance of some of these in preparing him for the mission which was to come.

On Roseberry Topping he received revelations about this exceptionally traumatic happening, which was strangely enough to become a fulcrum point for the success of his mission to Earth.

He kept tape recordings of his experiences throughout the mystical pilgrimage and the following is an excerpt from these:

> It was pointed out to me that this happening had to take place. If it had not done so at that time, a similar happening would have taken place later on and the full reasons for this were given to me. I now understand things far better and I also understand that, to a certain extent, I have been manipulated, as you might call it, through life in order to bring about a very definite result.
>
> The revelations concerned with the happening at Littleham, and the long-range repercussions of this, are absolutely staggering and almost unbelievable but are true. I know them to be true – I lived through the experience...
>
> The happening in that tiny little village to a very young child...had repercussions later on which to a great extent altered the course of world history. As strange as that may sound on the face of it, it is absolutely true. It is a fact and not fiction that if the great ones decide that a master plan will work out, it does work out. This aspect of my life is living proof of this statement. Even though the results of this happening brought me feelings of sadness throughout the years, I felt that there were reasons behind it; when I took to serious meditation I began to trace my life back to this very, very important crossroads.
>
> It seems that if you are chosen for a specific mission, your own likes and dislikes are not in any way taken

into consideration. Since the full explanation has been given to me, I do not feel any loss regarding the incident and am getting used to the fact that I was used as an instrument in order to bring about a very definite result – a good and beneficial one. But for that, the whole of world history as you know it today, and enjoy it today, would have been changed completely for you all...

A small incident to a small boy brought about a definite change so that 40 years later a mission to save mankind could be successful. That is the statement I am making, and before God, that statement is absolutely true. It does not in any way make me feel great or in any way fully satisfied with what I have done – in fact the opposite. It makes me feel very small and in comparison with the really great ones very, very humble.

It was the very illness of Dr. King throughout much of his childhood that forced him to go within, thereby developing his mental faculties in a way he would otherwise not have done. It was deemed essential by the great ones that he should learn from a very early age to rely upon his own mental deductions and inner resources – to think strategically rather than focussing on mainly physical attainments as he might have done had he been more healthy. From a young age he would ponder the possibilities of a situation and formulate a plan of action to achieve his determined goals, partly because his limited bodily strength made it necessary for him to do so.

There is a vast difference between a cosmic avatar being confined to ill health and an ordinary terrestrial person being in the same situation. We on this Earth are all working through our karmic limitations and tests in order to develop and evolve. This may require at any stage in our lives trials of health, as well as finance and general well-being, in order to gain essential experiences – albeit at times, very difficult ones indeed.

A cosmic avatar, on the other hand, does not have karma upon this Earth except for the karma he has taken on our behalf. These are not essential experiences that he needs to advance and evolve back to God, but they are necessary in order to pay the price for his mission. They also determine, to some extent, the expression of his personality and the specific abilities required. It was not until Dr. King climbed Roseberry Topping, which he renamed 'Realization Point' in 1978, that he had the realization of just how much his life had been manipulated by the great ones in order to bring about an essential result: 40 years later his strategies would save an entire planetary race.

*　*　*　*

When he was seven, the family moved to the Yorkshire Dales where his father had been offered a better paying job in a small school. The tough, no-nonsense manner, so typical of this region, left its imprint upon him and remained with him throughout his life. He always valued honest, plain speaking which character-ized his manner, both on and off the platform.

The Kings moved to an area in Yorkshire called Wensleydale, home of the famous cheese which became a lifelong favourite with him. They lived in a cottage attached to a small schoolhouse in Lunds in the parish of High Abbotside, a few miles from the village of Garsdale. Young George became a train enthusiast, learning the timetables by heart and often waiting for the massive Royal Scot steam locomotive to pass by. His health improved in the bracing air of that tough, barren landscape. As he recorded:

> As a small child, I was ill and sickly and had a very slow start in life because of this. But living up in the fells in that very bleak, stone-cold schoolhouse helped my health very much indeed. When I left there I was a lot fitter and more robust than when I went there.
> (Mystical Pilgrimage, 1978)

His sister, Mollie, fondly recollected in her latter years the time she spent with him in Lunds. She said: "Always as a child he seemed to have inspirations for different things. His mind was always in, somehow in space, or other I can't quite imagine, but we had a lot of fun together."

She cannot have realized then just how spiritually elevated

her brother was. He in turn was not able to share his inner experiences with those around him. In a lecture on November 23rd, 1962, on mystic yoga breathing, he revealed:

> I don't know about other people but even when I was a child when I closed my eyes it's always been blinding light, you know, and I couldn't understand it for many years. People would say, "close your eyes and it's pretty dark", and I have never known what it is to be dark. Go in a black, dark room, you know, and you look around, I mean it is light – it's more light than if the light was on. But it's a very different kind of light of course.

This gives us an insight into the inner state of this avatar in boyhood. Those around him could not have perceived the full extent of his innate awareness, but they did recognize his spiritual qualities in other ways. Mollie's daughter Pamela recalls her grandmother, Mary King, telling her how well-behaved he was as a small child, saying: "He was a perfect boy."

It was not long before the family was on the move again, something which young George experienced too often for his liking, and which affected him throughout his life. Many years later he would find packing a suitcase distressing, even though it was something he frequently had to do. When he was 10, the family moved some 60 miles east to Hutton Gate in the North Yorkshire Moors as he recorded:

> I cannot help but admit in all modesty that it is a long way between a young, small, sensitive boy walking the fells of North Yorkshire alone, and the glories of Operation Sunbeam[1]; between the same child, rather sickly at that, trudging through the oozing, wet fields and staggering back, carrying a metal bucket filled with drinking water from a spring about half a mile away, and witnessing the most elevated initiation offered to earthman – that of ascension[2] on a giant spacecraft 1,550 miles from Earth.
> (Mystical Pilgrimage, 1978)

One of the highlights of this period in his life, was his proximity to his maternal grandmother who lived in Redcar on the North Sea coast. She was now only a long bike ride away and he could visit her frequently. There he would spend the mornings flying kites, or sailing his model boat, *White Heather*, in the local pond. He also enjoyed helping in her herb garden. He always admired her and never forgot the fond memories he had of these visits. His niece, Pamela, remembers her great grandmother as: "a wonderfully calm influence…she gave that aura of total peace about her."

As well as being a medium, who had been consulted before the First World War by Lloyd George, who would later become Prime Minister, she was well known locally as a healer and herbalist. He experienced his first séance with her as she entered trance in his presence. He received psychic insights from her, including her vision of a bookshelf filled with books written by George King. One specific premonition she gave him was that he would have a serious accident between the ages of 20 and 21, but that he would do something just before the accident to save his life. He said of her spiritualistic accounts:

> I found them very exciting and quite easily
> understandable – quite understandable that a medium
> should be able to communicate with discarnate entities.
> I found nothing difficult about it at all. The difficult thing I
> found, by the way, when I was a child was that everybody
> couldn't do this. That I found a very, very difficult truth to
> swallow. But when I met a person who could and talked
> about it, I found it quite normal, which of course it is.
> (Mystical Pilgrimage, 1978)

The Kings' new home was larger but, as was common then, there was no electricity. Behind the house there was a forest for firewood, but to Dr. King it was more than that. He recorded:

> I somehow seemed to be in my own small, childish way,
> a master of those woods and indeed I was. I knew every
> tree and if some of the trees, which probably were not,

**but if I felt they were a little sick I would actually hold my
hands on them and give them healing.**
(Mystical Pilgrimage, 1978)

Nearby was Roseberry Topping, which was to become so
important in his life. He would spend many hours there exploring
the terrain, finding peace and sometimes pondering the meaning
of his life. Though he had friends with whom he played from time
to time, he always had a loner streak within him. As his sister
said of him later: "He made friends to some extent, but wouldn't
be jolly in a crowd. There was always something about him, that
little bit as if he was thinking things through...he'd disappear
into his room and be hours on his own, and it wasn't that he was
unhappy...he seemed as if he wanted a different direction from
all of us somehow."

It was very disturbing to him that those around him were
so ignorant about the things that really mattered, such as how
to pray. As he said many years later in an address on June 30th,
1979:

> **Another thing that amazed me was the ignorance
> about prayer. That absolutely staggered me. I thought
> everybody would know about prayer. As a child I knew
> about prayer and I thought, 'well, other lads don't seem
> to know about it,' although I did. 'Maybe when I grow up
> adults will know about it,' but they didn't and they had
> to be taught how to pray properly. I'm not going to say
> everybody... but the majority of people I met did not know
> about prayer until they heard the difference. And when
> we were able to demonstrate what prayer was, 'Oh my
> God, that is it!'**

His inherent knowledge of prayer was demonstrated while
at Hutton Gate in an outstanding experience, which he later
recorded in the following words published in his book, *You Too
Can Heal*:

> **When I was eleven years old, I gave my first demonstra-**

tion of spiritual healing.

My mother had been very ill for some time. As a matter of fact, too ill to be moved to the local country hospital which did not offer much of a service anyway, especially in those days in the very remote northern part of England in which we lived. Although, naturally, the doctor had been called and made frequent visits, he was baffled by her symptoms. It was then that he wisely suggested a second opinion, and another practitioner was called in from the nearest city some twenty miles away. As it happens, there was a delay in transportation and the second consultant could not come until the next day. As a young boy, who had been brought up in the belief of psychic phenomena, I felt, in my own adolescent way, that she was getting worse throughout the night. All local help available had been offered and appeared to be of no avail and my father was anxiously awaiting the visit of the specialist the following day. It should be remembered that all this happened 46 years ago on the outskirts of a very small village in the north of England. There was not the speed of travelling in those days as there is today. To make a journey from the city in bad weather conditions was something not to be taken too lightly.

As time went on, I had a strange urge to at least try to do something about her condition. The urge was so strong that despite the howling wind and teeming rain outside, I left the house, climbed over a fence and walked in the pitch blackness, guided by the feeble flickering light of an oil lantern, into the woods which I loved and knew so well. I came eventually, soaked to the skin, to a little clearing where I used to play very often. When I arrived there, I had no idea of what I was going to do or even why I was there, except that I had the tremendous urge to visit this place. I set the lantern down on the wet, muddy ground and stood shivering with cold, wondering what to do next.

Then suddenly the thought struck me that I

should say a simple prayer. Although, in every way, as boisterous as any other lad of my age, I nevertheless was then a keen churchgoer. Not that I believed everything I heard in church, but something about the atmosphere of reverence I felt in a church had a strange fascination for me. I liked to sit in the small country church on a Sunday morning and concentrate on the light shining through the different colours of the stained glass windows. I did not look at the stained glass windows as a whole, but concentrated on the different colours of the leaded glass which made up a picturization of the Mother of Jesus or something similar. This too, seemed to give me an inner peace which was difficult to find in other places. In fact, it was the same type of inner peace which I experienced when I used to sit alone on the top of a small mountain a few miles away from where we lived.

My thoughts went to this stained glass window and I tried to visualize the beautiful greens and blues and reds of the ancient leaded lights. Then I began to pray.

It is as though the next thing had to happen.

The old oil lantern finally 'gave up the ghost' and with one last puff, went out – enshrouding the whole scene in the blackness of a wet, blustery night. I felt an immediate fear arise within me, as indeed would most eleven year olds in the same conditions. However, I kept my ground and decided, come what may, I would at least say my prayer before I left. Dimly in the back of my mind was the agonizing thought of how I would find my way back in the pitch blackness, but even that was dispelled by some basic childish courage which I seemed to invoke from deep within myself.

I started my prayer in a weak trembling voice, which I am sure would not have carried more than a few feet above the eerie sound made by the wind as it caressed the branches of the trees, shivering as the wind blew the rain drops into my face and down my neck from a large copper beech tree some feet away from me. But spiritual determination is greater than any other determination and this overcame my immediate desire to run – and keep running.

I noticed, as my prayers progressed, I became braver, until at the end of saying what the church terms as 'The Lord's Prayer', I was fairly detached from my wet, cold, dark and miserable surroundings.

I then started to pray with greater earnestness and express, out loud, the thoughts which entered my mind and at the same time tried to visualize a picture of my very sick mother lying in her bed, pale and worn. The visualization came quite easily, and when it did, I felt that instead of putting my hands together as I had been taught in church, I should lift them in front of myself with palms facing the general direction of our house, which was some distance away from me. I found it easier to pray in this way. There was no restriction as there had been with the hands clasped together. I continued my simple prayer, praying to God that my mother would be made well again.

And then the vision came.

Gently, at first, I became aware of a presence, unlike any other presence I had come into contact with. My eyes were tightly closed and whether I went on praying out loud or not, I do not remember. But I do remember vividly that I felt a tremendous urge to open my eyes and at first fought against it, but then curiosity or fear, or a mixture of both, took the upper hand of my shivering frame and I opened them and for a moment stared wildly at that which I saw.

Standing about ten to twelve feet away from me was the figure of a man. He had a flowing robe and long hair and seemed to be illuminated in some mysterious way from within, for he carried no lantern in his hand and yet I could see him very plainly indeed. I closed my eyes tightly and opened them again, and the Being became even clearer to my normal vision.

To me he looked gigantic, but I feel that this was part imagination and part fear. However, he was tall, with long brownish hair and wore flowing robes which seemed to be luminous in the darkness. By this time, I suppose I was shivering with another feeling besides the cold. He looked at me and smiled a wonderful, all-knowing, fatherly-type of smile which gave me an inner reassurance as would the knowing, understanding smile of a parent. He made no attempt to announce his identity, but pointed with his right hand, index finger outstretched, and simply said:

"Go, your mother is healed."

And then as rapidly as the Being appeared, he dematerialized in front of my shocked eyes and left me alone to the darkness of the storm.

I moved around quickly and kicked something on the ground next to me and almost tripped over it. It was the lantern. I searched for the handle on the top of the lantern, could not find it, and decided to leave it and make tracks for home as quick as my eleven-year legs would take me. Had it not been for the fact that I had been to this particular part of the woods very often to play and climb trees – as any healthy boys will – I think I would have been lost that night, but I knew my way home. Actually, I am not saying that I could see in the dark, but apart from the one mishap with the lantern, I managed to avoid the obstacles of the forest, like fallen trees and branches laying on the forest floor. As though I had an uncanny sight and sense of direction, I made my way right to a small ivy covered gate at the side of the old country mansion, through it and around to the back door, opened it – and I knew before I did so, what I would see.

I was right.

For the first time for days, my mother was downstairs and being served food. When I walked in, she looked up, her blue eyes becoming reddened by emotion as she struggled to keep the tears from flowing. She lost the battle and they did flow; and she arose, held out her arms and held me tightly. When I could get away, I started to stammer out my experiences, although there was no need for explanations. My mother said immediately, that she knew I had gone into the woods, was praying for her and had a vision of, what she called in those days "an angel". When her thankfulness had died down, she ate her food and then walked, unaided, up the narrow staircase to her bedroom again.

The next morning the specialist arrived with our own doctor, who was dumbfounded to see my mother up and preparing to mix a large Christmas cake. My mother was a very forceful, outspoken woman, and she did not hesitate to tell the doctor that where he had failed, her son had succeeded. I kept out of the way while she extolled my virtues, which were undeserved by the way, to the amazement of the two doctors. They did not 'pooh-pooh' the idea. As a matter of fact, if I remember rightly, they stayed and had lunch with us and enjoyed a glass of old sherry while my mother related many psychic experiences from her childhood.

After all, they could not 'pooh-pooh' the fact that a healing had taken place by some means which was not described in their medical text books. As a matter of fact, more than once after that, our old country practitioner consulted my mother about other patients who were desperately ill, and together we would send them healing and some of the results were quite startling.

Dr. King later said that there was far more to his boyhood experience in the wood than he had realized at the time. It was not an angel that he had seen, but it was in fact a physical contact with a cosmic being. This was the first of two great cosmic contacts prior to the commencement of his mission to Earth.

* * * *

For all its challenges, Dr. King had a very active childhood indeed. At the age of 11 he obtained a scholarship to the local grammar school at Guisborough. He soon established himself, by dealing with a school bully in no uncertain terms. He was very good at English and science subjects, but disliked Latin. Significantly he was very poor at history, mainly because he found it very difficult to believe! He was not good at art, but had a good singing voice and was a member of the choir. He always remembered his first experience of singing in public a solo from a Gilbert and Sullivan operetta which he described as a very difficult experience, but which became easier the more he had to do it. He was also an enthusiastic bell ringer at St. Nicholas Church in Guisborough. He excelled at poetry recital including poems such as 'If' by Rudyard Kipling. Referring to this during his mystical pilgrimage, he said: **Even in those days I knew what dynamic prayer meant far better than, I am sad to say, the majority of the world does today.** In fact, throughout his life he could quote lines from classic poems and would do so from time to time in conversation.

He was good at sports – as a goalkeeper in football (soccer), a spin bowler in cricket and a long-distance runner. He joined the Officer Training Corps and became a crack shot on the school rifle range. Another sport in which Dr. King was highly proficient was the use of the quarterstaff, a traditional fighting technique which originated in Europe, and especially England, in the late Middle Ages. He was taught by his father to use this straight wooden pole, about six feet in length, demanding fast reflexes as he whirled around at high speed. He also became a very competent fencer, using the sabre, and at the age of 15 was invited to join a team of Yorkshire schools, taking part in a fencing competition in France with French and German schoolboys. He was also taught boxing by his father, who had been a champion boxer in the army, and he shone at this in his new school.

Despite the hardships Dr. King had fond reminiscences from his time in North Yorkshire. His sister remembered that: "he had a good sense of humour – we used to laugh." One mischievous incident involved a friend who had discovered that the sound of his harmonica could mesmerize sheep and that they would follow him. Together they herded a flock of sheep into the centre of town blocking the traffic for hours. Ironically in 1986 when he received the Freedom of the City of London[3] and discovered that he was legally allowed to do a similar thing in London, he mused how entertaining it would be to repeat this – though he never took advantage of this right.

His scientific aptitude was also becoming clear. After learning about generators in a physics lesson, he made a working generator at home, driven by a miniature steam engine heated by methylated spirits, winding his own coils and armature. Using his own pocket money he worked on this, unbeknown to his family, until he surprised them on Christmas evening when he showed them a model of a tower crane he had built and illuminated with dozens of tiny electric lights powered by his home-made generator. In an area without electricity this was indeed an impressive surprise.

He took an interest in meteorology, helping to establish the school's first official weather station. This reported directly to the Greenwich Observatory with daily readings of temperature, humidity and pressure. These readings had to be sent daily to Greenwich without fail. It also meant a daily release of a large weather balloon carrying a cluster of weather instruments. When relaying this story years later he used to smile as he remembered that he always made sure that his readings were taken at the exact time of either his Latin or history classes. His interest and knowledge of weather could be seen decades later during the spiritual missions he performed, including on Loch Ness where he would insist upon receiving daily meteorological reports from members of his team.

His writing abilities were also coming to the fore and one essay entitled 'Middlesbrough Market on a Windy Day' was so good that his headmaster did not believe that he had written it himself. Once it was established that he had, it was entered in a writing competition and duly won. His sister remembered: "Most of all he seemed to be keen on writing…he had a mind that was, I would say, different." She also remembered him as an avid reader.

Times were hard and Mary King moved to Redcar to open a confectionery shop on the seafront. Some months later they all moved to join her. Of this period his sister remembered: "We had a lovely house in Redcar and it had a nice woodland garden. I think my brother then started feeling – I don't exactly know whether he was meditating – as though he was into something apart."

In Redcar Dr. King had his first experience of motor racing – a car journey in a Bugatti at 90 mph which left an indelible impression upon him. He also remembered trips in a powerboat on the North Sea and in a stunt plane, which he had paid for with his pocket money. But, all the while, his mind was on higher things. As he would write years later in *You Are Responsible!*: **When I was 15, I knew that one day I would visit other worlds.**

His sister, Mollie, reflected on this period:

"My brother always could see something a little beyond, something in the distance which I could never quite understand at that time. Even at such an early age he was sort of in the world, if you know what I mean, but not of it somehow. He somehow seemed different...I think he was different from other children. I think his mind was way beyond the ordinary things that I could think about – being on the stage and being an actress and talking to the birds and talking to the flowers. I think he was probably, I was very much on the Earth, and I think he was elevated."

Later the family moved back to Hutton Gate, but a shocking incident would change his life. Now in his final year things were looking good for a successful result in his coming School Certificate. And then one day, in a physics lesson, everything changed.

*   *   *   *

Physics was one of Dr. King's favourite classes, taught by an excellent teacher who had a soft spot for young George, one of his brightest students whom he nicknamed with the endearing name 'Lamb'. The class was studying the science of mechanics. In order to show his boys how materials behaved under tension, the teacher showed the class a round, one-inch thick steel bar, about 18 inches long. This would be used in their experiments specifically because it was unbendable and other materials could therefore be tested in relation to it. He passed the bar among his pupils asking them to try to bend it, which of course none of them could. That is until it reached young George. To the utter amazement of the whole class, including himself, he was able to bend it swiftly and easily into a U-shape.

The teacher's face was ashen as the entire class reacted in stupefied silence. This was followed by an uproar among the pupils who moved away from Dr. King in fear. The teacher took Dr. King to the headmaster who was also shocked and immediately sent him home. The news spread like wildfire through the school and the whole community. His mother, however, came into her own at this moment of personal crisis and advised her son to pack his rucksack and spend a night on Roseberry Topping, advice for which he was always grateful. It would, however, be years before he would properly understand that the source of the super-human strength he had demonstrated was an early manifestation of the mystical power known in the east as kundalini[4].

His father and the headmaster agreed that he should stay at home for several weeks for his own safety and that of his schoolmates. In effect his schooling was ended. It was as though his very latent spirituality had prevented him from pursuing an

From left: George King Senior with his son.

academic route knowing that he would find an infinitely greater wisdom through his own path of realization than anything the academic world could offer.

On the face of it, this was a disaster for any aspiring teenager. But could there be another reason behind the timing of this pivotal event? Was he being directed away from the life which might have followed from a successful School Certificate towards a greater reliance on his own innate knowledge and abilities?

The family soon moved again, this time to Cleveleys, a small coastal town near Blackpool in the northwest of England, where Mary King purchased and ran a small hotel. Dr. King would have happy memories in this popular seaside resort. He took a job supervising a pinball machine arcade on the promenade, and when necessary repairing the machines, which helped with the family income, as well as keeping him in cigarettes. Life was more comfortable with running hot and cold water and electricity in the home. He also put his marksmanship skills to profitable use by entering rifle shooting competitions at the fairground. The prizes could be spectacular and on one occasion, though still too young to drive it, he won a brand new saloon car (sedan).

When the season finished, his parents and sister moved back to Redcar and he fended for himself, earning money by delivering books to local libraries. The following year he was back in Middlesbrough working for a department store until in 1937, at the age of 18, he left home and moved to London. Here he would have many and varied experiences, working in different trades and living in different places. As he recorded during his mystical pilgrimage: **You may be amazed at the different jobs I have done throughout my life; probably even at an early age I realized that all experience was essential.**

At first he stayed with an aunt in Mill Hill, a suburb of London and worked for a leading firm of butchers, often rising early to obtain produce from Smithfield Market in the City of London. In the spring of 1939 he visited his parents who were running a small-holding in Gammaton Cross, Devon, in the south of England. It was there that the prophecy made by his grandmother some 10 years earlier came to pass. In Dr. King's own words:

I was in Devonshire at the time and I had gone to the local farm to pick up some milk. I was very friendly with the local farmer of course and I picked up this milk. I was driving a small saloon car and it was drizzling slightly outside. It had a sliding roof and I opened it. I remember the farmer coming and leaning in the car – he was a big, tough Devonshire man – and he said, "what have you opened the roof for? It is raining and you'll get wet." I said, "I don't know, I just want the roof open." Anyway he wished me "cheerio."

The car skidded very badly on the wet, rough road and, being a small car, it ran up the bank and turned over on its side. My right hand was badly injured and was in a sling, off and on, for some months before it got right again. There are times when I still feel it today. But I think and I am absolutely positive that if I had not opened that roof I might quite easily have broken my neck when the car turned over on its side, because as it was, of course, my head stuck out of the roof. I rolled out of the car through the roof and actually physically pulled my hand from underneath the side of the car which was laying on it. I don't know how I did it, but I did do it.
(Mystical Pilgrimage, 1978)

Maybe this experience, coming just months before the outbreak of World War II, came at a pivotal moment. To convalesce from his injuries, he stayed with his parents in Devon and was working as a poultryman when he received his call-up papers for military service from the government. Like his father, who had taken a non-combatant role in the First World War, Dr. King would, by nature and upbringing, follow the same course. However, in his case it went much deeper for spiritual and, especially, karmic reasons. He was pursuing the Quaker faith with its belief in everyone's potential to experience divinity, and its commitment to pacifism.

But for Dr. King, it may have gone further even than his abhorrence of violence and the belief he held that it was wrong for any man to take another man's life. Although he had no idea of the extent of it then, it must have been hard-wired into his system that he had a mission to perform. The karma surrounding him was entirely different from that of an ordinary terrestrial person who had been called to arms.

It was also in this period that he had a profound experience which took place while staying with his parents when they lived in another house nearby at Great Torrington. As he recorded:

> One incident that did take place there was similar to the one that took place so many years before in Hutton Gate, when I went into the woods to pray and I had a visitation from what I thought was an angel in those days. I had a similar experience while staying in this house and I understood it a lot better. This was in the early part of the war – it could have been just before the war – and that too had a great effect on me. It made me think very, very deeply about the really serious matters connected with my life. It was an extremely elevating experience and one which is very close and very dear to me, and one which is of a most positive and uplifting nature, and that seemed to happen just out of the blue, as it were. Of course I know now that that too was a part of the great plan.
> (Mystical Pilgrimage, 1978)

In the Hutton Gate experience he had gone out as a young boy to pray for his mother's health. On this occasion, near Great Torrington, he went out to pray for world peace and, as before, received a visitation from a most elevated being from another world.

* * * *

On June 4th, 1955, the following fascinating answer was given in a cosmic transmission by the Master Aetherius[5] to a question about how young people, especially those in their early 20s, can help the world today:

Do not forget the lesson of your elders. They have had war after war; every war is due to be the last and it never is. Try to say to yourself, "well, where they have failed, surely I can succeed", and the very age, my dear child, will help you. You are looking out upon an uncertain world; a world which could be torn to hell by foolishly used atomic weapons, or a world which could be made into a peaceful, beautiful world by real understanding. Try to cultivate this understanding within you, and it is not impossible. May I use an analogy? I must apologise for doing this, and I am sure my present instrument will be most annoyed when he knows I have done it, but he, at the age of 20, had to make a great decision in his life. One part – the main part – wanted great excitement: but the other part – the God part – wanted real truth and wisdom. Now that decision cost him quite a lot: a career, degrees, a tremendous amount. But he took it, and the only reason that I can use him today is because he took it.

At this crucial point in his life Dr. King chose the pursuit of truth over excitement by becoming a conscientious objector[6]. In those days, such a decision would be frowned upon by most people, and would most definitely hinder his educational and employment prospects. Following the victorious outcome few in Britain had time for vocational non-combatants.

Although Dr. King kept his cards close to his chest where personal spiritual revelations were concerned, the timing of the experience near Great Torrington was highly significant. Was he instructed not to fight in the war? Or, did the guidance he received lead directly to him making this decision himself? Or, did it confirm what he had already decided? As he said in a lecture on January 17th, 1959:

A part of me wanted to join in the adventure. I was afraid of nothing in those days – maybe it was because I hadn't the common sense to know what fear was! But a part of me said: thou shalt not kill, this is against the Law. So I let that part win.

The pacifism of Dr. George King was considerably removed from that of many others. He was highly skilled as a boxer, sharpshooter, and in many athletic activities. As he said during his mystical pilgrimage: **Although I abhorred violence even as a child, as I do now, I nevertheless was quite good at what may be called belligerent type sports.** Although Dr. King, at great material cost to himself, took a pacifistic stand, his natural disposition was very different. In a lecture on May 23rd, 1961, he said: **I am a born fighter. I was put on this Earth for one reason: to fight.** His mission to Earth bore this out as we will see later in this biography. As he recorded:

> **I maintain that any man that states that he does believe in pacifism, unless he is an expert with a weapon, is slightly hypocritical. If you are an expert in a weapon and you still believe in pacifism, I maintain that is the real deep pacifistic conviction. You know, a young man might say he is a pacifist because he is afraid to fight. I believed in pacifism, not because I was afraid to fight or unable to fight, afraid to shoot or unable to shoot, but it was a deep spiritual conviction formed within me.**
> (Mystical Pilgrimage, 1978)

He determined to engage in the war effort as much as he possibly could without joining the fighting forces. He had already enrolled in the Auxiliary Fire Service (AFS) and he now joined up full time and soon became a section leader. He would often use his psychic abilities to help locate trapped bodies in the rubble when the devastating blitz occurred in London. It was a task as full of danger as many on the front line. He would later say that he wanted to fight, but all he had to fight with was a hose! As his sister put it:

"I think he picked one of the most dangerous jobs in the fire service, and he really came up against some harrowing experiences and was so brave through it all. I stayed in London and would go to the shelter, but my brother was nearly always on duty and though he didn't talk too much about it I think lots of things happened to him during the fire service that made him realize that he wanted to do so much more in life…He was never afraid. He was never afraid to be the first in when the going got tough. He wouldn't run away and hide. He would go in there and I think that had an influence on his life somehow."

For light relief he would demonstrate to his fellow firemen at the AFS sub-station at Edgware Road, his ability to identify serial numbers on ten shilling notes which had been placed in a sealed cardboard box. This was the type of psychic feat that he would later reject in favour of true spiritual realization.

Though Dr. King was a declared conscientious objector, his ability and bravery soon set him apart. He trained up and became an expert in deadly mustard gas, so that he could train others to protect themselves if necessary. His driving skills were also put to good and sometimes dangerous use. For example, when Coventry, a city about 100 miles northwest of London, was heavily bombed with many civilians killed, he was given the task of driving a mobile operating theatre into that city to bring relief to the wounded.

Near the end of the war his abilities came to the attention of the intelligence services, and he was assigned certain classified and risky operations. He was one of a multi-service team set up by Sir Winston Churchill to investigate arson and sabotage and was a member of a special intelligence unit. He could see then the dangers of communism, which he felt were not sufficiently recognized at that time by the authorities. He retained an antipathy towards communism for the rest of his life, largely because of its atheistic affiliations.

As the war came to a close Dr. King's burgeoning quest for truth, self-realization and oneness with God accelerated rapidly. He knew that orthodox religion was not the answer. As his sister put it, "I think probably he thought that going to church wasn't quite the answer. I think probably George felt that he had a mission to fulfil. I don't think quite the mission was to go to church on a Sunday like I did!" For him a leap of faith would not be enough. As he said in his book, *The Three Saviours Are Here!*:

I have never asked anyone to have a blind faith in
anything – neither can I myself. My faith has to be built
upon experience, logic and common sense.

*   *   *   *

He was now working as a driver in the luxury end of the market,
chauffeuring in Rolls Royces and Daimlers, a job he got through
the intelligence service connections he had made near the end
of the war. In 1952 he was a driver for royalty during the state
funeral of King George VI. He developed a passion for motor-
bikes including his newly purchased 500cc Norton OHC. He
acted as a Marshall at the famous Isle of Man TT motorbike races.

His driving became ever more versatile and he worked both
as a stunt driver at Ealing Studios, and a test driver of racing cars
for Jaguar Cars, including the Jaguar C-Type, on such premier
racing tracks as Le Mans. But, driving was just a means to an end
and later, when driving London taxis, he would frequently tell
his passengers that he was paying his way through university –
the university of life.

Through his sister he met Billy Wallace, a successful medium
who was known to levitate while in trance. With Billy he would
frequently attend séances being held by a variety of mediums.
On one occasion a Native American, called Grey Fox, used a
medium's finger to point directly at Dr. King and shouted out
"you". Later Grey Fox would indeed speak through Dr. King
impressing him with great physical strength. Among those he
met in the spiritualist movement was Lord Dowding, the Air
Chief Marshall of the RAF Fighter Command during the Battle of
Britain, who was a firm believer in contacting his deceased pilots.
Interestingly in the 1980s Dr. King would also meet the war hero
Sir Douglas Bader, made famous by the film *Reach for the Sky*,
when he dubbed him into an order of chivalry.

In addition to mediumship, his main psychic focus was
healing. Often the two would coincide. He had contacts with Sir
William Crookes, Sir Oliver Lodge and Sir James Young Simpson,
all of whom, along with Grey Fox, wished to help in this healing
work. Sir James, the celebrated Scottish physician who had

discovered the use of chloroform as an anaesthetic, would later perform psychic surgery through Dr. King. The main aim was to treat and, if possible, cure cancer using healing methods including colour. He established a small healing circle which would meet often at his bedsit at 18 Clifton Gardens in Maida Vale, or at the home of other members of the circle.

Dr. King's skill as a writer was also coming to the fore and he authored a number of short stories covering a variety of topics including science fiction, animals and spirituality. Some of these were published in magazines including the spiritualist journal *Two Worlds*. One of them, 'To Arms Ye True', is an appeal to spiritualists to rise up to the challenge of facing the atomic threat with spiritual solutions. Its closing sentence is: **We, as mortals who believe we are serving our apprenticeship in immortality, can provide that answer.**

His enquiring mind led him to what was in those days in the west a little-explored field: yoga. It was through this ancient science that he would find the answers he sought.

Nowadays this sounds perfectly normal, but then it was a ground-breaking departure for a man living in 1940s England. His sister recounted an incident which was very prominent in her memory when they shared a flat in St. John's Wood:

"One particular evening he came into the kitchen and said: 'I've met somebody who is very interested in yoga and tonight I've had my eyes opened...tonight has changed my life.' And, believe me, that was a changing path in my brother's life...he just became so dedicated and he studied with this yoga master from Chelsea and did an awful lot of healing. He was a very, very good healer. I received healing and my friends, some of my theatre friends, and they thought that he would really go places which of course he did, didn't he?"

We do not know the exact date or even year that this seminal conversation took place, but it certainly illustrates the unconditional commitment Dr. King made as soon as he found the yoga path.

Throughout this period of his life he would practise for an average of eight hours a day the most gruelling and advanced branches of yoga, including Raja Yoga (mental and psychic control), Gnani Yoga (wisdom), and Kundalini Yoga (the mystic serpent power). He performed intensive Pranayama (breathing exercises), Mantra Yoga (Sanskrit chants), as well as the physical asanas of Hatha Yoga, which so many people mistakenly believe to be yoga's sole purpose. Among others, he studied under the advanced yoga teacher Dr. Hari Prasad Shastri, who had moved to London from India in 1929. In fact Dr. Shastri may be the yoga master from Chelsea referred to by Mollie, because he founded a centre in Notting Hill called Shanti Sadan in 1933, which is still active today. Notting Hill is in the Royal Borough of Kensington and Chelsea in west London.

These were transformational years during which Dr. King threw down a bridge across the chasm of human ignorance and crossed it through sheer effort. They could also be lonely years. His sister, who did not really understand Dr. King's quest for enlightenment in that period, nevertheless made the following poignant remark many years later: "I think George was one of the loneliest people I have ever met. I think he had an inner loneliness…there can be loneliness and inner loneliness, and I think George had more than his share of inner loneliness."

He had many exceptional and, sometimes disturbing experiences. On one occasion he levitated at his bedsit in Maida Vale in North West London leaving hair cream stains on the ceiling, much to the amazement of his landlady. On another, he attended a metaphysical convention in Brighton where, after practising breathing exercises very intensively on the pier for some time, he became physically invisible to other attenders entering the building.

On another occasion, after a long night of spiritual practices, he left his hotel room the next morning and walked to a tobacco shop to buy some cigarettes. Entering the small shop, he could see a couple of people ahead of him in line, so he stood and waited patiently. The line moved forward, and another customer came into the shop behind him. The person in front was finally served and Dr. King moved forward. To his surprise, the shopkeeper spoke to the man behind him, then sold him his cigarettes. When this happened even again, Dr. King felt he needed to speak up and spoke sharply to the shopkeeper, who jumped back in surprise

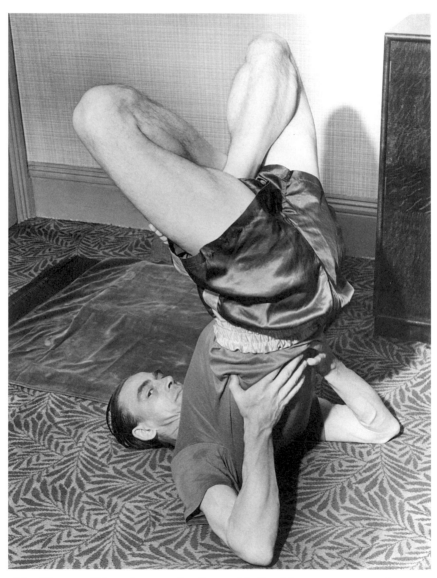

Dr. George King demonstrating a Hatha Yoga posture at home in London.

and turned chalk-white. Dr. King had been invisible to him until he spoke. The others in the shop were also visibly shocked, as Dr. King seemed to just appear from thin air. He quietly paid, picked up his cigarettes, and walked out. In later life he would use smoking and drinking deliberately to lower his vibrations and avoid this kind of problem in company – one which, it must be said, very few of us have to wrestle with.

He became an expert in psychic self-defence and took part in rescue work to protect people from interfering forces. On one occasion his sister was attending a séance at a luxurious flat in Kensington, London, when the medium started to lose control, and slipped into a coma. It was clear that she had been possessed, and now the entity was trying to strangle her, as bruise marks started to appear around her neck. As she collapsed to the floor, everyone present panicked, except Mollie, who immediately phoned her brother, who drove there as fast as possible.

Arriving at the flat, he soon contacted the malevolent entity, and told it to leave the medium. The entity refused to go, so Dr. King told it again to go, or he would project from his body to confront it. The malevolent entity apparently realized this was a fight it was not going to win and decided to let go, but not without making its point. In the room was a heavy marble fireplace, in front of which was a plate-glass fire screen, with the glass enclosed in a brass frame. As the entity left the medium, Dr. King described it as mentally spitting into the room, and the glass screen shattered into powder – such a very fine dust that it covered the whole room and everyone in it. It took many days for everyone to get this glass powder out of their hair and clothes, and out of the apartment.

Another power developed by Dr. King in this period was that of astral projection[7] which, like his skills in psychic self-defence, would be crucial when his true mission came into force. His astral travels were not always to heavenly realms above, but also to the hellish lower planes where he witnessed the depravities of humanity. He also astrally travelled to a physical location, an example of which he described vividly in an address on September 15th, 1985:

Many years ago I worked for a large company – I won't mention any names – working as a security officer, and I had to know everybody in the place. Some of it was open work, some of it was classified work they were doing, so I had to know everybody in the place, at least if not by name, by looks. I was familiar with all the employees and there were quite a lot of them.

In those days I used to receive what is called cosmic teaching. A being would create, through thought, maybe even a City of London, maybe a temple, maybe even something else – build it up through thought – and would teach me various aspects of it. I started to think really deeply about this and also some of the psychological implications of these teachings began to dawn on me very deeply.

So one night I projected from the human body and went back to the firm that I worked for in the daytime. It was filled with people. All the people there, most of whom worked during the daytime, were there at night. But they were a little different. Some of them floated around in a kind of a dream state, others were conniving, lying, trying to cheat one another, and, as you might say, 'get in with the bosses.'

I was so annoyed that I used my powers and cleared the building. I cleared everybody out. Of course nobody could stand against me – they were draughtsmen, technicians – when I was in a projected form. They all went home. Next morning, I went to work. People still treated me with the same kind of respect they did before, but there was a barrier there and especially some of the bosses were afraid of me. You know you can sense when a person is afraid of you. They didn't know why. I hadn't injured them, I hadn't hurt them in any way. I probably made a mistake by interfering with their night prowlings, but they knew, somehow, deep down that this incident had taken place without knowing how it had taken place, where it had taken place or when it had taken place. But they knew that it had taken place.

*   *   *   *

As Dr. King continued his rigorous yoga training – which included complete celibacy – he started to receive advanced initiations. Many, of course, he did not speak of, however there was one which he chose to share some details about. It took place in London in the spring of 1954 and concerned the power we are all on Earth to activate and control – kundalini. It happened in the flat of his parents who, in their seemingly constant process of moving home, had by then relocated to Waterloo Road in London. His mother had entered a deep mediumistic trance and Dr. King, who knew that he was to receive an initiation through her, was dressed in a white robe. He had not expected though that the initiator would be none other than Saint Peter himself.

As the power of Saint Peter surged through Dr. King, the kundalini was activated at the base of the spine and rose up each chakra[8] in turn, at least as high as the throat centre. His mother was not able to cope with the power surging through her and could not return from the trance condition she had entered. Dr. King, now an adept in yoga, and filled with the tremendous power of kundalini following his initiation, could now handle even this emergency. He explained later that when he had the powers he could bring a corpse back to life. Indeed a rare feat but one known to have been performed by masters of old.

Following this initiation, Dr. King struggled to control the enormous power of kundalini and bring it fully back down his spine so that normal bodily functions could resume. He found himself filled with such extraordinary energy, that he ran approximately four miles from Waterloo back to his bedsit in Maida Vale. Wishing to phone his mother, he went to a phone box to call her, but to his amazement, the heavy, almost indestructible, cast iron door ripped completely off its hinges as he opened it. Somehow he managed to get the coins in the slots and spoke to his mother to ascertain that she had now fully recovered.

From the supernormal strength he had exerted on the phone box, he realized that the kundalini was still active, and that it still needed to be returned in its entirety to the base centre. He ran to Regent's Park nearby, and continued to run until well after dawn. Even after returning from work that evening, the power was still active and he felt he needed to run the following night until it finally settled. This first experience of such a complete rise of kundalini had brought with it the exceptionally demanding task of controlling it, which he gradually learnt to do as he grew to become a true master of this ancient science. He later explained that this was the first time he had experienced a complete rise of kundalini to this extent and therefore, did not yet know how to control it. He subsequently learned how to do this, and indeed to master it.

The term 'master' is abused so badly in the spiritual movement that it has all but lost its real meaning. People claim to be masters who have barely activated the kundalini, never mind controlled it. Dr. King was explicit on what mastery meant which he knew from personal experience. A master is no longer limited to believing, thinking, feeling, or even psychically sensing – he or she is a person who actually knows. Meditation reveals the unquestionable certainty and deep significance of whatever the master chooses to meditate upon.

In a lecture given in June 1973, entitled 'A New Yoga For A New Age', Dr. King said:

> Gnani is my favourite form of yoga. This is the yoga of wisdom. It is not only a philosophical form of yoga, it is a vitally important one, and when one has raised the power of kundalini and gained the state of meditation (I'm talking about true meditation by the way), when one has done this then one enters into the field of gnani – or he becomes a knower.

Favourite or not though, gnani was not to be the yoga which would dominate Dr. King's life. His mission would take Karma Yoga to a whole new level of world service.

Chapter Two
THE MISSION BEGINS

It is attributed to Mark Twain that the two most important days of your life are the day you were born and the day you find out why. Dr. King was soon to discover the second of these. Where most people spend their twenties and early thirties preoccupied with establishing themselves in the material world through a career, and possibly a relationship and family, his focus had been primarily internal. Even towering 20th-century spiritual figures like Mahatma Gandhi and Swami Sivananda had to concentrate in their early life on learning and practising the worldly skills of law and medicine respectively. Dr. King, on the other hand, was perfecting mediumship, healing, exorcism, astral projection, the invocation of devas[1] and, along the way, manifesting an array of undeniable powers including levitation.

His niece, Pamela, saw him levitate in the 1950s when she was still a child. She said that the incident lasted for about 10 minutes and that he rose just over a foot above the couch. Many years later she described the incident: "He was sitting cross-legged and then he stretched his feet out on the long couch…we were talking about Yogananda and all this sort of thing and he then levitated above the couch…he uncrossed his legs…and rose above the seat."

Pamela developed a deep respect and complete faith in her Uncle George with very fond memories from her childhood.

He rejected the limiting idea that you could not heal without the help of a spirit guide. His yoga training had taught him to stand on his own two feet, a quality he maintained throughout his life. He had raised the kundalini to the highest chakras and, even more importantly, controlled it. He had entered the deepest states of meditation, known in the east as samadhi. But he had not yet been given the mission for which he came to Earth.

As a medium he had moved beyond basic spiritualism, which generally concentrated at that time on contacting deceased loved ones and could foster a weak-willed dependence upon guides. The records of his healing circle reveal an outstanding ability to act as a channel for communicators from higher mental realms. In the first recorded meeting on May 17th, 1953, Dr. King entered a trance condition with three others present during which a Tibetan adept called the Master Chang-Fu and Sir James Young Simpson, spoke through him. They are referred to as his guides indicating that this was not the first time he had been in rapport with them. Later communicators through Dr. King from the other realms would include Sir Oliver Lodge, the physicist and renowned spiritualist, and Grey Fox.

As well as mediumship and individual healing, circle meetings included healing thoughts for the world as a whole and prayers for peace. A visionary revelation was made on November 18th, 1953, as a result of a samyama (deep yogic meditation) Dr. King entered. He wrote in the minutes: **It is my earnest opinion that we will be able to form a society successfully after proving ourselves in healing.** This healing work included on one occasion a spirit operation performed by Sir James through Dr. King.

On February 2nd, 1954, a very prescient statement was made through Dr. King by the Master Chang-Fu:

> **This is a year when very important steps can be taken, which in later years will be seen to advance one to a particular goal.**
> (Healing Circle minutes)

Later, on April 3rd, a mystic from Rishikesh, India spoke these words:

> **The hand of science has gone mad, and the time is fast coming when the alleged wise men of the world must be shown that they have again to attend the infants' class in the school of common decency. For those who would help in this, gird up your loins. Concentrate, meditate, pray, control your mind and be ready. Those beings who have watched us from outer space for many years**

have discovered that it is up to us who have residence in this world to take the initiative. We can all help in this initiative by showing spiritual initiative ourselves.
(Healing Circle minutes)

This is the first recorded communication through Dr. King which refers to extraterrestrial beings. With hindsight, it is obvious that it was all leading up to a great event. Earlier in the message the mystic had said:

If you would help yourselves and the whole world at one and the same time you will work now towards the light of your own advancement, and when you are ready for your commission this will be laid upon you; but we who operate in the higher sphere cannot lay a commission until we are satisfied that you are ready to execute it.
(Healing Circle minutes)

On April 11th, Dr. King was the channel for a guide, described by the Master Chang-Fu as 'the very learned counsel', who stated:

The time is coming when this world will see a new kind of battle – not new, but new in your lifetime. Never before in the history of this planet have the dark forces and the light forces so come down to Earth. Everything that happens in heaven has its reflection on Earth. The dark will come to grips with the light – there will be a spiritual battle, the greatest spiritual battle that the Earth has ever seen. The plans are in the making now and they will be put into operation before long...
The time is short come when the bugles of declaration must be blown; the time is short come when some of the shrouds of secrecy must be lifted. You will help to lift, you will help to blow the bugles and you might suffer as a result but you will take little notice of this...
Before the moon gets round into the same place as it is today, many of you will be richer in wisdom.
(Healing Circle minutes)

No member of that circle could have known just how prophetic that message would prove to be in describing the future mission of the cosmic avatar, Dr. George King. Nor, how accurate the final statement would turn out to be. For the moon would return to the same place on approximately May 10th, and two days before that things would change forever for him and the planet as a whole.

*   *   *   *

Just prior to this on May 5th an interesting entry in the healing circle minutes reads as follows: "Absent healing circle cancelled as Mr. King was still supposed to be in Cornwall. He returned unexpectedly and accompanied Mrs. D'Arcy and Mrs. Bayliss to Caxton Hall[2] to hear Desmond Leslie lecture on flying saucers." It was he who co-authored with George Adamski the UFO classic *Flying Saucers Have Landed*. This may have been a follow-up to the hint given by the mystic on April 3rd since, aside from this, Dr. King had no particular interest in the subject at the time. He would certainly have been drawn to Leslie's reputation as a noted theosophist[3].

Whatever was revealed at that lecture would be as nothing compared to the voice he physically heard three days later on the morning of Saturday, May 8th:

> **Prepare yourself! You are to become the voice of Interplanetary Parliament.**

Later he would see that his whole life had led – had been virtually engineered – to arrive at this point. But then it was very different. What could it mean? And how would he be able to explain it to even the small number in his regular spiritual group, never mind to the world at large? From the records available to us it looks as though he decided not to publish the full story for almost two years.

He first published it in the April 1956 Issue 5 of *Cosmic Voice*[4]. In the editorial he said:

In my little ashram in Maida Vale, I had the most wonderful revelation of my whole life. A revelation which could not be disclosed to you, dear friends, until the right time. That time has now come. No longer need I remain silent about such matters. A great weight has been lifted from my shoulders, because I am now permitted to share my joy with you all.

This is the opening of the article he wrote under the headline, 'The Command', which followed this editorial:

In answer to numerous requests, I will relate the astounding happenings which led me into the field of flying saucer research.

It was about 11:00 a.m., on a Saturday morning, early in 1954. As is my usual practice on a Saturday morning, I was busily engaged in household chores. Not that you could call my present domicile a house – for if you wanted to swing a cat around within the yellow papered walls, then it would have to be a manx cat, and a little 'un at that! I was performing a tricky feat at the time, trying to dry four plates by shuffling them about rather in the same way that one shuffles a pack of cards. May I warn any 'independent bachelor-and-proud-of-it-laddie', that such a procedure – when you come to consider the frequent breakages – costs almost as much as a wife. And this, chaps, without the other amenities which are a part of matrimonial union. If it is any consolation, however, I will say that sweeping up the pieces of broken china can be a very good exercise.

My window was open, and the pale sunshine streamed through. The noise from the busy street below, blended with the tinkling of plate against plate in such a way as to form a symphony of materialistic activity. The type of activity, the type of noises you could hear in any town or city on the globe on a Saturday morning.

It all stopped. It stopped with the startling suddenness of a pistol shot.

"Prepare yourself! You are to become the voice of Interplanetary Parliament."

This was the alien sound which struck my ear drums with a somewhat gentle firmness. The ensuing silence was broken only by the shattering of plates as they slipped from my useless fingers to the floor. I cannot describe the tonal qualities of the voice which uttered this Command. It came from OUTSIDE of myself – from the empty space of that tiny room, into my mind with a numbing suddenness which made me grasp a chair for support.

I may have sat there for one or two hours – I do not know. The room did not seem to exist during that period – neither did time itself. My world of awareness revolved upon a central axis and that axis was a vital, living, vivid

Dr. King outside his bedsit at 18 Clifton Gardens in Maida Vale, in the 1950s, where 'The Command' was given.

memory of 'The Command' which had been given and the way it had come.

The following week he experienced such terrible loneliness that he almost wept. Nobody he knew could explain what it meant. As he put it in a lecture in Kansas City, Missouri on July 3rd, 1959:

> I was not due to find out, save by my own efforts. I knew many people who were so-called mystics, occultists, yogis, clairvoyants... I tried to gain information from them, but everyone agreed on one thing. Something had happened to this chap they knew as George King, but what it was they did not know. So we had total agreement on not knowing!

The following day the healing circle met as usual and no real answers were forthcoming from the small group who attended or the guide who spoke through one of them. In fact there is no specific reference in these minutes to 'The Command' which could indicate that Dr. King did not feel able to reveal fully the experience to the others. Another meeting was held on Wednesday, May 12th, and although there is reference to flying saucers, there is again, no direct reference to this pivotal event.

* * * *

The next great occurrence in relation to 'The Command' took place on Sunday, May 16th. Dr. King described it in his article on 'The Command' in *Cosmic Voice* Issue 5 as follows:

> It was eight days after this event, when I decided to listen to the most eloquent voice of all – the educating voice of silence.
> After very careful practice of pranayama – a system of yogic breath control – I settled down with a firm determination to stay there until some further explanation was forthcoming. I did not have to wait long.

For the second time, during that short period, I was shaken to the core by an amazing happening.

A man walked THROUGH my locked door, across the creaking boards beneath the faded grey carpet, and sat down opposite to me! The battered old chair creaked as it supported his weight! He was dressed in spotless white robes, which seemed to gleam in the green meditative light I was using. But they were real enough. I had heard the faint swish they made as he crossed the room. I recognised my visitor immediately as a modern leader of spiritual thought in India. He is very much alive at the moment – living in a somewhat rotund physical body in the Himalayas.

I am not permitted to give the name of the saint, but I feel sure those of you who study the all-embracing philosophy of the east, will have guessed it easily. After all, the world is one unit of experience and a study of a part of its philosophy is incomplete. It takes two halves to make a whole.

My yogi visitor smiled and I was submerged in a sea of peace which cleansed the wounds of frustration.

"It is not for you to judge whether you are worthy to be chosen, my son!"

Oh, my dear friends – and those of you who have read this narrative of my unique experience so far I trust are included in the category of my friends – how can I explain the joy in my simple heart at that moment? My mind was stripped naked and read and understood by this saint! My unworthiness for what was obviously a great task, had troubled me all the week. But there were greater beings than I who had pronounced judgement upon this. It was as though I was a living pawn positioned upon the chequerboard of life, and some master chessman had gained my consent before making his move. Submerged as I was in that still, deep lake of peace, my soul signified consent to the move. A move, which – in those days – was hidden by the opaque curtain of my simple ignorance. Despite myself, or because of my REAL SELF, tears of joy and gratitude trickled down my cheeks.

His voice was gentle, but held a peculiar penetrating property, as he continued:

"The real necessities of the age – brought about by the unfeeling march of science into the realms of the atom, and the wrong thought and action of the masses – can be met only by those few who are ready to tune in to those emanations now being sent to this Earth, and become the servants of the cosmic masters. You are one of many called upon to prepare yourself for the coming conflict between the materialistic scientist – who has arrived at his conclusions by the cold application of mathematics – and the occult 'scientist', who has arrived at his conclusions through the recognition that GOD IS ALL. Pray, be still, meditate and open the door of your heart and mind to the precious waters of truth."

After delivering this wonderful message, my yogi visitor gave me detailed instructions in certain practices. He also told me that those people best equipped to help me would be brought into my orbit.

The swami, having imparted this information, bowed with the politeness of a race which enjoyed an advanced culture when ancient Britons still painted themselves with woad. Then he made his exit by walking straight THROUGH my locked door! I jerked it open immediately, but the long corridor beyond was deserted. My initiator from the Himalayas had departed into invisibility.

The rest, some of you know. A group was formed and yoga was practised very diligently – until I was able to lift my mind into a higher framework of vibration, in order to tune in to the mental relay being radiated by the great Master Aetherius.

I know now that 'The Command' was given by Aetherius himself, in such a way as to leave no lingering doubts in my mind as to its authenticity. Also, I know that my visitor from the east – coming as he did with instructions soon afterwards – must have been in communication with Venus.

During a BBC TV interview on May 21st, 1959, Dr. King revealed that although this yogi visitor was alive in a terrestrial physical body, he came from the planet Venus. On July 3rd of that year during the lecture in Kansas City, he elaborated further on this historic encounter:

> Suddenly, out of blackness, out of frustration, came one strong, lasting light – a light that I was due to follow. I recognized my visitor immediately as a man living on Earth at the moment in a physical body, as a master of yoga, as a person who had written many books in the English language and circulated those books throughout the world; as a person resident, for some of his time, in northern India.

Dr. King revealed later to a few close followers that the yogi who had visited him in his room on Sunday, May 16th, was none other than Swami Sivananda. He had not disclosed this before because he had been asked not to do so by the great Swami himself.

The lecture continued:

> This master went on to give me precise instructions as to what I should do in order to make myself a channel for the intelligence conveyed by beings now resident upon other planets. He also went on to give me other instructions – little things about how to leave the physical body and pre-determine an objective, and go to that objective and return to the physical body again.
>
> Among many things, the master told me I would receive a communication from an Indian in this country. Shortly after this, I received a letter from a Sri Nandi in London and Sri Nandi informed me that he was setting up a yoga class – would I care to attend? If so, he would like me as a student. When I went along to see Nandi and asked him how he got my name and address, he said: "Oh, my secretary gave it to me." Well, his secretary

didn't know how she got my name and address! It appears she found a piece of paper on her desk with a name and address on it, and she felt she should write to this unknown George King.

Sri Nandi, by the way, had practised yoga under the same teacher that Mahatma Gandhi had attended, and also was a friend of Paramhansa Yogananda. I'm sure most of you are familiar with that wonderful book, *Autobiography Of A Yogi*, written by this modern Indian saint.

Our research indicates that Sri Yogacharya B.C. Nandi gave talks in London in this period. He also instructed qualified students at his residence in Hampstead on various yoga methods including concentration and advanced meditation. In a lecture on mystic yoga breathing on June 23rd, 1960, Dr. King said of this instruction:

During the attendance at these yoga classes, I learned these simple breathing exercises, which I modified slightly after gaining permission from those who count of course, making them very, very simple and easy and safe for the west. After I practised them for some time, I discovered that I no longer needed to attend the classes of Sri Nandi, but could practise these breathing exercises.

In his Kansas City lecture he said:

Things like that happened in the following two weeks so that I could set up a specialized group, and after diligent practice of yoga for some nine to ten hours a day for some time, I was able to gain telepathic rapport with intelligences living physically on other planets.

* * * *

On Saturday, May 29th, three weeks after 'The Command', at a healing circle attended by four people including Dr. King, the Master Aetherius for the first time spoke through his chosen medium. A series of questions were directed by attenders to the Master Aetherius, which he answered in a personable manner, understating his profound wisdom. The same format was used in subsequent meetings and many of them were reproduced in Dr. King's classic, *You Are Responsible!* which was published in 1961.

On July 10th, Dr. King's Tibetan guide, the Master Chang-Fu, requested that the new Venusian communicator be called 'Aetherius'. When asked a week later how his name should be spelt, the Master Aetherius referred the matter to the Master Chang-Fu, who obliged accordingly. The Master Aetherius amplified:

> My advisors have not yet thought it fitting that I should divulge myself fully. I am here to help you with any information I possibly can. Anything apart from that, and above that, will come when we consider the time is ripe.
> (Healing Circle minutes)

During the remainder of 1954 regular circles were held and, although still small, the group was starting to grow to, sometimes, 17 or 18 people. Among the numerous questions, one concerned a trip that two people in the circle were planning to make to Santa Barbara, California. In an answer given on September 25th, which perhaps revealed the shape of things to come decades later, the Master Aetherius replied: **The fact that both of you are going to a part of the Earth in which we too are interested – that is not by chance.** For Dr. King would himself reside in Santa Barbara in his latter years. It was also later revealed that there is a psychic centre of the Mother Earth just off the coast from Santa Barbara.

As well as the Master Aetherius, the Master Chang-Fu was a regular communicator. Unfortunately no recordings exist of these transmissions although there are a few written records. Occasionally Dr. King would receive a transmission on his own and keep his own written record.

There was an essential experience that Dr. King was instructed to go through during this period, one that has been necessary for many of the great avatars to go through. In Dr.

King's words during the Kansas City lecture:

> Shortly after the initial contact, I was given two very
> definite experiences. One was to reduce my possessions
> to nothing. Despite the fact that I lived in a dilapidated
> place, I did in those days have quite a well-paid position.
> I could afford to run a couple of cars and also I was fool
> enough to race a motorcycle – and anybody who's fool
> enough to race a motorcycle on the continent has got
> more money than sense, and I belonged to this category.
> So again, quite unemotionally and coldly, I began to
> reduce my possessions to nothing until I had one suit,
> a pair of shoes and that's about the lot! This was an
> essential experience. I recognized it as such and abided
> by it absolutely.

New ground was broken on January 29th, 1955, when the
Master Aetherius spoke through Dr. King at a public meeting in
London's Caxton Hall, not far from the Houses of Parliament.
However this brought the second difficult and very poignant
lesson for Dr. King as he explained in his Kansas City lecture:

> Another experience was this: I had to start, for some
> reason best known to the great ones, at the bottom. I
> was informed that the trance condition must be done
> in front of the people of London. When the whole of my
> group, just on the verge of this first transmission going
> before the public, walked out and left me absolutely
> and completely alone, it was like adding insult to injury.
> But you see, this was another essential experience. I
> will never forget my feelings that night when I walked
> into Caxton Hall, London, a lone little figure. I looked at
> the audience, went up onto the platform and thought to
> myself: "how in the name of the Lord can I get this very,
> very difficult trance condition under these conditions?"
>   You see, one flashbulb at the wrong time would have
> killed me; one noise at the wrong time might have given
> me internal haemorrhage. This I knew and appreciated

very definitely. There I was, completely alone – or apparently so. However, Aetherius – a Venusian communicator – was able that night to speak to London for the first time.

Despite his controversial claims, people were being convinced by the oratory and presence of the Master Aetherius in these early Caxton Hall meetings. They became known as 'Aetherius meetings'. Very few written records exist until the publication in June 1955 of the journal which later became known

Dr. George King receiving a cosmic transmission in a samadhic trance condition at Caxton Hall in London.

as *Cosmic Voice*. If tape recordings were made in this period they have been lost or erased by other subsequent transmissions.

The Aetherius meetings were attracting considerable interest and support to Dr. King, very much in contrast to his first public transmission. As he put it in Kansas:

> Since that time those conditions have altered quite considerably and other people, recognizing truth, came to my side and gave me great assistance. It was not long before The Aetherius Society had to be set up in order to handle the numerous letters that were coming to me from all over the world.

In his yoga years it had not been his goal to form an organization in and among humanity. As he revealed in a lecture on May 19th, 1961:

> At one time, my dearest wish was to have a class of crack students who could work together to give various information to mankind, but not to be attached to mankind. To be detached from mankind, but have channels through which various information could be given to mankind, such as books and so on, but without becoming attached in any way. In other words, go in to some retreat in some way and become self-supporting, that was my dearest wish. But I had to face this fact in myself that it couldn't be done. That the way of the monk is not the way; the way of the yogi who retreats is not the way; the way of the fakir who stands gazing at the sun is not the way. You have to be all three – you have to be monk, fakir and yogi and yet work in among mankind. And this is the most difficult thing to do, but this is the way in these days.

And so he set about officially establishing a society to do just that.

*   *   *   *

The Aetherius Society was formally started on August 2nd, 1956. The following is an extract from an article in the November 1956 Issue 8 of *Cosmic Voice*:

"On Thursday 2nd August, 1956, The Aetherius Society was brought into being. This move was brought about in answer to a directive given to us some months ago. We live in a world of labels and trademarks and although our "advisors" do not themselves wish to add to these new nameplates, they did, however, see the necessity to bring into being an organization based upon spiritual belief to promote the teachings of Aetherius and other great masters.

"The Chairman of the Society is Mr. George King and the Secretary-Treasurer Miss Grace Abercrombie.

"The aims of the Society are as follows:

1.   To spread the teaching of the Masters Aetherius and Jesus and other cosmic masters.
2.   To administer Spiritual Healing.
3.   To prepare the way for the coming of the Next Master.
4.   To organise the Society so as to create favourable conditions for closer contact with, and ultimately for physical meetings with, people from other planets.
5.   To tune in and radiate the power transmitted during a Holy Time or Spiritual Push[5] in order to enhance all spiritual practices irrespective of religious beliefs.
6.   To form a brotherhood based on the teachings and knowledge of the cosmic masters.

"It is agreed that the official organ of the Society should be the magazine COSMIC VOICE."

In later years the question of when exactly The Aetherius Society was formed would be raised from time to time. Dr. King was always adamant that it was some time during 1955, even though it may not have been referred to as such. The launch of

Cosmic Voice was certainly a pivotal event which suggested that an organizational framework existed, albeit a small one. On November 22nd, 1960, the Society was officially incorporated as a non-profit organization in the USA.

The need for a Society, however, had been identified by Dr. King from the very beginning. On Sunday, May 16th, 1954, the same day Dr. King was visited by the swami, the healing circle records quote Dr. King detailing the kind of organization that would be required. He wrote:

> It is up to us, who are forming this circle, to open our hearts and our minds to the teachings, and to the teachers who await us beyond the spheres. We must light the lamp of spirituality within ourselves, so that this cool, all-absorbing, never-flickering flame may shine through all the world into the very darkest corners and remotest recesses of this Earth. So that consciousness is risen, and man no longer becomes a selfish thing, but he becomes a worker for all the rest of the human race.
>
> We who form this circle will be a cog in a vast machine, in the vast but very delicately balanced machine.

(Healing Circle minutes)

It was seven years later on April 1st, 1961, that the Master Aetherius described The Aetherius Society as: **an essential part, an essential cog...the Master Cog.**

'The Command' changed Dr. King's life dramatically. To us, it sounds incredibly exciting, to be able to control great powers of healing and white magic, to be chosen to deliver messages from advanced masters from Earth and even beyond to the world, in this time of great need and change. Yet to Dr. King, a shy man in his mid 30s who had settled into a life of helping others through healing and psychic work, it must have seemed very lonely and demanding.

In late 1956 Dr. King moved from Maida Vale to Fulham where he took up residence at 88 The Drive Mansions which became the headquarters of The Aetherius Society. One member who stayed there with him overnight during this period in order to attend activities, described him as kind and affable. Another member from that period, Tom Curtis, recalled his first meeting, accompanied by two of his friends, with Dr. King in September 1957:

"We went along to 88 The Drive Mansions and I must say at this point that unlike other people around at the same time who were claiming contact, writing books...these people were not even interested enough to meet face-to-face. They said they were too busy with their publications, in other words to me it meant they were too busy making money. But it was quite different when I met George King. Here was a man who was willing to take the trouble to spend a lot of time with people who were strangers to him in telling them about his contact and many other aspects relating to flying saucers...Dr. King spent from 8 o'clock in the evening until, I suppose, about 2 o'clock in the morning with us. Never once did he show a sign of an attitude of 'well, you are keeping me up', and I found it so interesting."

He was, though, sorely tested: having to reduce his belongings to the bare minimum, delivering messages from a master from Venus to a very sceptical world in public; and then at the height of this difficulty, having those closest to him abandon him on the verge of the first public meeting. Sadly, Dr. King was to suffer many more examples of those close to him leaving his side at difficult times. Yet despite this, he always managed to accomplish what he needed to, and then some. He would always find the people to help him and support his mission, and he would build The Aetherius Society into a worldwide spiritual brotherhood capable of being the 'Master Cog'.

*   *   *   *

It is fitting that the mystical symbol for this unique Society had an interesting birth as well. Dr. King devised the symbol for The Aetherius Society in the summer or autumn of 1955 in St. Mawes, a small town on the coast of Cornwall, the southwest tip of England, when he was working as a chauffeur. It first appeared on the cover of the November 1955 Issue 3 of *Cosmic Voice*, which was also the first issue which bore its name. The story behind it reveals a very profound experience. In 1978 during his mystical pilgrimage he visited St. Mawes again and recollected the experience in these words:

> We were set there for two weeks with nothing to do in St. Mawes so I thought the best thing I could do was to retire to my hotel room and start some quite serious breathing practices which I did. When I got into the breathing practices I felt that I should slow them down and make a very long session of it. I don't know where the feeling came from except deep within me but I felt that is what I should do...
>
> I couldn't tell you what day it was but supposing it was a Monday, probably about 4 or 5 o'clock and I slowed down, slowed down until I could tune in easily to the activation of each psychic centre. Then I consciously manipulated the power of kundalini up through the spinal column and lodged it as far as I remember in the heart centre. Sixty five hours later I came out of meditation. I was very, very cold, very stiff indeed – as I had been sitting in siddhasana[6] on the bed – and it took me some time to bring the circulation back to normal. I walked around the room and I had no idea that I had been out for that length of time. I could tell it was early morning and I thought it was the early morning of, shall we say, the Tuesday. I got a surprise when I found that it wasn't, that I had been in meditation for at least 65 hours. And I found this out when I went into the lobby of the hotel and saw the date on the newspaper...
>
> The main thing that resulted from that tremendously elevating experience was the fact that I knew that The Aetherius Society should have as its symbol the mystical name for God together with the triangle; and these two symbols had a tremendous power, had a great inner meaning of such depth and profundity that the real secret of the amalgamation of these two great mystical symbols can only be given through initiation.

However to put it very simply, as all of our members
know, it signifies God manifesting Itself as wisdom.
But there is an awful lot more to it than that. Those 65
hours of meditation taught me more about the mystical
name for God than I have ever seen in print since and of
course than I ever knew before. As well as that the whole
wonderful meditative experience gave to me a deep inner
appreciation of what The Aetherius Society should really
stand for and the definite direction that it should take in
the future.
(Mystical Pilgrimage, 1978)

As it turned out the trip was cut short and very shortly
after this experience Dr. King had to drive his employer back to
London earlier than expected because the man's daughter needed
medical attention. As Dr. King reflected in St. Mawes in 1978:

One never knows just when the hour will come and
neither do we know the place. I had to travel all those
hundreds of miles from London to be on my own for a
few days down here, forced to be on my own for a few
days without thinking about my normal business life, or
without thinking and worrying about the small baby that
was The Aetherius Society in those days. I was forced
to be on my own. Conditions were brought about so that
I would be on my own and as soon as the main job was
accomplished, namely the meditation, other conditions
were brought into being to get me out of that area fast...
    If you were to ask me, did this happening take place
in St. Mawes because of the significance of the place
itself, I would have to now say, no. It took place because
of the conditions which were brought about and the time
that those conditions were brought about. Those were
the leading factors. A forced seclusion, with nothing
of a material nature to do, so therefore this forced me
despite myself, certainly despite my lower self, into very
definite spiritual action which resulted in 65 great, most
wondrous and glorious hours in my life. As well as that,

I do believe that this experience was a preparation for many things which were to come and which later did come.
(Mystical Pilgrimage, 1978)

It was later revealed that The Aetherius Society had been visualized by Saint Goo-Ling from the Great White Brotherhood Retreat within Mount Shasta in northern California, although we do not know exactly when. He is the Keeper of the Seal for the Spiritual Hierarchy of Earth and a member of the Executive Council, which makes him one of the most prominent masters on this planet. It is he who would later introduce two of The Aetherius Society's greatest teachings, 'The Twelve Blessings' and 'The Nine Freedoms'. On June 30th, 1958, he stated through Dr. King:

I visualized The Aetherius Society into existence...When I brought into being on behalf of the cosmic masters, The Aetherius Society, I also knew that great would be its task.

The Symbol of The Aetherius Society as visualized by Dr. King during a meditation in St. Mawes.

In later transmissions he also referred to this happening. On May 14th, 1960, he said:

The Aetherius Society, which I brought into being, has great opportunities to do good work throughout this Earth. There is no doubt that many of you will pull together as a united band of brothers in this spiritual task so that the great plans, which are now being formulated on higher levels for this organization, may be put into direct manifestation upon Earth through this organization. All those loyal to this spiritual cause will be given every opportunity to be of service in one way or another either actively, such as those directly concerned with the actual work to be done, or inactively, such as those who are able in this materialistic world to finance the workers in the field. Each one is given a great opportunity to be of invaluable assistance to a young but extremely active organization.

As you all know, before The Aetherius Society was founded, other organizations were closely examined with the idea of relaying the vital space message through these organizations. The examiners came to the conclusion that it was better to found a new organization, free from dogmatic limitation, rather than try to change an existing one bound by its own dogmas. That is why this organization was brought into being on the direct instructions from humble self, through George King, who is a direct channel connecting not only the Great White Brotherhood with ordinary man, but the cosmic masters with ordinary man. Because of this, you can all no doubt appreciate the great significance of this organization.

In fact, would like to make statement now: there is not another organization on Earth at moment, comprised of terrestrials, which has done as much for the Earth as The Aetherius Society since its birth.

Throughout the years Saint Goo-Ling has kept a watchful eye on The Aetherius Society giving invaluable advice including sometimes personal guidance to individuals within the organization through the mediumship of Dr. King. On July 8th, 1965, he stated:

I take this opportunity of speaking to you all. The Aetherius Society is near to me for many reasons, one of which was that, as you know, it was upon my directive that this organization was brought into being. I have more than a personal interest in your correct function.

Tom Curtis, who recorded many of the early cosmic transmissions, remembered being told that Saint Goo-Ling was the master of Dr. King's Tibetan guide, the Master Chang-Fu. If this is true, it may be that Saint Goo-Ling deliberately directed his advanced student, who resides on the highest inhabited realm of Earth, to overshadow Dr. King as a preparation for his great mission to come. It could also be that when the Master Chang-Fu selected the name, Aetherius, he did so with the authority of his master, Saint Goo-Ling.

The birth of The Aetherius Society and Dr. King's main mission to Earth was monumental. The contacts Dr. King was having were with some of the greatest masters on Earth and even beyond Earth. Because of this, there was a tremendous gulf between what Dr. King was experiencing and what the rest of the world was experiencing.

His lectures were delivered with a dynamic presence and uncompromising truthfulness – bluntness even – which always made its mark on those who heard him. He revealed later that he had known as a child that he was destined to become a public speaker and had visualized himself doing so. Through this, he overcame his natural shyness until it became invisible to many. The Master Aetherius, who must have known him better than anyone, stated as late as 1979: **George King is by nature a very shy person, although few people know this.** He exhibited in one persona supreme confidence, unadorned modesty and total fearlessness, a combination which could in itself be an indication of his alien origins.

Dr. King's life was a vortex of amazing happenings and mystical truths all with an urgency driven by the importance of saving a civilization. Even those close to him were not able to fully understand what was happening and certainly not its full ramifications. It is hard to imagine just how difficult it must have been for Dr. King to live his day-to-day life navigating between two very different worlds. Surely this must be one of the great tests for an advanced being: to understand and be able to work with the higher planes of existence and yet stay grounded and remain approachable to those still evolving on Earth. And this great gulf was due to grow even larger for Dr. King as the voice of the cosmic masters, Primary Terrestrial Mental Channel.

Chapter Three

PRIMARY TERRESTRIAL MENTAL CHANNEL - PLUPERFECT!

To describe Dr. King as a medium for the cosmic masters is to understate what he did. You cannot really compare any other form of mediumship to the techniques he used or to the results he achieved. Among the myriad claims of higher contacts through the ages which include the use of telepathy, remote viewing, clairvoyance, clairaudience and various forms of trance, no one in the public domain has attained both the elevated source and the high degree of accuracy of Dr. King.

In *Cosmic Voice* Issue 7, he described a communication from the cosmic and ascended masters as: **a transmission of a specific pattern of thought impulses radiated on a magnetic carrier wave.** He explained that to take a cosmic transmission he entered a samadhic trance, which he described as: **a positive yogic condition, self-precipitated by a control imposed upon the currents of psychic energy in order to receive and translate into sound these thought impulses.**

In this state his larynx was used as the voice for the communicator which brought not only accuracy but a wonderful individuality of tone. The sound and enunciation of the Master Aetherius, for example, is immediately recognizable in 1979 just as it was in 1955. The same consistency is true of Mars Sector 6 and other masters who spoke through Dr. King. In particular, the beautiful timbre and vocal character of the Master Jesus is such that some, without being told it was him, have recognized and identified his unique persona just from hearing the voice.

We can do no better than to quote Dr. King's description of the methods he used as Primary Terrestrial Mental Channel published in *Cosmic Voice* Issue 7:

The interplanetary communicators are able to transmit

their thoughts upon a magnetic beam which acts as a carrier wave. This beam or carrier wave can be directed by their applied mental pressures with almost uncanny accuracy towards any human being whether capable of conscious reception or not. The radiation is not limited to distance between transmitter and receiver, neither is it limited by differing vibratory octaves of existence. In other words, the Master Aetherius is capable of transmitting his thought waves in a predetermined pattern over great physical distances and from different planes of existence...

The yogic trance condition is employed by me in order to tune into and receive the mental stimuli directed by the interplanetary communicators. I have learned how to raise the psychic current (kundalini) from the lower centres and lodge it in a certain higher chakra in order to activate that centre to such a degree that prolonged concentration upon the actual carrier beam which conveys the thought transmission is possible. At the same time, I completely detach myself from the results of the sound translation to such an extent that my own pet likes, dislikes and opinions of the conscious mind cannot discolour the actual message itself. If I do fall short of this goal in any way, it can be put down to my personal imperfection rather than any fault occurring in the actual mental transmission originally received.

It is of course possible to receive a series of telepathic impressions while still being fully conscious of one's immediate surroundings. But to share an experience with others – at the same time – by translating the whole series into sound or speech, needs a positive type of yogic trance condition. Perhaps the greatest lecture I have ever heard was given to me by the Master Aetherius while I was travelling on top of a bus! And this stream of illumination lasted for two whole hours. During the time I was detached from, yet dimly aware of, my immediate environment. I was not in a deep trance condition. Yet I could not have spoken out

the words of the master for the whole period without
employing a deep trance condition. Maybe a phrase or
two could be spoken, but not the WHOLE MESSAGE
EXACTLY as received.

The technical precision of this explanation illustrates his level
of attainment. He was simply in a different league from other
mediums, of which there were many at that time. Nothing much
has changed since, except that mediumship is now generally
described as channelling. But he still stands out like a Rembrandt
at an exhibition of paintings by infants.

*   *   *   *

The most profound teachings by some of the greatest cosmic
masters in the solar system were channelled through Dr. King to
help mankind adjust our evolution towards understanding and
following the spiritual laws. There has not been a medium like
him before or since, as becomes clear when you study the content
and calibre of the transmissions he received, and those who
delivered them – with each communicator exhibiting distinctive
characteristics.

The Master Aetherius speaks in the style of a personable and
at times affable friend. He can deliver some of the most profound
revelations we have ever heard on this planet as though he is
reminding us of something we already know and have the
potential to understand fully. It is unlikely that we have realized
that potential, but it must be there and the Master Aetherius
always affirms his total belief in it.

In *Cosmic Voice* Issue 18, Dr. King described the Master
Aetherius as: **the Infallible One**. He stated that there were at
least two meanings in transmissions by this master. Study and
contemplation of them, as opposed to a light scan, always pays rich
dividends. The Master Aetherius speaks with a truthful directness
which, to anyone capable of self-honesty, can be simultaneously
uncomfortable and liberating. But his compassion always shines
through. It is as though he takes you into his confidence with firm
but gentle encouragement and, in doing so, he demonstrates an

extraordinary humility.

This is especially so when one considers his prominent stature. He is, we are informed, a Representative of Venus in Interplanetary Parliament. Of this, he said in a cosmic transmission which is published in the book, *Life On The Planets*: **I actually do represent the planet Venus but that is only part of my self-appointed task – note that, please – self-appointed task.** Mars Sector 6 separately revealed that such Representatives

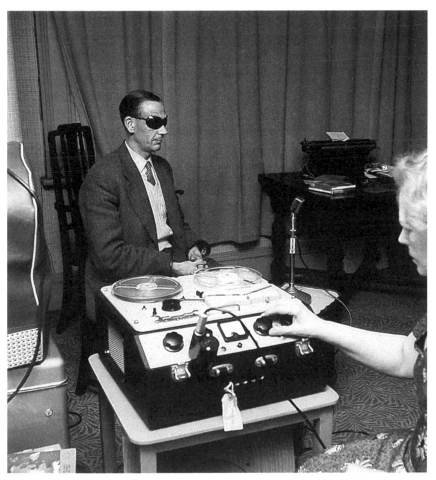

Dr. King, Primary Terrestrial Mental Channel, takes a transmission in the 1950s in London, which is tape-recorded for posterity.

are appointed by the most advanced masters on any planet in the solar system who are known as the Perfects of Saturn. Since the Master Aetherius appointed himself to this position, as he states, it could indicate that he is at that level or an even higher level. Years later in his book, *Contact With A Lord Of Karma*, Dr. King wrote: **we do not know exactly who the Master Aetherius is yet, except that he is an Advisor to the Karmic Hierarchy**[1].

His humility was commented on more than once by Mars Sector 6 who said in a cosmic transmission published in the book, *Life On The Planets*:

> **As you no doubt know, you have heard a message from an intelligence you choose to call – Aetherius. He spoke a word or two about the work he does. Did you notice something, Terra? Did you notice his humility? That is something that comes only in the wise.**

On another occasion, Mars Sector 6 stated: **Never have I met such a master of understatement as the great intelligence you call – Aetherius** (*Life On The Planets*). The relationship between these two masters must be not only highly significant but also extremely ancient. These are the two most frequent communicators of cosmic transmissions through Primary Terrestrial Mental Channel. They are the most likely to announce key developments in the Cosmic Plan[2] for our world about which they are far more than commentators – at times virtually its architects.

It became clear in later years that the Master Aetherius was Dr. King's own master who had arranged for him to come to Earth. It was also divulged that in his true being as a cosmic intelligence, Dr. King would report to Mars Sector 6 as his superior officer. Undoubtedly long before he came to Earth, there was a powerful connection between him and these two exceptionally prominent gods from space.

The admiration and esteem expressed by Mars Sector 6 for the Master Aetherius was amply reciprocated on several occasions. An example of this was disclosed by Dr. King on November 20th, 1993, in a fax he sent to members of The Aetherius Society about a response he received during a mental transmission:

Today, November 13th, the Master Aetherius answered me that I had gained the world record throughout all history for a fourth aspect intelligence living on level one[3] with the first transmission I took from Mars Sector 6 – never mind 'The Nine Freedoms'!

The transmission referred to was delivered in October 1955 during what was described as the second Spiritual Push of modern times. That this created a world record is an amazing tribute to Dr. King himself, but it also says something very telling about Mars Sector 6. It is a classic example of an apparently simple statement which contains different levels of meaning. The Master Aetherius chose to focus only on Mars Sector 6, and by doing so may have suggested his pre-eminence among the illustrious roll call of gods who have spoken to Earth through the ages.

This indicates two things about Dr. King. Firstly, that the lengths he went to on the inner planes to develop his abilities prior to 'The Command' in 1954 placed him in an exceptional category. It is possible that no avatar, never mind an Earth person, had perfected mediumship to this level, taking it to the zenith of its actualization. Who else has channelled by identifying an energy beam of consciousness on a specific chakra and then focussing upon it with unerring concentration? This is then translated by his brain into the English language because that is his native tongue, with the emphasis, feeling and energy of the individual communicator. This is far removed from a basic medium being overshadowed and impressed with particular wording, if they are able to or, in most cases, vague patterns of thought. To Dr. King it was an exact science involving the application of precise and discernible forces.

Secondly, must have been Dr. King's karmic position. Either because of his previous connections before he ever came to Earth, or because of arrangements made by his own master, Aetherius, or for some other reason, he was deemed worthy to be the channel for the cosmic intervention of a colossal intelligence who had never before been able to communicate in this way through any other avatar on this Earthly plane.

*   *   *   *

Dr. King recognized early on that Mars Sector 6 was in a different category from other communicators. On September 1st, 1963, he said in an address:

> This particular master is the most impersonal master
> I think that's ever used a channel on this Earth...He is
> interested not in personalities, not even in collections of
> personalities, but a planet as a whole.

As the years went by it emerged that he is one of the greatest strategists in the galaxy. He was described by our master variously as a supreme cosmic chess player; brilliant intellect in the fields of strategical astro-metaphysics[4]; and great karmic manipulator[5].

It became clear that the latter description was particularly apt when in 1988 Mars Sector 6 accepted an invitation to join the Karmic Hierarchy as a Lord of Karma. The ramifications of this are so vast as to be beyond our limited comprehension, never mind our literary remit. But whatever they are, it undoubtedly confirms his unique status in the cosmic pantheon as recorded upon our world. And, it was revealed that he could have received even higher initiations which he turned down in order to be of greater service. In Dr. King's words in *Cosmic Voice*, September 1988:

> He has not chosen to rise to his full unimaginable glory
> in the divine cosmic scheme so that he can still be of
> service to you and millions more. In my eyes, this indeed
> crowns the cosmic master Mars Sector 6 with the true
> essence of divine glory.

His transmissions are delivered in a voice of commanding authority and undeniable truth. He offers his wisdom as aspects of law and, like the Master Aetherius, with total confidence in our potential to practise them. From February 12th to March 15th, 1961, he delivered a set of cosmic transmissions called 'The Nine Freedoms' which spells out the path we must all take in our journey back to divinity as no teaching has ever done before. These were described by the Master Aetherius as: **the most important teachings yet given to Terra**. He further elaborated as published in *Cosmic Voice* Issue 25:

> It may be some time before these are fully appreciated by your Earth, but they will live throughout the centuries and the older they become, the more potent they will seem and with limitation, the more they will be adopted. It is seldom throughout the history of Terra that such profound jewels of wisdom are given openly. It was decided at this time that, being as it is **just prior to the Initiation of Terra**[6], the jewels be scattered among the populace so that those ready may pick them from the dust of your literature. From the worthless chaff of numerous incorrect statements and untrue relation of experiences, 'The Nine Freedoms' can be sorted as the true, living seeds of everlasting wisdom which have been scattered among you.

Advanced knowledge, never revealed to humanity before, is expressed in brief incisive sentences with as much simplicity as could possibly be wrested from the inner complexities of their meaning. It is the perfect complement to the other main set of Aetherius Society teachings, 'The Twelve Blessings', which had already been delivered through Primary Terrestrial Mental Channel by the Master Jesus on twelve consecutive Sundays from July 27th to October 12th, 1958.

* * * *

The Master Jesus, who came from Venus, was a relatively frequent communicator through Primary Terrestrial Mental Channel, especially in the 1950s in England. In fact, this period of Dr. King's mission was, among other things, very concerned with what might be termed 'New Age Christianity'. Most of the prayers used at Aetherius Society activities were channelled by this great master in those years, as well as some wonderful messages of love and selfless service, of which he is the very epitome.

His crowning teaching is 'The Twelve Blessings' which is increasingly studied and practised by thousands of people in scores of countries around the world. This was transmitted at Aetherius House in London, which had just been purchased by Dr. King with help from some others as the new headquarters of The Aetherius Society. He had left The Drive Mansions earlier in the year and, after a few months residing at 15 Fulham High Street, moved into this property at 757 Fulham Road. Tom Curtis who did most of the tape recordings of this sacred New Age scripture recalled:

"We had a special procedure during the giving of 'The Twelve Blessings', which took place in the hall of Aetherius House. Dr. King, prior to this time which was 6 o'clock in the evening, was not allowed to talk to conserve his energy. Also, until after the Blessings were actually delivered, he could only have a light diet. So whenever he wanted to communicate he passed little notes to us during the day."

The Master Jesus speaks in beautiful poetic language – some of it employing the phraseology of the expressive 17th-century English associated with the King James Bible and the works attributed (wrongly) to Shakespeare[7]. As a teaching it is a vast extension of the Sermon on the Mount introducing a cosmic concept to religious thought.

It is also the main spiritual practice performed at Aetherius Society meetings, including at outdoor locations, as well as online and at home. This is because Dr. King applied his own knowledge and innate understanding to the words he had received and brilliantly devised an effective way to use them. The Master Jesus must have known that he would do this and the credit for this practice should really be shared between the great master of love from Venus and the greatest avatar of these days upon Earth. It also illustrates that practicality is written in Dr. King's very DNA. Whereas the Sermon on the Mount is faithfully read aloud at Sunday services in various churches, the more evolved and mystical Twelve Blessings is lovingly practised at Aetherius Society meetings sending out great spiritual energy[8] to our needy world.

We can only imagine what it was like for Dr. King to take these tremendously important Blessings emotionally and physically. But this responsibility brought with it great danger, as there are forces on Earth that did not want such truths given. As he said during a lecture in Los Angeles on October 12th, 1959, the first anniversary of 'The Twelfth Blessing':

During the time that 'The Twelve Blessings' was given to this Earth through my very unworthy self, as a channel for Jesus – well, about half way through the Blessings – you know one Blessing was given every Sunday for 12 weeks. It was my responsibility to keep myself alive for 12 weeks. And it's not easy when you're really doing something of that nature. Try it some time, you'll see. I kept a very strict guard on any outside interference, except once when that guard was relaxed for a few moments while I was in a cinema. And the way the attack was made was quite brilliantly conceived.

The forces that made this attack knew that the battery of mankind is in the solar plexus region, and that is where you store the tremendous energy that you use for your everyday lives. If you inhibit the workings of that region at all, you cut off your source of energy. It's like cutting the wire to a battery on a car and then pressing the starter – nothing happens. If you inhibit the workings of that psychic centre, you cut off your battery or vital dynamo which is within you, and you have certain reactions: the first reaction is a gross loss of temperature, the second reaction is paralysis, the third reaction is death.

While I was in this cinema I must have lowered my guard for long enough for the attack to be made. And I felt as though a red hot needle was pushed from my side, from the left side, right the way across inside my body, the other side through the solar plexus region, and it came out to the right side. And I knew – and it happened like that [snaps fingers]. I of course, screamed and keeled over with the agonizing pain and I knew that

I'd been fool enough to leave my guard down for even a short time.

I managed to get out of the cinema, went home, and there were two people there. I said, "I want a hot bath, I should be paralyzed shortly, and I want you to massage me solidly until we fight it." As it happened it was the birthday, I think, of The Aetherius Society during this time and there was a good, old birthday party going on downstairs, I didn't appreciate it very much. The offset was, of course, that we managed to fight even this concerted attack.

Dr. George King in 1958 sitting behind a ribbon microphone in what is now known as The George King Chapel at the European Headquarters, in London during the period in which 'The Twelve Blessings' were given.

His work for the cosmic masters was indeed 24 hours a day and was a life and death mission.

Dr. King was very affected by his contacts with the Master Jesus at a deep emotional level. He was able to explain, as none had before him, the real mission of this master to Earth 2,000 years ago. That he came here deliberately and strategically to die and thereby take karma for humanity at that time, but not to forgive us our sins which is impossible. The crucifixion, engineered by dark forces, was anathema to Dr. King – he appreciated its outcome fully, but did not agree with the Master Jesus allowing it to proceed because of his deep love for this wonderful master.

Also during this period he received several cosmic transmissions from the chief disciple of the Master Jesus when on Earth, Saint Peter. Far from the simple fisherman we sometimes read about, or the weak, vacillating figure depicted in certain church writings, he is a Martian intelligence of fearless and exceptionally powerful character. His words delivered through Primary Terrestrial Mental Channel show a penetrating line of mystical thought which, with contemplation, brings profound realization. His are some of the most thought-provoking communications Dr. King received, often relating to aspects of Christianity.

* * * *

Dr. King's mother, Mary, was an ardent devotee of the Master Jesus, who played a significant part in the early development of The Aetherius Society. Amazingly she had a formidable series of close encounters in her own right. These were physical meetings with extraterrestrial beings which included, on more than one occasion, journeys in what was then termed a flying saucer. They took place over a four-year period in the late 1950s, possibly because of her unique karmic position as his mother.

One took place on January 25th, 1958. It was authenticated at the time by Dr. King and confirmed some days afterwards by the Master Aetherius himself in a transmission. She was visited by a Venusian master at her home in Barbrook, Devon. He answered many of her questions as reported in *Cosmic Voice* Issue 15. When this being left, she reported his parting words as: "I have done as my master commanded. Farewell, little sister of Earth". He then walked down the drive, leaving footprints in the falling snow, and on reaching the gate, disappeared leaving no further footprints on the path beyond.

An even more significant physical contact took place on September 15th, 1958, when she was invited by appointment into a spacecraft which had landed in a field a hundred yards from her house, following her recent move to Kentisbury nearby. She was shown around by the captain of the craft who, it later turned out, was an aspect of another very important contact of Dr. King's known as Mars Sector 8. He promised her a ride in this vessel at a future date.

This would turn out to be what the cover of *Cosmic Voice* Issue 20 described as "one of the most important physical contacts ever made with space people". As Dr. King wrote in this edition:

> On January 12th, 1959, Mary King telephoned Aetherius Society Headquarters and told me that she had been given a rendezvous but must keep the time and place strictly secret. She was also given the directive to... **"bring the Book. This must not be touched by any at Aetherius House, save our Mental Channel."**
>
> I packed up a new copy of *The Twelve Blessings* in a plastic cover, then in a strong plain envelope, putting this again into a larger envelope, marked with the title. This procedure was adopted with all Aetherius Society publications. I then sent these by registered post to my mother. She in turn took each publication, separately wrapped, out of their titled outer envelopes and took the books along to her rendezvous.

The Twelve Blessings had only just been published in book form. To be on the safe side, Dr. King had responded to this directive by including all the Society's publications, but he must have had more than an inkling that the reference applied to this New Age teaching of the Master Jesus. A week later between 12:30 a.m. and 3:40 a.m. on January 19th, the great happening took place. Mary King was taken by Mars Sector 8 and his crew on a journey in the craft she had visited a few months earlier, carrying with her the publications prepared by Dr. King including the all-important copy of *The Twelve Blessings*.

The climax of this visit came when the spacecraft went into a mother ship and she met the Master Jesus together with the Venusian who had visited her home the previous January. Her beloved Master Jesus, with whom she was informed she had been connected in a former life, then blessed *The Twelve Blessings* and placed it in a magnificent box which he took away. Before doing so, she said that he declared Dr. King as chosen to be "a leader among men of Earth, in this their New Age." This contact was unequivocally endorsed by Dr. King who included it in future editions of *The Twelve Blessings*.

She was to have one further trip in the spacecraft of Mars Sector 8 later that year when she met the Lord Babaji, Master of Earth, in the Himalayas and learned much about her son and his mission to Earth, which made her feel, as she put it, "indeed honoured to be his mother". It is clear from this encounter not only how well Dr. King was known to the great Lord, but also his very close connection with Mars Sector 8. In fact Mary King was reported to have said that there was a marked likeness between the aspect of Mars Sector 8 she had met aboard his spacecraft and the photograph of Dr. King which appears on the back cover of his book, *You Are Responsible!*, which is certainly food for thought.

*   *   *   *

Mars Sector 8 – General Information was one of the most frequent communicators through Dr. King. In later years there were also many mental transmissions from another communicator known as Mars Sector 8 – Special Advisor S2, who later became known as Sector S2. Mystery surrounds exactly who or what Mars Sector 8 is, but Dr. King once described him as a control point and a communications point for this solar system, which he said was located on the smaller of the two Martian moons, Deimos, subsequently moving to one of the moons of Jupiter.

His cosmic transmissions are usually given in a trenchant,

no-nonsense manner with a powerful monotone delivery. He supplies authoritative data on a variety of matters including the effects of nuclear radiation, government cover-ups of UFO information and specifics of spiritual energy radiation to the planet. He exudes a practical, almost down-to-earth approach, sometimes with a dry humour. He can launch into uncompromising spiritual, even semi-political, oratory when for example

The photo of Dr. King on the back of *You Are Responsible!* which Mary King is said to have described as a likeness of Mars Sector 8.

providing a forceful critique of what he called the silence group, for suppressing the truth from the people.

Perhaps the most idiosyncratic communications, at least in their tonality, are delivered by the intelligence known as Jupiter 92. There is a musical quality to these inspirational messages with breathing patterns which surprised even the BBC in respect to the lengths between Dr. King's inhalation and exhalation. They appeal to humanity to raise its consciousness from the mundane, lowly levels to which it has sunk, upwards and into the realms of glory. Perhaps the word which is used most in these beautiful exhortations is 'rise'.

The most elevated planetary intelligences in this solar system are from Saturn. Communications from these divine Lords are few and far between with only one teaching transmission of substantial length called 'The One Energy', which ranks as a high watermark in the oceans of wisdom delivered to our world through the millennia. The gentle voice of compassion which utters these timeless profundities, belies its vast authority and power. For at the same time as the Lord delivered these words he also transmitted communications to a thousand space vehicles spread throughout the Milky Way for reverent study by the cosmic intelligences within them.

There are a number of other cosmic beings who spoke through Dr. King from time to time – some from this solar system, including one from Neptune, and others from beyond it. One of the most notable is a transmission from an inhabitant of a planetary system towards the centre of this galaxy called Gotha. More will be said about this later because of its importance in Dr. King's mission.

In the 1950s particularly there was an emphasis on demanding the truth about flying saucers. In August 1958 Dr. King organized and spoke at a large rally in Trafalgar Square, London for this very purpose which must have been very controversial at the time and was certainly groundbreaking. Also public forecasts were given by cosmic masters through Dr. King, often at the Caxton Hall in London, detailing when and where these craft would be active. Very often these were observed by independent witnesses at the given dates and locations, and sometimes subsequently reported in the press, thereby confirming the forecasts. Some of these are published in the closing pages of *You Are Responsible!*.

Another topic which featured regularly in the early transmissions was the dangers of nuclear experimentation and radioactive release. The cosmic masters focused not only on its physical effects, which were disastrously underestimated by governments and scientists at the time, but also on its subtle aspects at different octaves of manifestation. These, they warned repeatedly, would have dire consequences including cancer and genetic mutation. As Primary Terrestrial Mental Channel, Dr. King was at the forefront of those campaigning to ban the bomb and reduce the release of radioactivity into the environment, at a time when its effects were little understood and its regulation was inadequate to say the least. At his own expense he sent copies of transmissions about the death-dealing effects of atomic radiation to prominent representatives of officialdom.

Dr. King was also a brilliant teacher in his own right. He had an uncanny ability to take the great teachings of the past, both from the east and the west, and explain them simply in a way the modern spiritual worker can use to help the world. He also demonstrated an in-built cosmic understanding of the great truths within teachings such as 'The Twelve Blessings', 'The Nine Freedoms' and others he was receiving as Primary Terrestrial Mental Channel. Certain of the explanations he gave were as perceptive and revealing as those contained in some of the great transmissions.

*   *   *   *

Arguably the most important announcements that were delivered through Dr. King from the 1950s onwards were the dates of what were referred to by the Master Aetherius as Spiritual Pushes and by Mars Sector 6 as Magnetization Periods. The first of these commenced on May 28th, 1955, and lasted for seven weeks. It was announced by the Master Aetherius a week later as published in *Cosmic Voice* Issue 3:

All spiritual exercises will be greatly potentized. This will

apply irrespective of class, colour, creed or religion. We advise ALL of you to cooperate and work hard at your spiritual exercises...

We are using between 20,000 and 30,000 mother ships, and between 180,000 and 280,000 remote controlled vessels, in an effort to pour into your Earth a great flood of magnetic energy of which you are in urgent need.

This stupendous cosmic manipulation initiated a pattern of regular Spiritual Pushes, generally four or five a year, throughout Dr. King's lifetime and for centuries beyond it. These took a historic turn from the second Spiritual Push, which started on September 18th, 1955, when Satellite No. 3 was put in orbit around Earth to manipulate and radiate these magnetic energies to the world. From this point onwards it seemed the need for so many vehicles to manage a Spiritual Push diminished, possibly because Satellite No. 3 is such an advanced and specialized craft. The controller of this Satellite, it was later revealed, was none other than Mars Sector 6 who thereafter took charge of these periods with his crew of advanced spiritual technicians. This was described in his first transmission to Earth in October 1955 which the Master Aetherius would refer to decades later as a world record. Further information was revealed about Spiritual Pushes in future transmissions including the fact that they potentized all spiritual actions performed by human beings by a factor of 3,000.

Another vital element was introduced by the cosmic masters known as 'the absorption factor'. This was a measurement of the spiritual power absorbed by mankind and sent out to others in need during these periods, which would be announced after them to indicate how effective human cooperation had been. A low absorption factor could signal great danger to the world as a whole and Aetherius Society cooperators would be urged to compensate for this by redoubling their efforts to radiate energy to humanity. Science and spirituality were becoming two expressions of the same force – a fusion that resonated perfectly with Dr. King's persona.

The enormity of his responsibilities as Primary Terrestrial

Mental Channel, which were becoming ever more clear, placed immense pressure upon him. The pinnacle in mediumistic terms was the reception of what were called 'Special Power Transmissions'. These took place at critical times for the benefit of humanity. During Special Power Transmissions the trance condition adopted by Dr. King was even more demanding than a teaching transmission. One reason for this was the speed and urgency of the communicators, and the other was the number of them – sometimes coming in so quickly that they appeared to overlap one another. For Dr. King this meant an extraordinary feat of concentration which had never been demonstrated by a medium before.

The following are extracts from a lecture given on November 23rd, 1963, in which he described this condition:

> It's a yogic type of trance which is brought on by a direct conscious manipulation of kundalini...I allow myself never more than two minutes to get into this condition...I can do it in thirty seconds if I'm pushed...I will not reveal the mechanics, even the mental mechanics, of this particular manipulation because it is dangerous...
>
> It has never been demonstrated before this type of condition...a beam is tuned into – now this beam...varies between the size of a half dollar piece; in England it would be about a two and sixpenny piece [approximately one and a quarter inches] to something about the size of a dollar piece which is...twice as big.
>
> Inside this beam appears to be quite a bright bluish pinkish light, and that is what I have to concentrate on for however long the trance condition lasts. If I lose that I lose the whole communication and the whole thing would then be jumbled...
>
> There's more than one beam existing at the same time. When there is a fluctuation between, for instance, Mars Sector 6 and another operator, I have to move quickly between a beam which seems to have a physical position about six inches in front of the head, to one that might have a physical position of...probably two feet...

to the side of the head. So it's an immediate switch of consciousness from one to another. Such a switch could not be done by the conscious mind so it is...brought about more by the super-consciousness.

Nothing like this had ever been heard of before. Charles Abrahamson, one of Dr. King's leading early disciples in America recalled that during certain Special Power Transmissions spiritual energy would be radiated through a cooperating group of members in the hall called a 'block'. He said:

"These operations were to put energy into the mind belt and to certain places...and these energies would be broadcast...I suppose they felt different to different people. To me they created an almost unbearable increase of tension...it was a pressure which was created deliberately...a level of a flow of energy through your subtle and physical nervous systems, and possibly circulatory and muscular systems, but the body was not used to it and the mind was not used to it."

But the most powerful by far of those sending this energy out to the world were not the humans involved but the cosmic and ascended masters who were used as channels. And the most important type of Special Power Transmission, referred to as 'Operation One One One', was not for the benefit of humanity but for the Mother Earth Herself.

Dr. King's move to Aetherius House in the Fulham Road put his function as Primary Terrestrial Mental Channel on an increasingly military-style footing. On October 11th, 1958, Mars Sector 8 said of this new location:

As this place will be a centre of very great importance, the organizers of The Aetherius Society will, in future, be prepared for a transmission at any time with only a few minutes' notice. If the operation we are now contemplating is to be really successful, this will need the cooperation of all. In future there will be no mistakes, no omissions...It will be essential in the future to prepare for emergency transmissions in less than 120 seconds; suggest continued practise until you can do this. We

> have been invited to use this place and this organization as a central transmitting station. We will do this, but if this operation is to be successful, then those people who have specific tasks to perform must do these correctly.

Tom Curtis commented on this directive:

"Indeed that did take place because Aetherius House was then operative. It virtually constituted a power centre; this was a facility to them; they took and made good use of it.

"In this respect they decided to institute a series of Special Power Transmissions, which would be given at very short notice – in fact 120 seconds' readiness. Because of this it meant that all people that cooperated at Aetherius House had to be trained to take care of this situation in their various capacities...

"Dr. King would get a 'pip', as he called it, which meant that it was imminent and he would, wherever he was situated, get up and sound the alarm system by just pushing a button. That's all he had to do and, when everyone heard this alarm go, they went to their pre-arranged positions to do their particular task...The very loud factory-like hooter would come on, which reverberated all through Aetherius House and, if one were asleep at the time, it would certainly wake one up...

"The whole procedure was worked out and we did successfully cooperate with several power transmissions at very short notice."

When he moved to America, this procedure continued as Charles Abrahamson described:

"Sometimes it would be 'transmission stations' and you had 120 seconds. He had 120 seconds to put his knife and fork down if we were in the middle of dinner, and by the time he got to the Transmission Room and behind his microphones and we had got to the tape recorders, that 120 seconds was gone. And he took a few deep breaths, he had a mantra[9] which he used to repeat out loud...and he had his orange juice and olive oil...What we heard as we got the recorders on...would be a sudden catch of breath and a sound as though he had swallowed and then within seconds, you would hear [the communicating intelligence]."

Dr. King was training his closest followers to operate not so much as devotees of old but as a spiritual commando force. This pattern would continue into the future when he would establish a mainly voluntary staff team around him. But demanding as this was for some of his disciples over the years, it was absolutely nothing compared to the strain he bore throughout his multi-faceted mission, and it certainly took its toll on him.

*   *   *   *

It cannot be stressed strongly enough just how debilitating and at times dangerous was the trance condition he adopted. As he wrote in *The Aetherius Society Newsletter*, August/September 1976:

> I am paralyzed during every transmission taken. After some of them I have had to be carried because I was not capable of walking two or three feet from the transmission chair to a bed in the same small room.
>
> I have had to have oxygen equipment to treat me and healing for some time before I was even capable of walking again.
>
> Anyone who treats their body like that and gets away with it is either a very fortunate man or a very knowledgeable one.

Another difficulty in the trance conditions Dr. King adopted related to the amount and quality of the spiritual energy sent through him. He at times had to make a special point of lowering his vibrations afterwards. He explained this in relation to one of the public transmissions by the Master Jesus titled 'The One Who Came In Grace' given in Caxton Hall, London, on September 14th, 1957:

> After nearly one and a half hours of exposure to the tremendous power radiated through me by the cosmic masters during these transmissions, it was necessary for me to practise certain yogic exercises which are specially designed to bring the pranic flow to a more normal level. After all, human cellular structure will only

stand a certain amount, even of the highest powers, before it develops a chain of physiological change, the results of which are a transmutation of matter. As wonderful as this condition undoubtedly is, my work in a dense physical body is not yet complete. Therefore, cooperation with known laws brings about a more lasting result than any attempt to try to force one's way from one realm to another, until the right time! Hence the necessity for the "de-tuning" or balancing procedure to be adopted after such a long period of acting as a radiator for the holy powers of the great ones.

Ray Nielsen, who was a new young member at the time, recalled his first experience of attending a cosmic transmission, in this case delivered by Saint Goo-Ling at Aetherius House on July 22nd, 1961:

"The hall in Aetherius House is quite small and it was packed. In those days there were small wooden chairs, and to get everybody in we were fairly near to the table behind which Dr. King was seated...the table was set...he would have a glass of orange juice and olive oil, which he would use to lubricate his voice box, his throat. And everybody was told to be very, very quiet and not to make any noises because the microphone would pick up this type of thing.

"Dr. King came down and he sat in the chair directly opposite me and he just straightened his back. The lights were fairly dim and he put on his dark glasses, took a sip of the orange juice and olive oil and started to breathe. This was the first experience that I had ever seen like this; as he breathed he became larger and larger and larger. Then I looked at his hands and he started to use various mudras[10]. After about two minutes of using various mudras his whole body shook and his face went into an expression of sheer agony and pain. It was all kind of screwed up and tense.

"Then Saint Goo-Ling came through and he said, something like: not possible to go into trance that quickly. That was the first sentence, and I might tell you the silence in that room was deafening. I was petrified, I was absolutely blown away, I mean I have never ever experienced anything like this...there was the master in trance and Saint Goo-Ling began his speech…

"After the trance condition he slumped forwards and Keith Robertson [his main assistant at the time] brought a little screen made out of cardboard that was placed in front of Dr. King so that you couldn't see him in the first stages of his recovery. Then after his recovery, when he was composed, he got to his feet and then he slowly moved back down the hall."

When he came to America, he was helped after each transmission, and sometimes before, by his leading female disciple, and later wife, Monique Noppe. Often she was the only person in the room when he received a cosmic transmission, and afterwards she would give him massage and healing. She was even commended by the Master Aetherius during a cosmic transmission on September 8th, 1962, for the healing she had given him prior to a Special Power Transmission. He said:

> To the early hours of this morning this girl worked very hard healing, comforting and attending your leader in the most professional and help-worthy manner. I would like to remind you all of this, because the success, to some extent, of the transmission today was dependent upon her efforts! She was sick herself during these healing administrations, but she did not leave her post until she was ordered to by your leader.

On at least two occasions Dr. King received cosmic transmissions on live television broadcasts. One of these was a programme called 'Lifeline' for the BBC on May 21st, 1959. During this programme the host was able to interview the Master Aetherius, who gave a very simple and succinct message of why they were communicating to Earth at this time. The following is an extract:

Questioner: When you come here, what is your purpose?

Master Aetherius: At the moment, Earth as you call it, faces a certain situation. This situation can be described as rather a dangerous one. You are liable to upset the balance of your Earth through number one, atomic experimentation and number two, your deviation from the spiritual laws.

Questioner: Are your visits designed to warn us against this?

Master Aetherius: Yes.

This short transmission, seen live by millions and many more in the years that followed, explained the core problem for Earth then – and now.

The other programme was the Tom Duggan Show on a TV station in Los Angeles on July 19th, 1960. Dr. King announced to attenders at a lecture soon after:

Dr. King being interviewed on the Tom Duggan Show.

History was made in America. As you know, the people from other planets have never spoken in that way over television in America before...so I was the first to do it in England and now the first to do it in America.

Dr. King gives a spiritual dissertation to an exclusive audience at the prestigious Hotel Bel-Air in California in 1959.

There was a significant interchange following the transmission by the Master Aetherius when Tom Duggan queried whether Dr. King had heard what this master had said. Dr. King responded, no. This was to guarantee accuracy – he could not possibly modify the energy beam he was receiving from the Master Aetherius with his own thoughts because he was not consciously aware of it.

Never before has there been such an audio record of interplanetary masters speaking to the people of Earth, comprising over 600 cosmic transmissions. The exact number he received is unknown because some of the early tapes in London were, unbeknown to Dr. King, either lost or erased by his assistants at the time. Extraordinary as this may seem to us now, it does serve to illustrate the lack of appreciation among even some of his close followers in those days. Thankfully we believe that this only applies to a small number of these priceless gems.

He could have done this in another way – one that would have been much easier and safer for him – namely, by only taking mental transmissions. In this case he would not be in a trance condition but would either write down the thought impulses he received or record them on tape. And at times during this period he did this in outside locations or in another unusual situation. He gave one example of the latter in a lecture in San Francisco when he described the communication he had received from a Martian intelligence, Zeme 85 Co-Efficient, on February 14th, 1957, at The Drive Mansions:

> I was in a flat, together with some more people. I said to them, "leave this room", and they went out. Now this flat had been burgled several times because one or two bright people in London wanted to get hold of my tape recordings. So, in order to frustrate their attempts – in a very amateurish way of course – we put a bolt at the top of a door, a bolt at the bottom of a door, a chain on the door, a mortice lock and a yale lock. All these bolts were drawn and yet the people in the flat heard that door open, heard the squeak of the hinges, it clicked shut. The being from Mars walked in. He said, "You will write". I wrote. He bowed and he walked out – the door opened

with a slight click and closed with a slight click and those bolts were in place. And that person was as physical as anybody here and he was heavier in physical weight than anybody here. And he was bigger than anybody here – almost seven feet in height.

But, for the most part, he endured the gruelling demands of a positive yogic trance condition for humanity, until 1981, after which he received all communications in the form of mental transmissions. Had he not used this form of trance mediumship for over 26 years, we and posterity would have been denied this priceless, unprecedented spiritual archive. As a result we have not only the words of the great ones, but also their energetic expression through sound. He took the mediumistic model he found upon Earth, which was unsound to put it mildly, and transmuted it into something truly magnificent. He was the master who changed mediumship from séance to science!

*   *   *   *

Why was such a superb instrument sent to Earth, and why now? For the first time in hundreds of thousands of years mankind had discovered the secrets of the atom, as we had in previous civilizations, often referred to as Atlantis and Lemuria. We had again developed weapons capable of destroying our entire culture.

The cosmic masters are limited in how much they can help us, due to the spiritual laws of God governing the universe. They were allowed to communicate through Dr. King, their Primary Terrestrial Mental Channel, strategic thoughts and truths that were crucial in those days and indeed for our future. These truths would go out to the mind belt of Earth and be able to influence the thoughts of those who were ready, including individuals in key positions.

A case in point was the transmission, 'You Are Responsible!', which was transmitted to Earth through Dr. King by Mars Sector 6 on May 7th, 1957, and published in *Cosmic Voice* Issue 11. It was given to inspire people to work to stop this seemingly unstoppable push for more and more atomic testing and more and more countries obtaining nuclear capabilities. The following is an extract:

> We have stated in the past that we have made many approaches to the governments of Terra. Yes we have approached Moscow, as well as Washington, but openly we have been turned down! That is why we now appeal to the ordinary man, for sooner or later ye brothers will rise! When you do, let us hope your protests will not come too late! If ever there was a need for national heroes, that time is now! If ever there was a need for martyrs to suffer for an honourable and just cause, that time is now! Where is the spirit of adventure? Did it die with television programs?
>
> Come on ye men! Rally! You, in this small country of the British Isles, are in a favourable position, for you can show the larger countries the way – the stony way – the way to your own spiritual progress. You can demonstrate, demonstrate, demonstrate your belief in God! You can demonstrate, demonstrate, demonstrate in a most practical way, your love of freedom by living the teachings of that master you revere so much! Even if you believe not in Deity, still can you take part in the great adventure to lead the Earth, as a unit, towards sanity. You can work for goodness, in this case. The men and women of the present generation have a moral and ethical responsibility to God and to the coming generation! If you allow this mad race into the weapons produced by nuclear fissionable matter, you condemn your own children!

Dr. King jumped into the anti-nuclear testing campaign with both feet. He used his journal *Cosmic Voice* to spread the transmissions of the cosmic masters. He also reported on detailed activity in the nuclear protest field, and made suggestions to his readers of why and how they can help in this dire struggle to end nuclear bomb testing. This pushed Dr. King, who was by nature a shy man, into a very public forum. Yet he knew its importance and that he was a key agent on Earth at a vital time.

He sent the recording of 'You Are Responsible!' to the Duke of Edinburgh, consort of the Queen of England, all the Members of Parliament, hundreds of world leaders and to the press world-wide. As a result he was on many radio and TV programs, and extracts from it appeared in numerous magazines and newspapers around the world.

Dr. King's efforts in spreading this truth, combined with the power of the cosmic masters, impressed the minds of open-mind-ed scientists with a profound effect. On May 15th, just days after 'You Are Responsible!' was given, Linus Pauling, an American scientist who had won the Nobel Prize for chemistry in 1954 and 1962, gave a speech at the prestigious Washington University in St. Louis, Missouri, urging the end of nuclear testing. The response was so positive that after dinner that night, he and another professor put together a petition from scientists supporting this cause.

Over the course of the next eight months, over 9,000 scientists in many countries signed this petition. It was presented to the United Nations on January 15th, 1958. This grass roots movement had gained a momentum that could not be stopped. After the expected ups and downs of the high-stakes, international politics – including a few self-imposed moratoriums on testing – the politicians finally signed the Partial Test Ban Treaty which went into effect on October 10th, 1963. Since then, 123 countries have become party to the treaty.

*   *   *   *

The crowning transmission in its importance to our world, occurred in Los Angeles on July 8th, 1964, between 10:00 p.m. and 10:57 p.m., namely the Primary Initiation of Earth. Charles Abrahamson recalled that, although Dr. King was expecting this event to come at some time, he did not know beforehand that it would be then. After receiving it and taking a very short rest, he went to see Charles who was still in the recording room and who vividly remembered it:

"He came down and he said 'Monique told me something about this transmission…she said that it might have been the Initiation of Earth.' And I said, 'Oh yes, it was all right!' So he said, 'I've got to hear that right now'. So we set up one of the original tapes and played it back for him to listen to, which was extremely unusual since he almost always left time for a copy to be made. He listened to one of the originals – that was how urgent it was to him."

This cosmic transmission is published in full in the book, *The Day The Gods Came*, which Dr. King regarded as the most significant of his or any other authors' books ever written upon Earth. Because of this, and the degree of appreciation which should be given to its contents, he later determined with the full authority of the Master Aetherius, that it should only be available to members of The Aetherius Society. The tape-recorded transmission, which is played annually to members, is a formidable demonstration of his sheer prowess as the voice of the cosmic masters. During one revealing exchange, Mars Sector 6 requested a report from one of his cosmic associates of the mental capacity of Mental Channel Number One. The one-word answer he received from this all-seeing source, could be applied to the totality of Dr. King's trance mediumship and the vast untrammelled regions of the wisdom it brought to Earth: **Pluperfect**.

On July 21st, 1964, Mars Sector 6 stated:

> **Search as you will throughout the world we refer to as Terra, you will never find greater teachings, more simply given, a greater truth with less distortion than you find in and through Mental Channel Number One.**

Great as some of them undoubtedly are, the spiritual works of the past do not come close to 'The Twelve Blessings' delivered by the Master Jesus, 'The Nine Freedoms' by Mars Sector 6 and teachings by the Master Aetherius and other cosmic masters. These are pure, undiluted truths of the highest calibre which increasing numbers of discerning people around the world are starting to recognize.

However, this statement by Mars Sector 6 is not just referring to wisdom delivered *through* Dr. King as Mental Channel Number One, but very significantly *in* him as well. His own advanced knowledge, combined with an innate understanding of the needs of humanity, was a key factor in his role as Primary Terrestrial Mental Channel. It was known that he would be able to not only receive these transmissions, but also leave in-depth explanations of their inner meanings for posterity. Had he not brought the messages of other intelligences to our world, he would still be in his own right one of the greatest teachers ever to walk our Earth. This is something he did not stress himself, tending to defer to other masters, but it became increasingly clear to his students in his lifetime and especially since. He was not just Mental Channel Number One, he was Number One.

Chapter Four
NUMBER ONE

As the 1950s progressed it became ever clearer that Dr. King's mission was about even more than acting as Primary Terrestrial Mental Channel. As early as March 14th, 1959, Mars Sector 8 had described Dr. King as: **our Primary Agent upon Terra** and stated:

> I would like to say this: your leader was chosen a long time ago for his task. He was approached and volunteered for this task. He has now his instructions. He will go forward.

It was spelt out again on April 21st, 1959, and published in *Cosmic Voice* Issue 21 when Mars Sector 6 described him as: **Primary Terrestrial Mental Channel and our Primary Agent upon the planet Terra.** He was not only the voice of the cosmic masters; he was one of them.

We do not know exactly when the great realization dawned on this apparently terrestrial man that he had come, like the Master Jesus, the Lord Buddha and others before him, from another planet. A significant revelation and prophecy was made on December 23rd, 1956, in a transmission from the interplanetary master, Saint Peter, which was published in *Cosmic Voice* Issue 15:

> When the one called Jesus chose his followers, chose he not haphazardly but did recognize that those followers themselves, had travelled through the skies before him – even though the followers knew naught of this in those days.
>
> But there cometh a day of realization and a day of dawning and the dawn hath come.
>
> Praise be to God on high, for this flash. For this hope. For this expression of love.

There is one among you who shall shortly look into
his heart and there will see what he too has been. Then
will he rise in completeness.

Coming from one who had 'been there', having suffered
the pain and limitation of incarnating upon a backward world,
this statement by Saint Peter gives us a profound insight into the
condition such great ones endure. He explains that he and one or
more of the other disciples had not realized their cosmic origins
when they were first called to follow the Master Jesus. But, as he
put it: **there cometh a day of realization.**

When this 'day of realization' came for Dr. George King has
not been stated or published anywhere on record but, based on
this transmission, it must have been some time after December
23rd, 1956. Undoubtedly Dr. King would have understood
immediately that Saint Peter was referring to him – it certainly was
not anybody else in his circle at that time – so one must assume
that he would have known it, at least intellectually, as soon as
these words were played back to him. The full inner knowledge
of his identity must have come sometime later though; with his
powers of perception as an advanced master, probably not very
much later.

*   *   *   *

A seminal event in this unfolding realization occurred on May
16th, 1958. He vividly described it in *Cosmic Voice* Issue 17 in an
article called 'The Spiritual Nature of Man', though arguably it
would have been more aptly titled 'The Spiritual Nature of Dr.
George King'. These are some extracts from it:

Sometime in the afternoon I was informed that I had to
leave home at 10:30 p.m. to keep a rendezvous on Putney
Common with a being from the planet Mars! It started to
rain earlier that evening and by 10:30 p.m. had become
a veritable downpour. The dimly lighted streets seemed
to be carpeted with a shimmering screen of rushing
waters as I splashed my way – on foot – towards the

rendezvous point. Before I had covered half the distance the persevering raindrops had gained a good measure of success in their campaign of – penetration! Drop after drop gleefully followed one another down my neck and through a gabardine raincoat which now hung limp, like wet blotting paper, as though, in surrender to the forces of nature, the material had taken the only course left open to it – that of inaction! The rubber boots, worn for the first time on this occasion, kept my feet dry – but at what a cost! An ankle, damaged previously, rubbed into anger by a boot, began to throb. Every step became an agony. I plodded on in the knowledge that the way to truth is oft-times painful – but rewarding.

I passed over Putney Bridge and looked in the direction of the common and there, at an elevation of about 60 degrees, was the sign that he would be awaiting my arrival. I saw three bright golden pinpricks of light in the black sky, which formed the outline of a triangle. They remained for about one second then went out. I limped on eagerly and some twenty minutes later approached the point of meeting.

I was directly under the glare of a yellow sodium street lamp when I became aware of a – presence – invisible yet so definite that I could have touched it. A great wave of vibrating power swept through my body. I could feel my spine as an ice-cold rod under the interplay of these forces. I became aware that these vibrations took on a certain pattern. The power, which I could feel the full length of the spine, began to pulsate. Words, more real than those spoken, flashed across my mind. The skin over the forehead tightened as though I wore a band of metal around it.

"I will now enter your consciousness, my son."

The pain went instantly from my ankle. I knew that I was now soaked but could not feel it. I walked slowly on, unaware of the torrential rain – aware only of the pattern of pulsations caressing the whole length of the spine with ice-cold fingers. Of the tightness across the forehead which came as a reaction to these forces and then the translation of these impulses into understandable language. For what must have been in our time, about 35 minutes, the two-way telepathic conversation continued. During this time I asked many leading questions and even before I could put most of them into coherent form, the answers came. I would start to form a mental question – would feel a rapid increase of the pulsations through the spinal column and the answer would be there – simple, definite, profound...

Many revelations were given to me during that walk, which upon later reflection, caused me to gasp in wonder. These – in the main – may not be revealed until the right time. However, one of the most staggering, almost fantastic revelations, I will give to you...

I asked my nameless Martian guru, "Do you on Mars have communication with your etheric realms?"

His answer staggered me, as it will all those readers who are ready to appreciate a revelation of such magnitude as this. For in this answer, dear friends, is a profound truth hidden from modern man until this time. I maintain that here is one of the most important revelations in the annals of all mysticism!

The pulses of energy along my spine became more pronounced. My forehead seemed to shrink under the tight band across it and the shattering answer came.

"My son, we live in our etheric realms at the same time as we inhabit the physical aspect of our planet."

The wise one told me that every person on Mars is fully aware of his etheric counterpart, which lives in the subtle realms [Spirit World]. The etheric dweller is called – ASPECT NUMBER 1. This ASPECT NUMBER 1 is joined in spiritual union with its twin soul or opposite balancing counterpart. This perfectly balanced pair have their secondary aspects, ASPECT NUMBER 2, which – as twin souls – live in physical bodies, beneath the surface of the planet Mars. When a Martian visits Earth for a short time, the pair of twin souls bring into being

ASPECT NUMBER 3 – male and female. Sometimes this is manifested as a single entity, containing the positive/negative poles or sometimes two separate entities, male and female, are formed. This decision is made when a full knowledge of the purpose of the visit has been ascertained.

I was further told that if it is necessary for a Martian to take permanent or semi-permanent residence upon Earth, another body is formed, referred to as ASPECT NUMBER 4. As with ASPECT NUMBER 3, this also could be two separate intelligences – male and female – or one intelligence, which was male and female, energetically balanced in such a way as to enable it to perform a specified psycho-spiritual function[1]. Sometimes this ASPECT NUMBER 4 – either as two separate entities or a single one – is introduced into the cycle of terrestrial life, for one or more incarnations.

Although the twin souls forming ASPECT NUMBER 3 have a full realization of their higher counterparts, often the lower ASPECT NUMBER 4 has but dim knowledge that he or she is part of a greater whole, although this awareness is now gradually dawning on these beings.

* * * *

This was not the first time Dr. King had experienced a contact with this Martian intelligence and it would not be the last. On each occasion he had similar internal reactions, as precisely described here by Dr. King, accompanied by a statement to the effect that this intelligence would attach itself to his consciousness. These were interesting words with a different implication from the other cosmic masters who communicated through him. It is as though this particular intelligence was becoming one with him for the duration of the experience.

Dr. King would sometimes refer to this Martian intelligence as his master, but it was later revealed that his master was in fact the Master Aetherius. One possible reason for this could be that the Martian intelligence was a higher aspect of himself joining up with him in order to direct him in his mission. In this instance, it would have been connecting with its fourth aspect in order to explain to it the nature of its existence. Maybe because Dr. King would not reveal his interplanetary origin, he described this Martian intelligence as his master rather than as a higher aspect of himself.

On October 24th, 1962, Dr. King gave an in-depth explanation of this experience in his classic lecture entitled 'The Four Aspects of Creation'. He said:

> If it is necessary for some reason or other for a Martian to be introduced into the cycle of life on Earth, then the fourth aspect is divided off and this is introduced into a terrestrial body.

On the face of it this lecture is a highly metaphysical, somewhat cerebral discourse about a very esoteric topic. But when you realize he was talking about his own life, it becomes very moving and takes on a whole new level of meaning. In this respect it is rather like certain alchemical texts which mean one thing to an ordinary reader but far more to a mystic who is 'in the know'. Interpreting this revelation of the four aspects of creation as being given by a prominent Martian intelligence to its own lower aspect, separated from itself with all the poignancy that suggests, gives flesh to it.

Despite this information probably being given to him in the dawning awareness of his true being, his selfless nature was such that he chose to share this teaching as widely as possible. He did it though in such a way as not to disclose his identity, and he emphasized that it had never been given to Earth before. As he said in his lecture:

> Nobody has ever come near this secret. Although people have spent years in research into the subject of the true nature of the people from outer space, they had not begun to come near to it until May 16th, 1958, when this information was first, first, first committed to paper. It was actually in the early morning hours of May 17th.

You cannot understand Dr. George King fully until you recognize him as a fourth aspect interplanetary intelligence. This explains his completely alien approach to human existence – one that was driven by the passionate desire to serve for 24 hours a day, without a thought for himself, and with a spiritual brilliance that is in a different league from any terrestrial genius or even master. It also explains the psychological pressures he was under, and the sense of total isolation he felt at times.

The Master Jesus expressed this beautifully in his heart-rending Blessing for the planetary ones – fourth aspect intelligences. After all he knew about it from his own tragic personal experience. In it he said:

> These are the ones who have left their homes – their spiritual homes – who have left their brothers – their spiritual brothers – in order to watch over you. These are the ones who, day by day, suffer the unspeakable hell of terrible aloneness, in order to give you their hearts. These are the ones who suffer, day by day, in a thousand psychological ways, so that – the dark little Earth may make its revolutions through evolution.
> (*The Twelve Blessings*)

In the light of these words Dr. King's lecture on the four aspects of creation, takes on an emotional resonance as in the following extract:

> You imagine a Martian intelligence running anything on this Earth like it does on Mars. Everything around would be burned out because it would not be able to stand the full impact of this type of concentration – this urge...So it is tuned right the way down as far as it can be tuned down and yet it is there. It's a higher consciousness than any on Earth. It can be used, information can be fed through it and so on.

The necessity to be, as Dr. King put it: **tuned right the way down as far as it can be tuned down**, was a source of excruciating frustration to him. Perhaps it is one reason he went out of his way to conceal his true identity wherever he could. He would adopt human traits and modes of behaviour as the years went by which enabled him to blend in and relate to those around him as far as possible.

He must have been talking about himself when he continued:

> There was an aspect number four Martian in a certain place and this aspect number four realized its Martian connections but, of course, tried to keep them secret. A direct physical contact to a relative of this aspect number four gave this relative the greatest shock of their life when they were told that so-and-so comes from the planet Mars.

The relative in question must have been his mother, Mary King. In more than one of her physical contacts, the true identity of her son was made known to her.

He continued with some words which could only have been spoken by someone who had experienced it:

> Gradually when this awareness has to dawn on aspect number four of its true spiritual nature, then this awareness dawns directly to that person in one of many ways. Maybe by a physical contact, maybe by other ways, but it will dawn on them in a very, very definite manner and they will not declare this fact. But sometimes it is very difficult for them to keep this identity closed. Some people with great awareness can recognize it even though the aspect number four might put on an act to try and cover it up. So the awareness dawns when it has to dawn so that it can go forward and do its particular job, its particular mission on Earth whatever it might be.

* * * *

This dawning awareness was accompanied by a brand new mission, Operation Starlight, in which Dr. King was directed to climb 18 mountains around the world so that they could be charged with spiritual power by the cosmic masters. Nine of these mountains were in Britain, starting with Holdstone Down in North Devon which was charged by the Master Jesus on July 23rd, 1958. Some three months later Saint Goo-Ling confirmed that a highly significant offer had been made to Dr. King, which he explained in a transmission on November 8th:

> Now few days ago did offer to your leader special operation. He has considered this for past few days, and has decided to accept personal responsibility for the execution of this very vital operation. Thousands of years ago the adepts upon Earth knew the secrets of charging the mountain tops by the invocation of great power. This ancient science is now to be re-introduced to present age through your leader adept. The July 23rd operation proved to us, beyond all doubt, that he was capable of doing this, indeed did do it very successfully. This particular operation, upon which you will now embark, will necessitate much trouble, both in Britain and other countries.

Dr. King accepted this mission. With his growing awareness of who he was, he realized that as he was their primary agent on Earth and was responsible for the success of his mission he felt enabled to request changes, even from the cosmic masters, if he felt they would help ensure success. This can be seen from the following transmission from Mars Sector 6 delivered in the autumn (fall) of 1958:

> We are prepared to grant the request of Mental Channel Number One when he asks for an extension of his time in the terrestrial country of Britain. As you know, you were informed at the beginning of this present year that the presence of our agent would be needed in the Americas before its close. However, we have taken into consideration his request and have granted it.
>
> In the meantime, we have imposed Operation

Starlight upon our agent. This operation will be, in certain phases, strictly secret. The Aetherius Society will be given certain information regarding this operation as it continues. We will leave this to the discretion of our agent upon Terra. Operation Starlight has already successfully passed through its first phase and will shortly enter its second phase.

The other mountains charged in the British Isles were: Brown Willy in Cornwall; Ben Hope in the Scottish Highlands; Creag an Leth-choin in the Cairngorms; The Old Man of Coniston in Cumbria; Pen y Fan in the Brecon Beacons, South Wales; Carnedd Llywelyn in Snowdonia, North Wales; Kinder Scout in the Derbyshire Peak District; and Yes Tor in South Devon. His request to delay his scheduled journey to the United States had paid off in that the last four of these were charged in early 1959.

On each mountain it was necessary for Dr. King to climb to a particular place, which became the 'charged spot', where he would enter an elevated state of consciousness. This enabled a charge to be put in the mountain by one or more cosmic intelligences. Pilgrimages would then take place to these now holy mountains

Dr. King during Operation Starlight on Carnedd Llywelyn in North Wales.

– and still do regularly to this day – during which pilgrims could tap into the inexhaustible supply of spiritual power within them. This is sent out for the healing, upliftment and peace of the world as a whole.

The Master Aetherius gave a foreshadowing as to how important Operation Starlight would be on March 14th, 1959:

> **In this Aquarian Age, as you call it, the practice of The Twelve Blessings upon the charged mountains and hills, is the most potent practice you could perform. This is the new yoga of this present age.**

He also stated that this practice had been given 52 years early which implies that either 'The Twelve Blessings' or Operation Starlight or both would not have happened when they did had Dr. King not been available to the cosmic masters. Perhaps Dr. King took the karma to enable the charging of these mountains to take place earlier than originally planned. This meant not only that more power could be sent out to the world sooner, but also that they were available to him to interweave into his karmic magic as would become evident later.

A highlight of these early phases occurred on Brown Willy on November 23rd, 1958, when a Lord of Karma delivered what became known as 'The Lord's Declaration'. It was already an aim of the Society to prepare the way for the coming of the Next Master, but this declaration spelt out how it would occur. It was not delivered as a transmission but by a great and audible voice which Dr. King compared to the voice that delivered the Ten Commandments to Moses on Mount Sinai thousands of years before. The Lord made it clear that the Next Master will come openly and with full powers, doing whatever is necessary to prove to Earth leaders his credentials. As published in *Cosmic Voice* Issue 19, he stated:

> **There will shortly come another among you. He will stand tall among men with a shining countenance. This one will be attired in a single garment of the type now known to you. His shoes will be soft-topped, yet not made of the**

skin of animals.

He will approach the Earth leaders. They will ask of him, his credentials. He will produce these. His magic will be greater than any upon the Earth – greater than the combined materialistic might of all the armies. And they who heed not his words, shall be removed from the Earth.

This Rock is now holy – and will remain so for as long as the world exists.

Go ye forth and spread my word throughout the world, so that all men of pure heart may prepare for his coming.

This coming will signal the final sorting of 'the wheat from the chaff' as prophesied throughout the ages, and only those ready to act accordingly will remain upon this planet. This is not

Dr. King on Brown Willy in Cornwall, the mountain on which 'The Lord's Declaration' was delivered to him by a Lord of Karma.

to punish those who do not, but because they simply will not be able to adjust to the immense spiritual and physical changes to come. Instead they will continue to gain experience upon a planet in this solar system – as yet undiscovered – with conditions more conducive to their evolution.

For Dr. King, Operation Starlight was as gruelling and demanding, as it was momentous. With limited resources, and very small, ill-equipped teams to support him, he climbed the mountains as designated to him by the great ones. In fact he went above and beyond their expectations by speeding through the first phases in Britain. As the Master Aetherius put it on December 14th:

> My dear friends, now I have but few words to say to you this evening regarding the last and next phase of this present most vital operation. First of all, I would like to congratulate you all on the way you performed phase number three and it is worthy of mention too, that because you threw the whole of your energy into that particular operation, we were able to speed it up a little, so to speak. This was very good.

And he added four days later:

> I would like you Operation Starlight organizers to discuss ways and means among yourselves, and to be ready to carry on the next "leg" – usual inverted commas there of course – of this operation as soon as possible. You decided to speed it up you know. So therefore, you have made your bed, without a mattress, so therefore, my bonny lads, you must lie on it!

By pushing through these early phases Dr. King was able to manipulate even more karma for mankind under the most arduous of conditions. For example, he climbed the third mountain, Ben Hope, with a severe injury to his hip, in bitter cold, through deep snow on December 10th, 1958. Only four days later he was on Creag an Leth-choin, still in pain from his hip, having spent the previous night in a small hut trying to keep some semblance of warmth in his chilled body. Dr. King knew the karmic price which had to be paid on behalf of mankind as a whole for the successful performance of such a mission, and he was willing to pay it.

Many years later, upon the advice of the Master Aetherius, Dr. King revealed that Kinder Scout had been charged by himself, and that he accomplished this with the guidance and assistance of the Master Aetherius. For someone in an ordinary Earth physical body to accomplish such a feat was extraordinary, to say the least. As usual, he kept it hidden until his latter days when it was deemed necessary to complete the record of which master charged which mountain.

The ninth of these mountains, Yes Tor, was successfully charged on February 25th, 1959. The British aspect of Operation Starlight was completed in just over seven months despite – and from a karmic perspective because of – the agonising hardships which were endured. During an address at the Society's third Annual General Meeting, on March 14th, 1959, Dr. King made this remarkable statement about a message he received about Operation Starlight:

> I asked again "what shall we say to the unbelievers?" I was given this answer which absolutely staggered me – so much so, by the way, that I was quite ill afterwards. The voice said: "Ask them if they have ever created a world and when they say 'no' say that which spoke to you created this Earth." That should give you a little idea of the great importance of this Operation Starlight, which we have just concluded in England.

This probably referred to the Lord of Karma who spoke to him on Brown Willy[2].

Dr. King's cosmic identity was becoming increasingly known among those around him. A file from this period which was titled, 'Special Directives, Instructions and Reports for the London Committee', is open and candid. It was dated 'early 1959'; its subject was marked as 'General (confidential)'; and the communicator was named as Saint Goo-Ling. There is no audio record of this transmission, which must have been a series of directives given by Saint Goo-Ling to the Committee at the time, but there are some notes. These cover a variety of issues and projects including the addition of a seventh aim and object of the Society as the performance of Operation Starlight.

The notes which leap off the page as being the most relevant to his identity, are as follows:

- George King came from Mars – volunteered for his mission 100 years ago
- He has had no previous terrestrial incarnations
- Has considerable cosmic status
- Soon in C.V. everyone will see reference to Martian individual

C.V. stands for the journal *Cosmic Voice* but there was no reference to Dr. King being a Martian individual in any subsequent issue. There is an obvious reason for this – he was the editor. He chose, seemingly in contrast to statements made through him by the masters, to hide who he really was as far as he possibly could.

*   *   *   *

On April 11th, 1959, something happened, which would make it very difficult for him to remain undercover. It occurred on one of the holy mountains which had recently been charged in Operation Starlight, Carnedd Llywelyn. Some 20 years later he spoke these words during an address at Aetherius House in London, which were published in *The Aetherius Society Newsletter*, October 1979:

> Carnedd Llywelyn is also very dear to my heart in that I **was physically killed** on that mountain on April 11th, 1959, in a battle to the death! I mean **killed**, I mean **dead** in a battle to the death with the black magician who arranged the murder of Jesus. That was in the early days when I was still a relatively young lad; if not young in mind, younger in body than I am today. The Master Aetherius gave a running commentary of this terrible battle which

gave me excruciating pain: **the type of pain which none of you have ever suffered because you could not suffer that type of pain and live!**

I had the choice then whether to remain on Earth or whether to leave it. I decided to remain on Earth and the Master Aetherius himself joined the cord between life and death, so I regard my life, since that time, as borrowed time.

This could be taken as the date from which the combat mission for which he came to Earth commenced, namely the transmutation of the most dangerous forces of evil upon Earth. And it started with the defeat of the foul entity who had been responsible for whipping up the ignorant mob who called for the crucifixion of the Master Jesus. During this conflict Dr. King technically died but, with the help of the Master Aetherius, he was returned to life again.

The whole battle was described in vivid detail by the Master Aetherius through him in the presence of a number of attenders, who were shocked to their very core by this completely unexpected and traumatic experience. Tom Curtis, who had been on the team for the charge of this mountain earlier that year, described later how he felt as the person who recorded this transmission:

"Up until this time we had been cooperating with the Special Power Transmissions and, on this occasion, we settled down to what we thought was another of these power transmissions. But it didn't turn out to be exactly that. Without going into detail, which I cannot do, Dr. King left the physical body and projected to the Carnedd Llywelyn area, and then ensued something which to me was absolutely fantastic. Something! An experience which I will never forget, although I cannot recall it now in exact detail. It really left one speechless in the finish you know. One was lost for words, rather like I am now, actually…

"Had they not put a beam on Dr. King, or the physical body anyway, it would then be thrashing about all over the place because he was virtually dead…

"The whole thing came as quite a shock, I must tell you that, because it was totally unexpected."

Another attender was Hazel Moody, who had been a member for only a few months, but would soon start a very important branch of The Aetherius Society in Barnsley in northern England. She recalled:

"When we entered the transmission room there was already an atmosphere of very tense energy. Dr. King was sitting in his usual chair behind the table with its microphones, and after donning his dark glasses went into a trance condition…

"After a gruelling battle that lasted about an hour, followed by a short power transmission, Dr. King slumped forward in his chair. Helpers ran to his aid, or he would have fallen to the floor, and carried him out. His body was soaked in perspiration, including the clothes he was wearing. We were told to sit and remain quiet while they worked on reviving him."

One of his aides on this occasion was Keith Robertson who later remembered:

"Agreeing to return, enabled space intelligences to carry out the necessary healing to mend this lesion [the cord between life and death] – thus causing 'resurrection'. However, injuries caused to the etheric structure could not be healed before it had produced its effects upon the carbon-based structure. The injury to his physical body was subtle enough to be noticed only by those who knew him before this particular engagement."

It is as though Dr. King had to conclude an aspect of the mission of the Master Jesus while simultaneously commencing his own. Perhaps he had to die and virtually resurrect in this battle in order to transmute the very entity which had caused the physical death of the Master Jesus followed by his glorious resurrection.

Now Dr. King had demonstrated who he really was and what he was born to do, but a pattern was emerging. The cosmic masters would allude to Dr. King's cosmic origins, and he would try to hush them up. On April 21st, Saint Goo-Ling delivered what was introduced by Mars Sector 6 as:

The commendation from the Great White Brotherhood for the operation successfully brought to a conclusion but a short time ago.

Saint Goo-Ling stated:

> Sir, you have done well. Your choice was good. Your
> actions were framed in accordance with this choice, and
> wisdom used in this manner did prevail. The Earth owes
> to you a great debt. It will not repay this for some time,
> but look ye towards the face of that which speaks in the
> tongue of resonance, and you will learn of your nobility.
>
> Be prepared to work in this most exacting of all
> ways, for you are one of the few capable of such a
> gigantic task. Karma lies balanced in this extent and you
> will see this and gather your force accordingly, for it is
> known within our centre that you are prepared.

Dr. King did not wish to publish this but he did so at the
behest of Saint Goo-Ling himself. However, he played it down in
his introduction by saying that it was given to him: **In recognition
of his tireless work and individual devotion to duty in the
service of the cosmic masters for and on behalf of the peoples
of Earth.** But the real reason must have been the battle on Carnedd
Llywelyn. Combat with the dark forces was the "most exacting of
all ways" referred to by Saint Goo-Ling; and the "gigantic task"
would be the transmutation of centres of evil upon Earth.

After this commendation from Saint Goo-Ling, the Master
Jesus spoke and he too made an explicit acknowledgement of Dr.
King's interplanetary status. He said:

> Even in the midst of your trial, you too will be filled with
> the light of God and you will be elevated by this mighty
> flame. This will make you choose to go forward among
> the strangers – alone yet never lonely. My son, you are
> now one of us and we now declare this to all men.

Against his wishes Dr. King did publish this unequivocal
statement about himself, but he avoided making the claim in
public wherever possible.

*   *   *   *

He was a spiritual warrior and he had come into his own, but more was to be revealed about his mission as a cosmic adept and it would come soon. On the last page of *Cosmic Voice* Issue 20 under the heading 'Stop Press News', the following announcement was made:

"Attention all Cooperators

"At a special power circle[3] at Aetherius House on Sunday, 17th May, the Master Aetherius, in a stirring appeal for spiritual cooperation, informed mankind that there were three specially trained Adepts upon Earth whose mission it was to transmute the black magicians who manipulate the evil forces upon Earth. If these Three Adepts were taken from Earth for any reason, then humanity had no hope of survival.
        "Aetherius went on to say that because of this move on the part of the White Brotherhood to transmute evil it was essential for all spiritual workers to radiate an unconditioned spiritual energy into the subtle realms of Earth.
        "This great release of power could then be used by the Three Adepts in their coming conflict.
        "Cooperators should, as often as possible, visualize a white light leaving their heart centres out into the Earth.
        "This procedure will help the Three Adepts in the mission to save Earth."

Once again Dr. King as editor withheld his own identity as one of these three. Yet in this transmission, which he never published, the Master Aetherius had disclosed it beyond doubt to the attenders present:

You have been used in a certain way this morning so that spiritual power, as you call it, may be radiated outwards into your Earth. This power radiated outwards in an unconditional manner will be used by certain terrestrial, or apparently terrestrial, Adepts in the next great phase

which is soon due to start – indeed for one prominent
Adept has already started, but will start for the rest in the
very near future...

The prominent Adept was Dr. George King himself and the
next great phase, namely the transmutation of evil forces upon
Earth, had already started on Carnedd Llywelyn. When decades
later full details were given about which cosmic or ascended
masters had charged which holy mountains, another dimension
to the all-perfect plan emerged. For Carnedd Llywelyn was
charged on January 9th, 1959, by none other than himself as
Adept Number One[4] in full aspect.

The Master Aetherius continued:

It is vitally essential that the Adepts who do this task,
and there are but three upon Terra capable of such a
task – the main one as far as ordinary man is concerned
is the person you call King – it is vitally essential that
these people be given power radiated outwards in a very
unconditional manner. So that they may draw upon the
reserve of this power to help them in their battles, and I
mean battles, which are to come.

This is indeed the greatest service of all. It is the
unsung service, for few will ever hear what these ones, or
these three, will do. I can tell you now that if these three
were suddenly taken from Terra then terrestrial man has
no hope of survival.

In the light of this, the meaning of Saint Goo-Ling's statement
on April 21st that Dr. King will gather his "force accordingly",
becomes clear. It must have been a reference to him joining up
with the other two Adepts.

On May 30th, Mars Sector 6 reinforced and amplified this
announcement in a transmission delivered to a packed hall at
Aetherius House entitled 'The Plan'. He said:

These Adepts are among you this night. Some work in
silence. Others, obeying their orders to the letter, work

more openly. These Adepts have taken the limitation of a
terrestrial body so that you terrestrials may see that you
too can tap the source of wisdom within, as these can do.
   Among these Adepts are three who are specially
trained to deal with centres of black magic now being
practised upon your lower realms. One of these Adepts,
as you already know, you know!

If there were such a thing as cosmic nonchalance, the last
sentence of this excerpt would have captured it. It is as though
this orator of divine proclamations took it as read that everyone
present would know that Dr. King was one of these Three Adepts.
It came just days before Dr. King was to start a new chapter of his
mission by travelling to the United States of America. The open
declaration of his role as one of the Three Adepts coincided with
his move to the country that would become his home base for the
rest of his life.

*   *   *   *

On a cold, damp foggy night, last winter, I was given the
direct instructions to visit America. The being from Mars
who gave me this command seemed to enshroud me
with his dynamic presence as he issued these precise
orders.
   "You will present yourself in the Americas. You will
give our true message to the people there. You will not go
so much as a converter, but merely to state our true case
as you know it. Operation Starlight will be extended to
these countries."
   Although I did not see how, from a financial point of
view anyway, such a long journey was possible, I made
up my mind quite firmly to carry out the orders of this
great cosmic adept.

Dr. King published these words in *Cosmic Voice* Issue 21.
They may refer to a contact which took place on Putney Common
at midnight on January 18th, 1959, with a Martian intelligence

who was described as a member of the Supreme Council. Could this be the one who had instructed him on the four aspects of creation in the same location?

On this dark, wet night Dr. King was informed by this cosmic adept that Operation Starlight would be extended beyond the British Isles and that he must be prepared to travel. And so it was that on June 6th Dr. King, accompanied by Keith Robertson, left England from the Royal Albert Docks on a freighter bound for New York called the *American Banker*. Keith described their journey:

"As the *American Banker* left its mooring, I was ecstatic with a feeling of adventure that only a young person can experience… After stopping off at Le Havre for a few hours, the little ship continued its 10-day journey across the vast expanse of the Atlantic. This was indeed a slow boat to the USA…It seemed the longest 10 days I ever spent. Then one day the New York

Dr. King on board the *American Banker* in 1959, headed for the USA as directed by the cosmic masters.

skyline appeared on the horizon and seagulls flew around us in ever-increasing numbers with their mournful cries of communication. New York!...The little ship had docked late. On the quay stood an Aetherius Society member waiting to rush Dr. King to The Philosophical Research Centre[5]. On the lecture platform he was electrifying from the start. I was always besieged by a sea of hands wanting literature!"

Dr. King explained:

> From that moment on, it was "go, go, go." Both myself and Keith Robertson were soon on our way across this vast country. I addressed audiences in Philadelphia, Franklin, Toledo, Kansas City, Chicago, Oklahoma City and then the great convention run by The Amalgamated Flying Saucer Clubs of America, in the luxurious surroundings of the Statler Hilton Hotel in Los Angeles.

It was at this convention that Dr. King would meet the twins, Monique and Erain Noppe, who would become two of his foremost disciples as well as later his wife and sister-in-law. In a conversation with Richard Lawrence in 2017 just months before her passing, Monique recalled meeting Dr. King for the first time at this convention.

Monique: As soon as I saw him I knew he was a very special guru or master.

Richard: Was that from his eyes or generally a feeling?

Monique: It just happened! And I think he said: "Ah, you've come."

Richard: Oh really, like he was waiting for you?

Monique: Obviously he recognized – whether that was especially for us or not I don't know – he knew immediately that we were going to stay.

Erain, who was the first of the two to meet him at the Society's convention bookstall, said: "He just looked and smiled. I've never seen anything like the expression in his eyes. It was a cosmic feeling. It was a love that you can't find on this Earth."

As instructed by the cosmic masters, Dr. King continued the performance of Operation Starlight in the USA. On August 9th, assisted by a small team of Keith, Monique and Erain, he climbed Mount Baldy in Southern California thereby enabling it to be charged. Shortly after this he met his other key disciple from those very early days, Charles Abrahamson, who recalled:

"He had every reason in the universe to be immensely proud, but I think few of us have ever met a more humble person than George King. He was virtually penniless. He didn't know where he was going to go virtually from the night that he left that flying saucer convention. Fortunately, the twins took care

Dr. King with Monique (middle) and Erain Noppe (right) at the TV studio in Los Angeles which broadcast the Tom Duggan show.

of that for him. He had almost no money, he had no prospects. Not only was he a very humble man, he was also a very practical man. So when people made offers to help him in his mission – and primarily he was here to spread Operation Starlight to the Americas and beyond – he leapt at the opportunity to take any help that he could get."

Sure enough he completed Operation Starlight in the USA with three more holy mountains being charged: Mount Tallac in Northern California; Mount Adams in New Hampshire; and Castle Peak in Colorado. From there he went onto Australia for the charging of Mount Kosciuszko and Mount Rams Head in New South Wales. Then to New Zealand for the charging of Mount Wakefield in the South Island, which took place on a bitterly cold Christmas Eve in 1960, despite the fact that it is in the middle of summer in the southern hemisphere. That night Keith, his only

Dr. King during Operation Starlight on Mount Baldy, California.

Dr. King surrounded by journalists in Australia where he
travelled to extend Operation Starlight in 1960.

team member, recalled:

"Dr. King and I were trapped between the summit and the
charged rock, hoping to survive exposure until dawn came when
we would attempt to get off the mountain. At one point I asked
him what would happen if we did not survive and were taken off
the mountain in body bags. 'Instant rebirth!' came the reply."

In 1961 Operation Starlight moved to Mount Kilimanjaro
in Tanzania, Africa. Dr. King was not required to perform this
charge due to his previous accomplishments in this mission, as
explained by Saint Goo-Ling in a transmission on July 22nd, 1961:

> Because of the tremendous effort put forward by your
> leader and those who gave him backing and support,
> both physically and financially, it will not be necessary
> for him to perform Operation Starlight in Africa.
>
> I have myself been enabled by cosmic karmic law to
> cause this mountain to be charged. As a result of this,
> the Great White Brotherhood have been able to move

into Kilimanjaro area. When Operation Starlight has been successfully performed in Europe, it will be finished. The pages of the Great Book of the Cosmic Initiation of Earth will be opened upon this gigantic task, which, throughout the coming ages, will have its repercussions throughout your Earth.

The two final mountains were in Europe: Mederger Flue (also spelt Madrigerfluh) in the Swiss Alps and finally on August 23rd, Le Nid d'Aigle in the French Alps. This concluded the colossal and, for Dr. King and his teams, harrowing mission for the benefit of the world as a whole. As well as bequeathing nineteen holy mountains to New Age pilgrims throughout the coming centuries, three of these enabled new Great White Brotherhood retreats to be opened by the ascended masters in locations nearer to civilization than they had previously been. These were: Ben Macdui which is connected to its neighbouring Creag an Leth-choin; Castle Peak; and Mount Kilimanjaro.

After Operation Starlight was completed, all the holy mountains were interlinked through subterranean channels. This meant that pilgrims activating the energies on one holy mountain through themselves, activated the energies in all. As a result of this, on July 27th, 1962, the Master Aetherius made the following astounding declaration: **Operation Starlight is the greatest single metaphysical task ever undertaken upon Terra in this Her present life.**

*   *   *   *

Dr. King kept his cosmic origins as hidden as he possibly could in the country which in time would become his place of residence. When asked whether Dr. King mentioned to her, when he first came to America, that he was Adept Number One, Monique answered: "I don't think he even knew". A study of the record indicates that he did know by then that he was one of the Three Adepts, but possibly not which one.

When asked the same question, Erain commented:

"He would not talk about that but all I know is, on his first trip to Oakland, California (August 26th, 1959), visiting a lady there, he was listening to Bolero by Ravel and afterwards he was glowing with so much pleasure. Now I don't remember exactly, but he said he had a revelation. He was told, as Number One, his code name."

On February 23rd, 1960, the Master Aetherius gave the first report through Dr. King of the Three Adepts in action together in a battle against powerful dark forces in the lower astral realms of Earth. Although his close circle obviously knew about his main mission to Earth by then, it was never discussed even in his presence. This was possibly for reasons of security, or just because he wanted to play it down or both.

In the meantime, Dr. King and his closest followers had settled at a property on Hobart Boulevard in Los Angeles, which de facto became the American Headquarters. The incorporation of The Aetherius Society on November 22nd, 1960, was very significant as the By-Laws state under 'Basis of Authority': "The Society acknowledges and proclaims the authority of Interplanetary Parliament based upon the planet Saturn." Inflexible officialdom in Britain did not offer Dr. King an equivalent registration in his own country, and the incorporation in America was indeed a very welcome and significant development for the Society.

He was operating simultaneously on different levels. On the physical, he was acting as a channel for, and delivering in his own right, the greatest teachings that have even been given to Earth. These would be spread to higher realms too for the education and enlightenment of the more advanced souls there. At the same time he was alert 24 hours a day to the lowest realms, where the most wicked forces in our history posed a dire threat to continued civilization.

As well as these momentous and unprecedented responsibilities, he had been performing Operation Starlight, the greatest mission upon the Mother Earth in Her present life. Even more than humanity, it was serving Her that would become his overriding motivation.

Chapter Five
WHY DOES SHE DO IT?

Imagine something as great as the Logos[1] of a world who knew that She would have to hold up Her evolution long enough for a race that had just killed a planet to evolve. Imagine giving permission! I don't think you can really appreciate this fantastic sacrifice – this true, true, true, true essence of love. Not the love you know, but the real cosmic love in action. It is one of the saddest things I have ever heard of, and I say in all truth to you that I cannot talk very much about it. It affects me greatly even though I am a trained yogi and I am trained to control my emotions up to a certain point. But I am afraid, talking very much about this tremendous decision does affect me emotionally and it should affect you emotionally.

These words, delivered in a lecture in Amersham, England, on 'The Cosmic Plan' in 1974, reflect exactly how Dr. King felt about the Mother Earth. This feeling had been with him since boyhood. In his book, *Visit To The Logos Of Earth*, which is among other things a beautifully devotional tribute to this Goddess, he wrote:

One lesson which I will never forget was, strangely enough, one which I have always known ever since I was a very small child, but this truth was brought home to me more forcibly than ever before. It is a simple truth and an obvious one, but has been overlooked by mankind for centuries. It is a truth which the more highly evolved beings, living on other planets in this solar system, have known about for thousands of years.

Very simply stated, the truth is this: **the most holy, the most sacred, the most godlike being you have ever physically touched, is the ground beneath your feet.**

Just as he had known as a child how to pray without being taught – a technique he later introduced to the world as dynamic prayer – so he knew and appreciated the divinity of the planet upon which he lived. It was inbuilt within him and would become his overwhelming passion.

* * * *

In 1963 he published in *The Nine Freedoms* an account of his experience of cosmic consciousness. This rarefied state is the ultimate meditative condition attainable upon Earth. Variously called nirvana, seedless samadhi and by other names, it is true oneness with all life in the universe. He did not reveal exactly when this experience took place – whether it was before or after his arrival in the USA in 1959 – but we are confident that there is no account like this one. Others have written of their mystical realizations and detailed the blissful, visionary rapture which accompanied them, but few, if any, have left a record of this level of divine becoming.

Possibly to express his total control over the state he had entered and his ability to detach from it at will, he wrote about himself in the third person. However his account takes, to the best of our knowledge, a completely new and certainly unexpected turn. For at the zenith of his soul-drenched immersion in spirit, rather than bathe in its continued emanations he went in an entirely different direction as the following extract elucidates:

> As the state became even more advanced, he felt as though he was above the world embracing it all, a part of it. Living with it in complete intimacy, knowing it, appreciating it, loving it as he had never felt love before. He became one with that upon which his super consciousness[2] dwelt. He became detached from this oneness when he felt he should, in order to learn from the experience of detachment and attached when he wanted to in order to learn from the experience of attachment.
>
> He became existent in timelessness.

He became vitally aware of the dimensions in which
he existed and knew them – aye, all seven of them. He
became as tiny as a molecule when he wanted to and yet
bigger than a world when he wished. He looked down
from his lofty position high above the Earth, appreciating
Its great glory, Its power, Its supreme light; perceiving
the limitations It had put upon Itself in order to allow
lifestreams, like him, to gain the very experience which
he was now living through in almost godlike ecstasy. It
was then, when this realization dawned, that he stopped
short.

Here was the very power which he had sought.
Power beyond the wildest dreams, beyond the most
imaginative conception of mere man; power to know
what secrets he wished; power greater than that needed
to move any mountain, anywhere, at any time. But yet,
he stopped short as though strangely disappointed with
himself. Beneath him, beneath the crust of Earth, within
the ancient globe dwelt a greater being than he or all
men. A Being which had imposed upon Itself, crushing
limitations, so that the mass of men could crawl through
existence upon Its back in order to gain experience,
knowledge and eventually – even wisdom.

It was as though he had learned the great lesson
brought about by striving for this, what was to him then,
an ultimate state of being. The lesson of detachment
from even the greatest states he learned and gradually
he came back.

Those writings of which we are aware – probably describing
a lesser but still profound state of oneness – do not emphasize
the necessity to leave it, never mind this reason for doing so. It is
simply wrong, Dr. King realized, to remain in such a condition,
while the living planet is enduring such limitation on our behalf.
To Dr. King complete detachment from suffering humanity was
tantamount to a moral and spiritual crime, but detachment from
the sacrifice of the Mother Earth was far more heinous.

The need to remain grounded is understood in meditative

circles. Paramhansa Yogananda, who was greatly respected and highly recommended by Dr. King, described the disappointment he felt after his experience of cosmic consciousness. This was caused by his return from such an elevated condition to a basic conscious state – a sentiment which chimes with those expressed by other mystics when comparing such sublime realities with worldly existence. His guru Sri Yukteswar did not allow him to dwell on this but directed him to fetch a broom and sweep the balcony floor, through which he learned the need to remain balanced. This incident, which could virtually be taken as a parable for would-be initiates, epitomises the traditional approach to self-realization which has been adopted through the millennia.

But we feel sure that Yogananda himself would be the first to admit that this approach is not in the same league as that of Dr. King, who was disappointed for another reason. It was not caused by his personal loss of the blissful state he had chosen to leave, but a disappointment with himself – because he realized, as the fourth aspect intelligence he was, the full glory of the planet upon which we live and our indebtedness to it. Before he ever came to this world he must have experienced samadhic conditions way beyond those attainable by the people of this world. Compared to these, as extraordinary as it might seem, nirvana must be relatively lowly and heaven fairly mundane.

Even during this most sought-after of experiences, he was not focused on himself, not even his real self. His love for all life was as never before; he knew it absolutely and understood it completely; but he stopped when he became aware of the suffering of the Mother Earth. This was too much to bypass or ignore. He had to return to serve Her – an inner compulsion demanded it – and this would stay with him throughout his mission as the dominant impulse within his being.

We were informed that he and the other two Adepts came to Earth to transmute evil here. But this mission of salvation must have crossed another arc of ancient karmic delineation, wrought by a long-suffering, selfless Intelligence manifesting Herself in planetary form. It was Her time and a certain cosmic adept had to be here for that time. In earthly form, at least, his name was Dr.

George King.

* * * *

The concept of sending spiritual energy to the Mother Earth existed from the early days of the Society. It first emerged in a fascinating way on February 10th, 1957. Dr. King received a transmission which, it appears, was not intended for him, because a communicator from Satellite No. 3 stated after it:

> This is Satellite No. 3 now damping all terrestrial
> reception channels. Just before I do, might I point out
> that Mental Channel Number One was tuning in, rather
> as a pirate station. However, would like to say: God bless
> you all.

A pirate station in those days was a radio station, generally located off the coast in a boat, which was not legally sanctioned by the broadcasting authorities. This statement makes the point with characteristic dry humour, that it was not really intended to be received by Dr. King.

The transmission in question was a very revealing one from Mars Sector 8, possibly given for our benefit once realizing Dr. King was receiving it:

> This is Mars Sector 8 reporting from 32 miles above
> the surface of Earth, just over the Swiss Alps. We are
> carrying on a power impregnation in this sector, because
> of a certain magnetic belt, which actually goes right
> through the Earth. We are actually, at this moment,
> impregnating that particular magnetic belt with our
> energies so that these may travel right through the Earth,
> and may help the terrestrial Logos. This is termed as
> Operation Number One, for it takes priority over all other
> operations. Mars Sector 8 discontinuing.

This is a description of energy being transmitted by Mars Sector 8 into what must be a psychic centre of Earth located in

Switzerland. Years later in a lecture on November 30th, 1963, Dr. King revealed:

> **The position which holds the main psychic centre of this Earth, through which the Earth Logos Itself is charged, is somewhere in Switzerland.**

Mars Sector 8 is adamant that Operation Number One, as he calls it, takes priority over all other operations. Probably this is what later became Operation One One One, a Special Power Transmission in which the energy is directed to the Mother Earth rather than humanity.

The most significant Operation One One One by far was the Primary Initiation of Earth. It should also be mentioned that Dr. King, along with the other Adepts, actually took part in this monumental Primary Initiation. The more one studies his life and mission, the clearer it becomes that he was meant to be on Earth when this event occurred, and not only to receive the transmission. In fact this was delivered, as Mars Sector 6 put it on July 8th, 1964: **through the grace of Mental Channel Number One – through the grace of Mental Channel Number One.** The implication of this statement is that he did not have to take this transmission, even though he made himself available to do so. But he had to be here for the essential cosmic preparation for this happening, and after it for its multi-faceted effects upon every realm of the planet.

* * * *

One vital cosmic move was called Operation Bluewater. This was officially announced by the Master Aetherius on March 16th, 1963, and published in a special edition of *The Aetherius Society Newsletter*, March 1963. For the first time a transmission had to be delayed because of a torrential rainstorm breaking the guttering at the American Headquarters at 674 Crenshaw Boulevard in Los Angeles, to which he and his team had moved the previous October. But after this had been fixed, Dr. King proceeded to receive it.

It was delivered to an audience of over 50 members and sympathizers and began with the Master Aetherius complimenting Dr. King on his decisive ability in making the practical decision to postpone it. He then announced:

> At this time I would like to speak a little about the next mission to Earth as given to and accepted by your leader. I do not have to remind any of you that this mission was given to Mental Channel Number One because of his obvious ability to handle it.
>
> This mission was given to The Aetherius Society because no other organization approaching its kind was capable of its correct execution, without great internal upheavals within these organizations. We have not time for such house cleaning now. We must get down to practicalities away from the much used field of theory. The science of metaphysics is not a theoretical one but strictly a practical one. This operation will be strictly a metaphysical one and naturally very practical.
>
> It will be necessary for one or two short voyages to be made off the coast so that a certain pattern can be described in order that the radionic apparatus[3], to be built, may pick up very definite energy waves which will be beamed directly upon it at certain specified periods. This energy, after being picked up by this apparatus, will then be stepped up and released into the sea as the vessel is performing a specified and quite exact pattern. **The apparatus has been quite outstandingly conceived by your leader so that it will perform exactly this function.** The energy waves so potentized and released within a defined pattern, will then be projected through the intervening depth of sea so that they will impregnate the Earth beneath. The whole area will, of course then become highly charged with energies. But these energies will not be for the same purpose as were the energies in Operation Starlight. At this time it is not fitting that we divulge the full implications of this next vital mission to Terra.

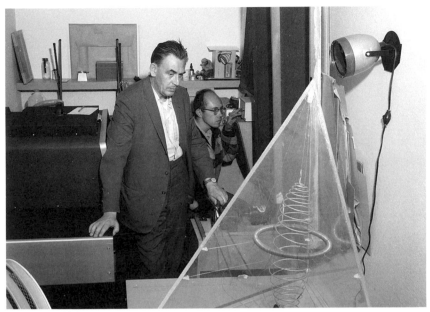

Top: Dr. King focuses intensely on apparatus he designed for Operation Bluewater, with Al Young in the background. Above: Dr. King steering the boat while maintaining telepathic rapport during a phase of Operation Bluewater.

In addition to his outstanding telepathic abilities, this mission would require two other major skills of Dr. King. He would have to skipper a seaworthy vessel over turbulent waters according to a precise navigational course; and he would have to use his knowledge of radionics – much of it gained in another place at another time – and devise effective, physical equipment to radiate powerful cosmic energies.

Boating was not new to Dr. King. He had been a member of the crew of a Thames fire boat of about 50 feet, which went to Dunkirk, France, to assist in the evacuation during the Second World War. After the war he had, with others, purchased a large motor launch as a business venture. It was a torpedo boat which they purchased from the British Navy, and which they took out to sea. Although this was not commercially successful he gained considerable experience of manoeuvring and servicing such a vessel. This would undoubtedly stand him in good stead for Operation Bluewater and other missions to follow which involved boats. Dr. King would later state that since the majority of the Earth is covered in water, to be occultly balanced no spiritual organization should be entirely land-based in its functionality.

Dr. King must have seen this coming as he so often did, and made sure his team gained the necessary experience. Perhaps he acted on a clue given to him by the Master Aetherius following the last of a series of emergency power transmissions from Jupiter on February 19th, 1962, when he stated:

> So you see that these operations have been of vital necessity. But before I do vacate transmission orbit may I say this in great, great secrecy of course – and only very few will understand it. And those who do will no doubt be very pleased...Now to give my little cryptic message to the choice few: fresh air is very good; sea air is very much better than the city air, you know. Do you see what I mean? Good hint? Good night.

Charles Abrahamson elaborated:
"Prior to this time, Monique, Erain, Dr. King and I had purchased a little, single-engine, plywood Chris-Craft powerboat

and had taken short trips – a few out to Catalina Island, off the coast of southern California. It was apparent to all of us that none of us were very interested in boating, but Dr. King seemed to feel that this experience was essential. So we went along with it and, of course, when this transmission was given we found out why that experience was essential. It is possible that Dr. King did have sort of an idea that some kind of a cosmic mission at sea might be forthcoming, and indeed that is where Operation Bluewater would be performed."

Al Young, who had now become a key member of Dr. King's inner team, remembered that the selection of this vessel for training purposes was assisted by a communication received through Dr. King from Sir Thomas Lipton, who had been a successful businessman and yachtsman. He also commented on Dr. King's outstanding skill as a skipper of this vessel: "Dr. King virtually took off from the word go at the helm, because he had the ability to man a craft like that and he was a superb driver in his own right."

Dr. King had already demonstrated a genius for radionics through his inventions designed to enhance the flow of spiritual energy out to the world. In the early days of the Society in England, two of these were lovingly nicknamed 'Gertie' and 'Gertina'. On April 22nd, 1958, he had been given specialized instructions by the Master Aetherius to design some radionic apparatus which would be used at special transmissions and power circles during Magnetization Periods. This was used to greatly enhance the output of energy. This new equipment, known as the 'King Pranic Concentrator', was connected electrically and radionicly to Gertie and Gertina to create the first Spiritual Energy Radiator. The following year on November 18th it started to be used directly and very successfully by Satellite No. 3 during Spiritual Pushes to radiate power to the world.

Operation Bluewater, though, was a new departure because it involved penetrating 2,000 feet of seawater with spiritual energy. Dr. King had been informed about it sometime before it was officially announced by the Master Aetherius and had not only accepted it but conceived the design of the necessary equipment. He revealed later that he had built it in mind-substance before it was ever physically constructed. Charles explained:

"He designed it in mind-stuff and we had to pick it out of the air and try to duplicate it...what he would do would be to make gestures and describe verbally what he had in mind, and of course we know that he was very good at describing things verbally...he obviously formed pictures in his mind and I know that I, and to some extent I guess Al, were able to pick these up. And we would go away and make something – usually a cardboard model."

Al, who would often accompany Dr. King on short walks in the evening, remembered:

"Walking around the block, Dr. King was working on this. What he was doing was constructing a model in the etheric substance. We couldn't see it, but he would construct these models and make them operational in that [higher] plane [of existence], then study the energy and how it functioned. Did they function the way our mission required them to? And he would reconstruct the equipment until it did."

At the same time Dr. King was looking for a larger vessel, capable of carrying a crew of six. He and his closest followers purchased a 37-foot Colonial at their own expense, which he named *Sea Deva II*. It required considerable rebuilding and maintenance to make it seaworthy for such a task. He then proceeded to train his crew in readiness for the mission which commenced on July 11th, 1963.

In his transmission on March 16th, the Master Aetherius had given further details:

> The new operation will be in accordance with the necessity to concentrate energy in specific parts. Only this time the energy will be for, as I have previously stated, a different purpose than that given to you and placed in the mountains in Operation Starlight through the unique abilities of your leader. The new operation also must be performed at this time as a definite function prior to the Cosmic Initiation of Terra...By Karmic Law you must perform the terrestrial part of this operation. The Law of Karma would not allow us, for instance, to land a vehicle at the bottom of the sea, which we could

easily do, and execute this radiation pattern. You must do that. But rest assured that we will do our part, which will be the transmission and some of the manipulation of the energy.

The four phases of this mission occurred before and after the Initiation of Earth and concluded on November 29th, 1964. Dr. King went to sea with his crew – their destination a psychic centre of the Mother Earth off Dana Point in the San Pedro Channel near Newport Beach, California. In this vicinity Dr. King manoeuvred the boat while simultaneously maintaining mental contact with the cosmic masters who relayed the precise navigational patterns for him to follow. This extraordinary and unprecedented feat enabled cosmic energy transmitted by higher powers to be radiated through a Spiritual Energy Collector and Radiator designed by Dr. King so that it could reach this sacred spot.

If Operation Starlight was too advanced for some to appreciate, Operation Bluewater was far more so. It was designed to send energy directly into a psychic centre of the Mother Earth which had been bled by humanity. It helped to bring an essential balance to this centre which was necessary for the Primary Initiation of Earth. It also included the vital element of karmic manipulation through terrestrial cooperation, as opposed to relying on the masters alone to perform such an elevated, metaphysical procedure. Representatives of humanity were now starting to stand on their own two feet prior to the dawning of the New Age.

After the completion of Operation Bluewater the Master Aetherius delivered a transmission on January 30th, 1965, entitled: 'This is the Hour of Truth'[4]. It is an unambiguous rebuke of humanity's vandalizing disregard for the planet upon which we live, as well as of those who could have helped with Operation Bluewater but did not do so. In it, he made the following most significant statement which would be a pointer to the future:

Operation Bluewater could only have been successfully executed by George King. There is no one else in a

terrestrial body who could have so quickly designed an instrument capable of the radiation of energies through quite a depth of coastal waters.

It was now on the record that as well as the unsurpassed calibre of his mediumship, and his unique credentials in spiritual combat, he was the only person on Earth with the level of radionic expertise required for such a specialized commission. It was obviously an innate knowledge that he had brought with him to this planet, because there was certainly no one here who could have taught him.

The principles behind Operation Bluewater were a trigger for Dr. King's genius. His love for the Mother Earth would lead to a new direction in spiritual practice throughout the realms of this Earth and beyond. For he would devise a mission to change the world and, extraordinary as it sounds, the galaxy.

*   *   *   *

In later years he would tell it this way. One evening in the mid 1960s he sat with a cocktail, looked into the sky and wondered to himself whether he would ever do anything really great. That one thought alone proves his alien psychology. By then he had already taken the transmissions of 'The Twelve Blessings', 'The Nine Freedoms' and others; he had already accomplished Operation Starlight and Operation Bluewater; and so much more. But still he was not satisfied with himself and those who knew him best would vouch that he never was. No matter what he had already done, he was always seeking to do more, to give more and to sacrifice more.

He looked up to the sky and the clouds appeared to form the initials of his name: G K. It was then that the idea for Operation Sunbeam came to him. He decided to take some of the energy placed in the holy mountains for the benefit of humanity, and send it instead to the Mother Earth through one of Her psychic centres. This would be a token repayment of the vast debt owed by humanity to the Goddess who, to quote the Master Jesus in his Seventh Blessing:

Did accept material limitation, so that you – the lower aspects of God – could walk through experience back to God again.

Now, humanity would be making a sacrifice of this energy on Her behalf.

In an article published in *The Aetherius Society Newsletter*, May/June 1966, Dr. King wrote:

> After Operation Bluewater, the Master Aetherius rightly admonished us all for not devising a similar mission ourselves. For thousands of years man has taken all he could from this mighty Goddess Earth without one thought of any repayment for Her sacrifice and indulgence. Seldom, throughout the countless centuries of man's habitation upon Earth, has even one of his number come forward to try to repay Her. Several times She has suffered near catastrophe, brought about by the microbes crawling upon Her back. Yet She has borne this with an infinite patience which only the gods understand. A patience born from the womb of vast cosmic experience. A patience, a divine love, an endurance which towers high above even the greatest beings who have ever come to Earth. **Never once has She ordered man to change or perish!**
>
> The karma of mankind has been in the balance over and over again – yes, in your lifetimes – **even a relative few months ago the karma of mankind was weighed in the cosmic scales**! Mankind tottered on the brink of his own destruction. The FEW came forward and almost sacrificed their all to save mankind from the inevitable fall. The karmic scales were balanced again, not by collective man's efforts, but nevertheless balanced – in his favour. He was **allowed** to remain on this beautiful, shining world. The Master Aetherius was right to admonish us for not thinking about a similar task to Operation Bluewater, in fact, he would have been right had he admonished us even more than he did.

Mankind deserves worse than the words of the admonishing master!

I was pondering these thoughts one day and came to the obvious conclusion that someone should think of some way, no matter how small and insignificant it was, to give back to the Earth some of the energy which man has pilfered from Her throughout the centuries. Then, as a great flash, it dawned upon me how this could be done. I almost cursed myself for being so utterly stupid – for not thinking about this before.

He may have described himself as utterly stupid but he was miles ahead of everyone else on the planet, and even certain avatars who had visited it in the past. He had taken his cue from his own master who had instigated Operation Bluewater and taken to heart the admonishment that we should have been able to come up with such a mission ourselves. Trying to do this would have left anyone else at sea – Dr. King came up with a plan to go to sea – and the rest is history.

Built into this strategic manipulation was the key element of terrestrials playing an essential role in this mission. Dr. King understood, possibly better than anyone before him, just how important it was karmically for a spiritual action to be 'touched by human hands'. This was the most precious artefact on his altar of transmutation.

He was enabling ordinary people to play a part in a spiritual initiative of such enormity which even the adepts of old had not performed, nor even the ascended masters themselves. This would start to turn the global karma of humanity from its destructive course towards a direction of light. He knew, though, that such ordinary people would not be able to generate spiritual energy of sufficiently high quality to be offered to a planetary logos – a cosmic source would be required for this. Even though the energy would be coming from the holy mountains, it would have to be invoked by a cosmic master. It would also be necessary for Dr. King to design a portable battery which could be physically taken up one of the holy mountains to be charged, and then later taken by boat for its discharge over water.

There were considerable problems to be solved and in some of them he was helped by Saint Goo-Ling. He explained in the newsletter:

> There are huge spiritual batteries in the Great White Brotherhood capable of holding spiritual energy for hundreds of years, if necessary. These batteries can be charged up and the energies released at any time by the operators, but we must realize that vast mechanism is used for the charging and discharging process. It should also be realized that it is one thing to charge a spiritual battery, but another thing to discharge it. This latter problem has been solved by consultation with that prominent member of the Great White Brotherhood – Saint Goo-Ling.
>
> At the same time that he helped us with our major problem of discharging the battery, this wonderful being also obtained the **sanction necessary to perform the operation**! In all matters of energy transference on a scale as big as this one, permission has to be given by the Spiritual Hierarchy of Terra before any move is made. On May 1st, 1966, the master Saint Goo-Ling reminded us of this point and asked the Lord of the Earth, the elevated Master Babaji for his permission. You will all be overjoyed to learn that the great Master Babaji made this statement: **"My permission is hereby granted."**
>
> This means that we are not contravening any spiritual, occult or karmic law by our intentions in Operation Sunbeam, and we can go ahead with a clear conscience in this respect. It also means that, **if we perform the operation correctly – with the highest spiritual motives possible**, motives which are unquestionable in all respects, then the operation may be accepted by the cosmic masters as an official spiritual mission. In which case it would appear to me that such a mission could continue for the **rest of the life of The Aetherius Society**! Such a mission need not even be confined to this present century, but could continue as

long as man continues to live on Earth!

*   *   *   *

Dr. King was now more than Primary Terrestrial Mental Channel, and more even than the primary agent of the cosmic masters. He was a self-directed instigator of a spiritual mission in his own right which did indeed receive the stamp of authority from the great ones. On May 21st, 1966, the Master Aetherius stated:

> I have decided to accept Operation Sunbeam as an official act within the confines of the Cosmic Plan for the evolution of the planet and those who reside upon Her.

It would have been amazing enough had Dr. King designed a mission for the benefit of humanity which was accepted into the Cosmic Plan, but Operation Sunbeam was also for the evolution of the planet Herself.

He was here for the Mother Earth, not only prior to Her Primary Initiation by playing an essential part in such actions as Operation One One One and Operation Bluewater, but after it too. She was holding back the energies, which had been given in Her Primary Initiation through a Solar Lord under the awe-inspiring direction of Mars Sector 6, because of humanity. The people of this world simply would not have been able to handle its intensity and could not have continued their existence on this planet. Dr. King made a step in the direction of providing a karmic balance for this dire situation through Operation Sunbeam. He reversed – at a token level at least – the dynamic of the Mother Earth sacrificing for humanity, by taking energy intended for us in Operation Starlight and giving it to Her.

It can happen with epoch-making discoveries that their very greatness lies in their simplicity. History records that hundreds of years ago Newton discovered gravity through watching an apple fall; and thousands of years before, Archimedes discovered while bathing, in his famous 'eureka moment', a method of measurement in relation to volume and density. To metaphysics, Dr. King's invention of Operation Sunbeam as he looked into the sky, was as big as the discovery of the wheel was to physics.

On September 24th, 1966, the mission started on Mount Baldy with none other than Saint Peter charging the first two batteries. As Dr. King wrote in *The Aetherius Society Newsletter*, November 1966:

> My procedure was to go before the battery, standing very near the charged spot and through simple prayer and other yoga manipulations, bring forth the power of the great metaphysical manipulator – Saint Peter. This power went through me so quickly that the first time I physically collapsed afterwards and had to be helped into my tent.

Dr. King stressed the importance of the powerful force of Saint Peter in this charge, but with his trademark humility gave less attention to the fact that he too had added certain attributes into the energetic patterns, as well as power from Mount Baldy. The same procedure was adopted with the second battery.

Six days later on September 30th, these two batteries were discharged into a psychic centre of the Mother Earth off Goleta Point in Santa Barbara. Dr. King and his crew used a small boat which had been purchased specially for this mission through donations by members. Phase One of Operation Sunbeam had been successfully completed and a step had been taken into a cosmic arena of such vastness that it would surprise not only Dr. King but even the Master Aetherius himself.

The revelation came on December 18th in these words by the Master Aetherius published in *The Aetherius Society Newsletter*, January/February 1967:

> **Operation Sunbeam has triggered off a line of thought which has its repercussions from one end of this galaxy to another.** Many inhabited worlds in this galaxy have, in the past, made a token energy gift to the Logos which supports them, but many have not.
>
> The inhabitants of Earth are a very backward race, extremely primitive, and yet in the midst of such

savagery as that displayed by terrestrial man throughout his bloody history, has come an offer to give back to the supporting Logos an energy token in honour and regard for Her divine patience.

Believe me, ladies and gentlemen, it has triggered off a thought – even an ambition – throughout this galaxy. Races which, up to this date, had looked up to more advanced individuals than themselves in such a way that they felt that they were not worthy of making a sacrifice to their supporting Logos have, now that this has been done upon Terra, changed their whole concept...

If any operation, which has ever been designed, has taken the imagination of similar type races to those upon Terra, Operation Sunbeam is the name of that assignment. Even as I speak now to you, literally hundreds of worlds who before thought themselves totally inadequate, are now preparing, in their different ways, an operation similar to that that you know as Operation Sunbeam.

In fact, I would go so far as to say that here, upon Terra, in the mind of one individual was built a sphere which is liable to become one of the largest snowballs in the whole of galactic history.

It is absolutely fantastic, even to myself, when I receive reports from all over this galaxy how the imagination of individuals has been inspired by the idea which was born in the mind of a man who is now President of The Aetherius Society. He did not foresee this. Neither did I for that matter.

It all started in the mind of a man in an ordinary Earth physical body and that fact alone made it karmic gold. His master had laid down the parameters in Operation Bluewater and then unlocked the door by stating that others upon Earth should have thought of it. Dr. King pushed the door wide open and walked through with a handful of terrestrial cooperators who would otherwise not have even known that such a door existed.

Top: Dr. King on Mount Baldy during the charging of a battery for the first phase of Operation Sunbeam on September 24th, 1966. Above: Dr. King on board a boat, testing Operation Sunbeam equipment by hand.

                        *   *   *   *

The Lord Babaji, who is an aspect of an intelligence from the most evolved planetary race in this solar system, namely Saturn, gave permission for Operation Sunbeam to proceed. But there are three even greater intelligences who dwell not upon the Earth but within it. The ultimate authority for any action directly involving the Mother Earth is theirs to give, and it is possible that the Lord Babaji had obtained their agreement before giving his permission. They are known as The Lords of The Ineffable Flame of the Logos of Earth and sometimes as the Protectors or Keepers of the Flame. These Three are in their full aspect and have been termed as intergalactic. Their main task is the protection of the Logos of Earth Herself. If there is a need, they have the karmic permission to invoke tremendous power to do so.

The existence of these sacred beings has only been known in advanced and generally secret metaphysical circles. Though they are here for the planet rather than for humanity, the two are inextricably linked so long as the Mother Earth permits them to be. They were first mentioned in Aetherius Society literature during a series of power transmissions from Jupiter in 1962, when energies were directed through them to the Logos of Earth. It is extremely rare for any contact to be made directly with these intelligences by anyone on Earth other than the Lord Babaji. To do so would generally require not only the permission, but also the ability, to come into their presence. This entails projecting through the crust of the Earth Herself and deep within to their dwelling place at the centre.

It was therefore momentous both for the world and for Dr. King personally when on January 2nd, 1972, he did just this. After gaining permission from the Lord Babaji he projected astrally through a secret entrance near Avebury and not far from Stonehenge in Wiltshire, England, into their Holy Presence. He later described this as the most valuable piece of real estate upon the planet! To project through this entrance was no mean feat even for an adept with his capabilities. As he disclosed afterwards in *The Aetherius Society Newsletter*, July 1972:

Space is dangerous, friends, but it is just as dangerous to go down into the Earth as it is to go out into space. In fact, it has been said that exploration of the sea is more dangerous than the exploration of space. In a limited way, this is true. And exploration of the inner core of the Earth is even more dangerous. One has to know certain mantras in order to penetrate this barrier.

The Protectors will only receive an individual who is engaged upon a project of immense significance to the Mother Earth and, in certain cases, the destiny of mankind, and even then it may not happen. Dr. King's visit was made to discuss the construction of certain apparatus for the radiation of energies the Mother Earth received during Her Primary Initiation, upwards and outwards through Her realms. In the interview, which he said lasted about 15 or 16 minutes in Earth time, he received wise and helpful advice on this matter. However, the Protectors chose to spend most of the interview talking about the vast importance of Operation Sunbeam, which they considered to be the greatest single mission being performed on Earth by any organization or even country.

For Dr. King it was an outstanding honour to meet such illustrious Beings at all, and more so to receive from them such a compliment about a mission he had personally devised. It would not be his last audience with them. His next visit came on November 29th, 1979, during which he was invited to return again in order to know more about the Logos Herself.

And so it was that on January 20th, 1980, he received the following mental transmission from the Lord Babaji:

It is my pleasure to extend to you a further invitation from the Protectors of the Ineffable Flame of the Logos of Terra on January 23rd, 1980, at 2:00 p.m. your time.

Have an enlightened day on that which you call your birthday.

(*Visit To The Logos Of Earth*)

So profound was Dr. King's love for the Mother Earth that

he regarded the honour of receiving a birthday present of such magnitude as this to be more than he deserved. As understandable as his humility might have been, who upon Earth could ever have deserved it more? He was the master who had performed both Operation Starlight and Operation Bluewater; who had received the transmission of the Primary Initiation of Earth; and who had then devised and performed Operation Sunbeam, which inspired the galaxy. What credentials could trump these other than possibly those of the Lord Babaji himself?

As an aside, Dr. King mused on the Lord Babaji's comment about his birthday and questioned whether it implied that the date should have been registered in Shropshire as January 22nd. It is known that mistakes were sometimes made in those days in registering births. But that possible allusion was dwarfed by the overwhelming significance of this invitation.

This time his journey was not mainly to meet the Protectors even. It was to see a small part of the Flame of the Logos Herself. The whole experience is beautifully written up in *Visit To The Logos Of Earth* with the permission, and partly at the prompting of, the Protectors themselves. He witnessed the advanced lifeform of a planet manifesting as a wonderful living Flame at the centre of Her being, and he would never be the same again.

He wrote:

> I stood there transfixed – paralyzed – absolutely fascinated by the indescribable movement within this living Flame.
>
> Even as I gazed in fascinated awe at the stupendous power within this Flame, She seemed to change before my very eyes and, for a fraction of a second, She would take on a definite shape, like a large ovoid or part of an ovoid, and then a circle, and then millions of squares, oblongs, pyramids, hexagons, and then these would disappear and the Flame Itself would revert back to giant multicoloured fingers of mystic fire reaching upwards.
>
> I could view this through the large arch which must have been – and this only a guess – at least 150 to 200 feet wide and 200 or 300 feet tall.

I was gazing at the life form of a cosmic being, so advanced as to become the Logos of a planet!...

I had heard about Her before from high cosmic sources.

I had written about Her.

But now I was actually seeing Her in living, breathing action.

Despite the stupendous movement in those living, cycling Flames, I knew that She must be in a state of quiescence for, had Her full powers been released, even for one second, the energy discharge would have transmuted the massive body of the planet and She would be able to travel through the skies to whatever destination She so chose, instead of remaining here in supreme sacrifice for the sake of many far less evolved entities than Herself. I remember blurting through my tears and emotion:

"Why, oh why, in God's name, does She do it?"

The answer came, calm, gentle, like a cool breeze across a summer desert.

"In your own way, why do you do it – and others before you, why did they do it?"

A question, but so surely a complete answer to my emotional outburst.

Describing this as an emotional outburst would be like describing the Sermon on the Mount as a rant. Such emotions have never welled up within ordinary humanity because such an experience is beyond its reach. The very emotion that caused Dr. King to leave cosmic consciousness was again evident in this even greater experience.

To devise a mission like Operation Sunbeam he must have known about the logoi of planets, possibly intimately, long before he incarnated upon this one. He understood that She was holding back Her own evolution, and in some unfathomable way he understood Her psychology. He was going to do everything he possibly could to help Her at this time. When he asked the Lords why She does it, he received from them the perfect answer in a way that he could understand. He knew the impulse which drove Her because, at some level, it drove him too.

Some of the actions he took, such as Operation Sunbeam, were gloriously uplifting with an unmatched spiritual exuberance for all connected to them. But others were the exact opposite. Following the Initiation of the Earth, the best of the best had disturbed the worst of the worst in their hidden lairs of perverted evil. These dark ones decided to bring on the much-prophesied Armageddon, thinking that victory would be theirs and it probably would have been.

But three Adepts stood in their way including, as the Master Aetherius stated on May 17th, 1959: **the person you call King**.

Chapter Six
ALIEN ARMAGEDDON

Great changes are starting – even now. Great moves are planned – even now. Time is not on your side any longer. Make this known and those with true, loyal hearts will be inspired to come forward, and go forward, so that each will take his respective part in the great mission, in the next step of a mission greater than any other ever given to an intelligence within a terrestrial body.

These words delivered by Saint Goo-Ling on February 16th, 1965, heralded in phase two of the mission of Dr. George King. He announced to members of The Aetherius Society that phase one was almost complete and that phase two would soon begin. This he said would be more difficult and more advanced; and he went further by openly speaking of Dr. King's mission itself rather than of specific assignments such as Operation Starlight and Operation Bluewater. Above all he explicitly declared Dr. King's mission to be greater than that given to any other master or fourth aspect intelligence in history. This must have included such cosmic luminaries as Sri Krishna, the Lord Buddha, the Master Jesus and others.

What he did not say, however, because it was classified, is that a major aspect of this phase would be focused on the lower astral realms[1] and the transmutation there of the worst evil this world has ever known. For centuries, spiritual teachers had promoted a doctrine of detachment from these forces rather than one of dealing with them head on. Perhaps it was not the time, or they were not able to effectively combat these powerful centres of evil, or both. Even recent metaphysicians advocated not engaging with evil and effectively leaving the dark forces to it, but this would not have provided essential protection from such entities. In some orthodox circles there were those who ludicrously equated God with the devil, something these forces must have loved and probably encouraged. To suggest a parity between the two is like comparing the Sun with a mosquito!

Through Dr. King, the cosmic masters redressed the philosophical approach to evil. In a transmission delivered through Dr. King to a public audience in San Francisco on September 25th, 1959, entitled 'Fight Ye The Evil', Mars Sector 6 stated:

> If you allow evil to be brought to bear against that which is so obviously good and true, you allow too the evil one to involve himself in even worse evil. If, on the other hand, you block his nefarious schemes by truth, you stop this one from sinking so low. You must, oh brothers, be prepared to help the evil ones by transmuting their wicked schemes.

And the Master Aetherius succinctly added a new dimension to spirituality on October 18th, 1973, in his brilliant aphorism:

> No saint can ever be a saint in heaven unless he has been a saint in hell!

Just occasionally someone has put their head above the parapet. Dante tried to describe what hell was actually like in his *Inferno* in the 14th century. Perhaps his intention was to engender compassion for those who abide there, but it was certainly not taken as such by the Catholic Church which used it as a fear-inducing threat to those who strayed from their manufactured doctrine. But Dr. King made it clear that Dante's descriptions were nothing compared to the foul reality of these realms. And some hundred years ago the British missionary C. T. Studd expressed an unusual sentiment for the time when he said: "Some want to live within the sound of church or chapel bell; I want to run a rescue shop within a yard of hell."

Dr. King poured cold water on concepts of a fiery furnace from which no one can ever escape. His first-hand knowledge of human evolution at all levels resulted in the liberating teaching that the destiny of all life, no matter how low it falls, is eventually to return to God. Unlike anyone who had gone before them, he and the other two heroic Adepts were commissioned to transmute the worst in the hells and reduce the dangers they posed to this and every other realm above them. It was the karmic time for such battles, as stated by Saint Goo-Ling in his introduction to a transmission by the Master Jesus entitled 'The Three Saviours Are Here!', which was delivered on September 23rd, 1967, as published in the book, *The Three Saviours Are Here!*:

> Be ye prepared to work for right – for this is the hour! The hour of the prophecies.
>
> The hour of the turning point of evolution, or the hour of the defeat of all which is good and holy upon Earth.
>
> This is the hour.
>
> The hour of light or darkness.
>
> The hour of truth or lies.
>
> The hour when the foundation stones can be laid for the New Age or never can it be built by man upon this planet.
>
> This is the crossroad of evolution. It is the beginning of greatness, or the beginning of darkness.
>
> It is the hour of light, or a more stifling blackness than you have ever known before.
>
> You stand as helpless children in this hour.

This battle had been foreseen by the great ones, and the Adepts accepted this task, as the Master Jesus explained in the transmission:

> Many centuries ago the Wise Ones looked into time and there they saw apparently inevitable results brought about by the fall of man. They conferred together, allowing the shining oil of sweet compassion to imbue their negotiations. They took into consideration the deep karmic implications of what was to come. Then turned they to three devoted beings, and asked of these to give up the bliss of their advanced initiatory status and take gross bodies, bound by karma, held by the limitations

of man and come and live and breathe and eat and pray and suffer among ye.

The Three Adepts spent no time in consideration.

Their souls leapt within them, filled with compassion for a people who were helpless against the might which threatened to crush them, even as a great hammer crushes a lowly stone. And so it was they came and throughout the years that they have been with you, they have fought your greatest and most important battles.

Man, without the Three Adepts, you would have already been lost for a long, long time. Over and over again, these mighty beings came to your rescue. When you stood helpless – they fought against tremendous odds for you. When you played in the garden of your simple ease – they sweated blood on your behalf. When you rolled in the pleasant, warm sunshine caring not – they suffered excruciating pain and agony for each and every one of you.

The Master Jesus gives us here a rare glimpse into the psychology of these three intelligences. The Wise Ones he referred to were, Dr. King explained, the hierarchical Lords of this solar system. They must either be, or be responsible to, the highest beings of the system, namely the Lords of the Sun. When asked to take on this most gruelling of missions by their Lords, the Three Adepts did not hesitate. They were motivated only by compassion for humanity without a thought for themselves. Although he went out of his way to conceal his origins, this shows that the totality of Dr. King's life upon Earth was self-sacrifice – that was its essence and its reality.

How different he must have felt from the inhabitants of this planet who are predominantly self-centred. He could honestly say, as he did on a few occasions later to those closest to him, that his every breath was taken in service because he did not even have to be here. While the psychological make-up of most people is wrapped up in the pursuit of their own happiness, Dr. King's was cast in an entirely different mould – infused by the fire of the gods in the foundry of service.

* * * *

Over a dozen sorties by the Three Adepts into the lower astral realms were reported by the Master Aetherius during the early 1960s. Each one was a battle between these Warriors of Light and dark forces of varied pedigrees, all of them extremely deadly. While concluding Operation Starlight, performing Operation Bluewater, taking numerous transmissions including power manipulations, directing and running The Aetherius Society in actions such as Operation World Healing in 1963 to counteract an onset of a virulent disease epidemic, Dr. King was also on call 24 hours a day for such a sortie. At any moment he could be summoned to leave his physical body and travel to the most debased levels of our world, together with his two comrades, in order to engage in combat of the vilest and most lethal kind ever reported in our history.

They risked far worse suffering than even the wars on this physical realm can produce. One mistake could have led to the death of not only their physical but also their astral bodies, or to long-term captivity among the denizens of the underworld. More importantly to the Adepts, if such a mistake led to the failure of their mission, there would be nothing left to protect humanity and countless lifestreams would endure untold suffering and limitation.

Of Dr. King's many outstanding abilities, perhaps the most impressive was that he remained balanced at all. Although he hardly ever took a vacation, he had a bit of what might be called a 'hinterland' i.e. a range of interests and pursuits in addition to his work. He followed a variety of topics, as well as metaphysics and spiritual matters, such as boating, audio technology and later, chivalric traditions and modern democratic causes. He rarely dined out, but enjoyed good cuisine at home usually cooked by Monique or certain members of his devoted staff. He was an animal lover, as he had been throughout his life, and owned a number of pets including dogs, fresh and saltwater fish and even a much-loved monkey.

He was an excellent photographer, filmmaker and eagerly embraced the video camera and recorder when it became

Dr. King enjoys target practice at a shooting range.

available in the early 1970s. From time to time he went to the shooting range to keep his eye in. He would often on weekends spend a few hours on his boat *Fairseas* moored at Marina del Rey in Los Angeles County. Otherwise he did not pursue any sporting activities, but did have regular walks in the vicinity of wherever the American Headquarters was located at the time, and in various locations in England when he was there.

He watched carefully selected TV programmes, especially films featuring combat, police dramas, espionage, science fiction or some challenging accomplishment. The Second World War film, 'The Man Who Never Was', was among his all-time favourites. Amazingly he always maintained an outstanding sense of humour which he shared generously with those around him. In fact he could easily have them in stitches from the laughter and merriment that he engendered. He also greatly enjoyed being entertained by the repartee and witticisms of others. Interestingly he told Richard Lawrence that Adept Number One is known among the cosmic masters for his sense of humour – as is, he said, the Master Aetherius.

As the years went by, he increasingly enjoyed a drink and took to having a cocktail hour before dinner, sometimes in company but usually alone. He would generally listen to music during these times, particularly of the light orchestral and film genres, big band dance music from the 1950s or guitar music by groups like The Ventures and The Shadows. Rarely would he listen to any music with lyrics, since he used it as a backdrop to his thoughts and contemplations.

In the late 1960s he also started to play percussion instruments in a combo he formed called the Supersonics. This small

Dr. King displays his artistry as a percussionist with the Supersonics during a New Year's Eve party at the American Headquarters.

band consisted of some of his followers with changes of line-up over the years. It always included piano, bass and drums, a singer when available, sometimes a guitarist and on one occasion an electronic keyboardist. When in the 1970s a celebratory gathering of members was held at a west London hotel, rather than booking a band Dr. King's combo performed so profession-ally that it was offered a contract to perform on a cruise ship by another hotel guest. Unsurprisingly the offer was turned down, but it illustrates Dr. King's work ethic even in recreation. He usually celebrated Christmas, New Year and other holidays with parties, sometimes in fancy dress for which he adopted a variety of guises. Sometimes he would perform his own magic act, using as his alias the name 'Dandini', which was much enjoyed by the partygoers.

On closer inspection, though, it becomes clear that this was not entirely a hinterland because it nearly always related directly or indirectly to his mission. In the materialistic world we are used to the concept of work-life balance – a businessman who plays a few rounds of golf; a politician who has a night at the opera; a working mother who takes a spa break. But such a concept was alien to Dr. King because work was his life. A dinnertime conversation could turn in an instant from hilarious storytelling to high philosophy to a dressing-down of one of the diners if a mistake on their part had come to light. Even his cocktail hour was not just relaxation, but also a time in which he gathered his thoughts and could receive his highest inspirations. Even the parties at which the Supersonics would play were at times used as a diversion from the battles on the lower astral realms in which he was engaged, and to disguise from the dark forces his role in these battles.

He did occasionally engage in relaxation pursuits but even while watching television, a part of his mind could be engaged in solving complex, other-worldly problems. His viewing was frequently interrupted by work-related matters such as checking off the printing of an issue of *Cosmic Voice* which was underway on the premises. He insisted on being informed without delay of any world calamities and of any serious developments affecting The Aetherius Society. He was also told immediately about the death of any member of The Aetherius Society, even if it meant waking him in the middle of the night. He would ensure, in coordination with those on higher spheres, that they were helped during their time of transition to another realm.

Dr. King's stability amid constant ongoing pressure for 24 hours a day for over 40 years was a phenomenon of our times. Even presidents and prime ministers of major nations generally have limited periods of office as do those who hold high positions in other fields such as the military and business. And Dr. King's responsibilities were far greater than any of these.

On February 24th, 1978, he gave a classic address called 'The Men Who Won Operation Karmalight For You'. He spoke about the psychology of the Three Adepts and the fact that they were prone to the same impulses as any other men because they were in terrestrial physical bodies. He pointed out that a normal, human reaction after fighting the battles they had fought would be to call it a day, go off and 'kick over the traces', but the Adepts did not do this because of their inherent balance. He did not attribute this to any hinterland or to the lifestyle we are used to in this materialistic world, but to something very different, very revealing and to us very alien. He said about these three without admitting that he was one of them:

> I do not know what it is with these people that kept them so balanced, so straight, unless it is the love of God through realization. I think it has to be something like that. It has to be something above the norm, and the love of God through realization is above the norm because very few people have it. They say they love God but they do not really realize what God is to the extent that the Adepts must realize what God is. And that is why their true love, true love, true love, true love – not the thing you call love but true love – must be so much greater than the capabilities of a terrestrial. Because it is borne out of realization, out of a knowledge of God, a knowledge of God, a knowledge of God – and it must have been this. This must have been the potion that kept them along that straight and narrow.

*   *   *   *

The great ones asked the full aspect of Dr. King and the other two Adepts to come to Earth because they could see what was going to unfold, and what they saw must have made the Book of Revelation[2], with all due respect to its visionary author, seem childlike in its depictions. They knew that upon Earth there were countless wicked terrestrial people who had passed after death into the lower astral realms, and that these realms were ruled by exceptionally advanced dark forces with diabolical capabilities. But there was something even more sinister than that: a dormant and, for the most part, undetected alien android.

The teachings delivered through Dr. King to the public presented an inspiring picture of extraterrestrial life. All the other inhabited planets in this solar system are populated by technologically and spiritually advanced cultures of the most noble and elevated character. But elsewhere in the universe, this is not always the case as was now dangerously clear. An evil race from outside of this galaxy, who were motivated by interplanetary conquest at any price, had fabricated a non-human android millions of years ago and placed it in the lowest realms of this world for strategic reasons. Operating in a different time sequence from ours they awaited the moment to activate it with a goal of conquering the world. They could then use the Earth as a position from which to enact their nefarious schemes of domination in this part of the galaxy.

This was exacerbated on July 8th, 1964. The Primary Initiation of Earth meant that sooner or later such spiritual change would come to this planet and that their schemes here would no longer be viable. Unlike the vast majority of human beings, who were insensitive to the subtlety of the new vibrational radiations in and around the Mother Earth, the alien android was not. It was shaken from its dormancy and it started to move.

Saint Goo-Ling's prediction that phase two of Dr. King's mission would be more advanced was now apparent. These developments would have sounded to most people then, as they would now, to be the stuff of make-believe and science fiction. They were a million miles from the banality of what some would regard as real life. But the fact that they may seem unbelievable has no bearing on their validity, and it requires a certain advancement, a truly open-minded, intuitive perception, to grasp this reality.

Perhaps because of this, as well as the interference that too much publicity could attract, Dr. King did not at first disclose widely the fact that on May 30th, 1965, the Three Adepts commenced the first of the major conflicts for which they had been recruited to Earth, namely the Alien Mission. This consisted of 27 phases culminating in victory on January 22nd, 1966.

It coincided with a major move by The Aetherius Society into new premises on Afton Place in Hollywood. They took possession of the property on June 2nd, just three days after the start of this battle for the survival and sanity of the human race. In fact, the second phase in this conflict had taken place only the previous day. The new premises were far from pristine. Due to

Dr. King and Monique supervise the renovation of the new Aetherius Society premises in Los Angeles in 1965.

Dr. King in the Transmission Room at the American
Headquarters.

the scarcity of financial support in those days, The Aetherius
Society was forced to purchase a property in need of substantial
repair. There were times when Dr. King and the other residents
of the property had to be out of bed in the middle of the night
working in the pouring rain to prevent flooding to parts of the
property – while being on call for a phase of this intense battle!
The superhuman ability of Dr. King to operate on vastly different
fronts virtually at the same time came to the fore again in his
simultaneous management of a seismic occult challenge and a
demanding material one.

    One of the most pertinent benefits of this move was the
installation of a dedicated, soundproofed transmission room with
tape-recording apparatus of the highest specifications available.
This eventually included two Ampex 351 tape recorders and two
Telefunken ELA M 251E microphones which are, even today,

regarded as the gold standard by many. The timing of this enhanced facility was ideal for the remainder of the outstanding commentaries delivered by the Master Aetherius during the phases of the Alien Mission and all future transmissions received in America. These go down in the annals of metaphysical revelation as unprecedented in their content.

On August 26th, as this conflict raged, Dr King received a communication from the Tibetan adept on the higher mental realms who had communicated through him since prior to 'The Command', the Master Chang-Fu. He had witnessed preparations for a battle on the lower astral realms for himself and reported what he saw. His devastatingly powerful words, published in *The Aetherius Society Newsletter*, August 1965, give us a small glimpse of the eight horrific months this ordeal lasted:

> I stood upon a vast, level plain and from about one hundred paces in front of me, right away to the horizon stretched a vast army; a vast army made up of fighting soldiers, every one of them correctly equipped with deadly weapons; every one of them an expert! Behind the army was great armour. Projectors capable of completely obliterating the Three Adepts; that is, down to the soul-body. Behind the armour were mighty thought-forms of awe-inspiring power created by an **alien intelligence.**
>
> Ladies and gentlemen, upon that plane I stood in awe. Never – not ever, have I ever seen such a display of tremendous power and colossal might put on by the dark forces. It was as though the devil himself had brought into being a mighty force, greater than anything ever seen upon the surface of Earth. A force powerful enough, if they met in battle, to crush the combined armies of the United States of America, Russia, China, Germany when it was at the height of its power and Britain when it was at the height of its power. An army capable of crushing these into dust.
>
> And then, in my imagination, I saw standing upon the same plane, three solitary little white figures and beyond

them, from horizon to horizon as far as my psychic eye could see, mighty power – black as the heart of the worst devil in the worst hell.

On October 22nd, the Master Aetherius clarified the significance of the Alien Mission beyond all doubt:

This mission is more important than the mission to Earth undertaken by the Lord Buddha and the master you call Jesus. It is as important, in every way, as the mission of Sri Krishna. It is as important, in many respects, as the mission undertaken to Earth – note to Earth – by the interplanetary intelligence you call Babaji who, as you know, is Lord of Terra.

The key date in the Alien Mission was not that of its start or even of its conclusion, but of Phase 18 on October 26th, 1965, when the alien android was actually evicted from Earth never to return. Dr. King speedily released an edition of *The Aetherius Society Newsletter*, September/October 1965, in which he wrote:

Between 10:28 p.m. and 11:35 p.m. on October 26th, 1965, the Three Adepts led an all out attack on an alien intelligence which had hidden itself upon the lower astral realms of Earth for **aeons of time**! The Three Adepts were, in this operation, reinforced by two other specially trained interplanetary intelligences and all sections of the Great White Brotherhood plus the finest brains of the higher mental realms, together with certain other contingencies. This action ended in a victory for the forces of light inasmuch as the alien intelligence was forced to evacuate this Earth and indeed this galactic system. **The forces of light were acting under direct orders from the highest possible galactic authority.** Their orders were to bring about this evacuation with the forces and energy at their immediate disposal. **This action was truly tremendous and one which will be chronicled forever in the Akashic Records[3] of this**

galaxy!

As a result of this event, October 26th was later declared on the highest realms to be the second holiest day in our calendar, surpassed only by the Primary Initiation of Earth on July 8th.

* * * *

Thus, during the Alien Mission, the Three Adepts became the Five Adepts. Dr. George King, as Adept Number One, was their strategic leader. It was he who formulated their plans with the agreement of the other four. As such he bore, in many ways, the greatest burden. He was also among other things the main pilot of their craft – a skill which was perhaps reflected on this more basic level in his choice of driving as a career and his later expertise as a skipper of boats. He was joined in his gruelling commission by the pick of the cosmic elite in spiritual combat. Adept Number Two is an outstanding electronics and computer expert as well as being an exceptionally holy man. Adept Number Three uniquely manifests an extraordinary combination of immense physical strength, lightning reflexes and being probably one of the greatest marksmen in this solar system. It was Number One who called the shots in the Alien Mission, but it was Adept Number Three who usually made them.

In a cosmic transmission the following year, which was published in the book, *The Five Temples Of God*, the Master Aetherius made some significant revelations about these Three when he stated:

> Many times throughout history have they come upon Terra in order to perform tasks which could not be performed by individuals then upon Terra. One of them has been very frequently to this planet of yours; in fact, even Greek mythology writes about this one. He is known, or was known in olden days, as Hercules and has been known by other names since that time. Another one of these specially trained fighters for supreme light has been known by other names throughout history.

The other one has made more fleeting, but nevertheless essential visits to your world.

In his commentary on these words Dr. King wrote in the book:

The Master Aetherius refers here to the fact that Adept Number Three has been very frequently to this Earth and has lived in a physical body off and on throughout history. The reference to Hercules and his accomplishments here, although appearing in mythology and therefore apparently not correct in all details, nevertheless has its basis in truth. It is possible that the tasks of Hercules, graphically reported in Greek mythology, were a seer's idea of some of the lower astral realm sorties made by Number Three when he was on Earth in a physical body in those days. It is a fact that this same Adept was, at one time, known as Samson – a great manipulator who came to Earth in order to perform a karmic manipulation which was absolutely essential for the betterment of mankind. The history of Samson in the Bible is probably incorrect and certainly incomplete, except that whenever feats of tremendous strength, controlled by a unique intelligence, are needed, it is Number Three who is called upon by the Higher Forces to provide these. It would appear that his role as Samson was no exception to this rule. Even though history in the Bible is incorrect in many ways, it is obviously the history of an individual with a strange, out-of-this-world destiny and one controlled by the Lords of Karma.

The next reference is to Number Two, who has also had previous incarnations upon this Earth. Although he played a very different role, having specialized training in a different field than that of Number Three, he was, nevertheless, essential to the overall karmic balance which had to be brought about. Little information can be given, at this time, but it is a fact that Number Two was a holy man of exceptional abilities. His abilities, at the present time, are those of an adept in all spiritual and indeed, physical sciences.

The third reference is made to Adept Number One, who has also visited Earth at certain times, but in a more fleeting manner, so to speak. Although a great deal of information is available on this Adept, it cannot be revealed at this time, save to say that, in the major karmic manipulations dictated by higher authority, it is Number One who acts as the strategist – having had previous experience for many centuries in different parts of this galaxy, in this difficult, yet essential role.

When the Three Adepts operate together as a unit, there is a perfect balance brought into being caused by their different, yet equally essential abilities. Number Three – tremendous physical strength and energy with pluperfect mental coordination. Number Two – a master of the spiritual and physical sciences and all forms of advanced visualization. Number One – supreme strategist with knowledge in many essential fields of endeavour. A more perfect team for the difficult job at hand has never been put together at any one time on this Earth.

From this one gains an insight not only into Dr. King's calibre but also that of the extraordinary company he kept. As usual he played himself down in this commentary and focused more on the other two Adepts. It is, though, very notable that unlike them, he had not incarnated upon this planet before but had made more fleeting visits. In other words, he had not come as a fourth aspect intelligence before, so this was a new and excruciating experience for him. He had undoubtedly come to save us before without the gruelling necessity of being born among us, which explains a lot about the alienation he felt in his childhood.

The two other specially trained interplanetary intelligences who reinforced the Three Adepts, were designated as Adept Number Four and Adept Number Five. Unlike their three brothers-at-arms, these two were in the much more fortunate position of not being limited to terrestrial physical bodies. They

did however make the immense sacrifice of not being in full
aspect on this backward planet, albeit on the higher realms. Like
the others, they were outstandingly proficient in several fields of
combat and scientific endeavour. In later years, the bond between
Dr. King and Adept Number Five became very evident as he
communicated with this great Adept probably more than any
other.

In an address delivered on July 2nd, 1967, Dr. King illustrated just how unique the Five Adepts were, not only on Earth but
beyond:

> You know, it's one thing to have a master able to do this,
> that, and the other miracle; it's another thing to have a
> master trained in combat. They're two entirely different
> types of training. A miracle, so-called, is the manipulation
> of energies on certain levels, but to produce miracle after
> miracle after miracle, in your language, in combat, takes
> a type of mind, which is extremely rare – may I repeat – a
> type of mind that is extremely rare – even in this system
> – **system – not Earth!**

*   *   *   *

During the Alien Mission Dr. King had deliberately kept his cards
close to his chest. Charles Abrahamson remembered:

"He didn't talk about these things because – one of the
reasons – he didn't want us thinking about these things. We were
pretty much instructed during, whether it was a sortie or whether
it was one of the phases of let's say the Alien Mission, not to think
in between phases about what had just happened; not to discuss
it because this would attract unwanted attention [from the dark
forces]."

Less than a month after the conclusion of the Alien Mission,
a very unexpected event occurred at the American Headquarters
when Dr. King received a physical visit from a cosmic intelligence
from another part of the galaxy. Charles Abrahamson recalled:

"We knew that something was afoot because the previous
day on Friday, February 12th afternoon and evening, the staff

and members had come in and were cleaning up the entire property. This was a very extensive clean-up inside and outside, so we knew that something was up. It was about sometime after 7:00 p.m. on Saturday, February 13th after two days of work that we were told to vacate." It is clear from this that even his closest followers did not know what would ensue.

Dr. King summarized this physical space contact in *The Aetherius Society Newsletter*, March/April 1966 as follows:

Between 9:00 p.m. and 10:15 p.m. on February 13th, 1966, a very important and highly advanced space being visited The Aetherius Society Headquarters in Hollywood. This intelligence came from outside of the solar system thousands of millions of miles away from this Earth. He travelled from his own planet in a very large spacecraft which he left in orbit of our moon while the visit was made. This visitor was a male and appeared in a physical humanoid form.

At his request, I had the great privilege of showing him over our premises and explaining our operations here. He was duly impressed with the success of all the important missions which had been given to The Aetherius Society especially in view of the extremely primitive tools at our disposal. It must be pointed out that this great Adept was highly spiritually advanced, from a very ancient race of beings who had perfected certain metaphysical sciences into the realms of advancement far above our imagination. Therefore, to him the tools available to The Aetherius Society or any other terrestrial organization for that matter, must have seemed very primitive indeed.

This meeting was arranged on the Friday evening previous to the visitation. I made an inspection of the premises and found that many things had to be straightened up. I called upon the staff to put forward their greatest effort without telling them why I wanted them to do this. Other members were called in and came willingly in order to help. I was happy to be able to tell these people afterwards that the contact had taken place. Several members so rightly expressed to me that they felt it was indeed a great privilege to have the opportunity to smarten up the premises for such a very important personage as this.

There was nothing haphazard about this contact. It was very carefully prearranged so that the best possible use could be made of the precious time available to the visiting entity. A great lesson was learned from this contact. THE VISITATION TOOK PLACE IN PREPARATION OF A GIGANTIC EVENT WHICH IS SHORTLY DUE TO HAPPEN. **An event of such magnitude as to stagger the imagination of all people concerned.**

Several months later, on October 15th, 1966, a fuller explanation was given of this visit in a historic transmission from the very intelligence who had made it:

I came to Terra. I brought with me – I left them in orbit of your moon – some of the beings from our supreme council. I wanted to make a visit to a man upon Earth. I came to this Aetherius Society to make this visit. I asked this man many questions, he answered me. His answers to me were more holy than the words in our Book of Reverence. Every word that this man said was transmitted mentally, by me, to these members of the supreme council upon a spacecraft near your moon.

Once and for all I wanted to show them what could be done by an individual with courage, determination and true, true spiritual fortitude. An individual committed to the most primitive of worlds, your Earth; an individual who only had at his command the most primitive of tools; an individual who had performed for mankind many great earth-shattering tasks.

When I stood, physically, in your little holy place wherein you worship in The Aetherius Society in Los Angeles, California, United States of America, I felt my inadequacy as never before. I looked around me at the primitive squalor of my surroundings. I compared it with some of the temples upon my world, temples which could seat, as you call it, six million individuals. And yet the man in front of me, even though I could just see a part of him, had illustrated a greater spirituality than the high priest who led the metaphysical practice in such a temple as I have described. For, you see, I knew more about George King than any of you do.

I was also amazed that his few workers, with primitive tools, had been able to do so much. Not for their own development, not for their own enlightenment, not to give them superior powers whereby they might stave off disease and death for 25,000 years and even longer – no, work given to you.

I looked around and felt the minds of the population upon Terra. Even as I stood there I felt the savagery, the full apparent ignorance. They did not even realize what had been done for them. All this information was delivered through me to my friends. They, in turn, conveyed it to every intelligence upon our planets. A lesson had been learned.

This intelligence came from a planetary system approximately 36,000 light years away from Earth towards the centre of this galaxy called Gotha. He revealed that thousands of years ago its inhabitants had made a decision to focus exclusively on their own spiritual development and retreat from all involvement with other planetary races. They were now under threat from attack by the same alien race that had placed upon Earth the android just evicted by the Five Adepts. Because of their inward-looking, pacifistic approach the supreme council of priests was not willing to defend their two inhabited planets against such an attack. This intelligence, who disagreed with the high priests of his system, had become aware of the stupendous actions of the Three Adepts, and especially the role of Dr. George King as one of them. In desperation he visited Dr. King to demonstrate to those on his world the very essence of true service.

The Three Adepts had visited Gotha at his request and given all the inhabitants the following advice as recounted by this master:

> If you do not think about yourselves, then what about others? If this alien can successfully make bases upon your worlds, he can attack other less evolved, weaker people than you. You owe them your action.

These words had cut through centuries of frozen time – a wasted period of dormant regression in the name of spirituality. No wonder this master from Gotha held the words of Dr. King as being more holy than those in their Book of Reverence.

So only two months after the conclusion of the Alien Mission, the Five Adepts were propelled into action again in what became known as the Gotha Mission. Dr. King revealed very little about this to the members of the Society except that he was deeply grieved to have to inform them that these gallant five were once more in the throes of a very dangerous cosmic assignment. The Master Aetherius went further when he stated on May 21st, as published in *The Aetherius Society Newsletter*, July 1966:

> The Three Adepts are engaged on the most important mission ever to be performed in this galaxy. May I repeat – in this galaxy. A mission far bigger than any of you – than all of you. Far bigger than the Sun. Far bigger than the solar system.
>
> They are, of course, only cogs in the vast machine which is being prepared for its greatest test. At the moment, I do not feel that I should tell you any more than that as the mission is strictly classified.

These words would prove very prescient for the mission which culminated a year later on March 24th, 1967, with what Dr. King described as the greatest event ever reported. It would be wrong to give even a short précis of this stupendous happening here because we could not possibly do it justice. Rather, we refer you to *The Aetherius Society Newsletter*, July 1967 where he brilliantly describes it in detail.

The Gotha Mission, coming so soon after the Alien Mission, took its toll on Dr. King's health. Not only did he play an essential role as Adept Number One, but also in his physical body he acted as the channel for the brilliant commentaries by the Master Aetherius describing the mission as it proceeded. He had already been so ill after the Alien Mission that the Master Aetherius had ordered him off duty to recuperate for 60 days with the first 30 days to be completely undisturbed. It was hard enough on Dr. King's body to take a teaching transmission without the added strain of being engaged in lightning-fast combat during such a samadhic trance condition. However even this essential rest had been interrupted when he was contacted by the master from Gotha only days later and he unhesitatingly returned to duty. But, even in the midst of this dire conflict, fatigued and unimaginably stressed as he was, Dr. King brilliantly interwove another aspect of his karmic magic into this newfound connection with the Gotha Masters.

* * * *

To say he was always thinking would be the understatement of the century. His mind was ever alert to new possibilities to improve and initiate strategic moves within the framework of the Cosmic Plan. He was on call for 24 hours a day for the cosmic masters, but even that was not enough for him. He was always looking to extend the karmic parameters of his mission and to introduce completely new elements into the matrix of terrestrial salvation.

And so it was that while he was battling against a deadly foe in the conflict which swirled around the planetary system of Gotha, he was simultaneously developing the wonderful mission he had devised upon Earth, Operation Sunbeam. He knew that it would not be possible for ordinary Earth people to invoke sufficiently elevated spiritual energies for this purpose, hence he had performed this task in conjunction with the great Saint Peter. But this would not always be possible, because this aspect of the mission might need to be performed in his absence and indeed after his demise.

While most generals would only be focused on wresting victory on the field of combat in which they were currently engaged, Dr. King could also see fertility in the healthy vegetation growing there. The mistake made by Gotha of focusing upon their own spirituality to the exclusion of other planetary races also meant that they were truly elevated beings with outstanding proficiency, even by cosmic standards, in prayer and the invocation of higher forces. Also they felt an unbounded admiration and immense debt of honour to their saviours, the Three Adepts. As usual Dr. King had no interest in receiving any form of debt repayment himself, but he immediately saw a karmic opportunity for the people of this planet.

The result was best expressed by the Gotha Master himself when he spoke on October 15th, 1966:

> Already two of our number are living upon your Earth. These two have been accepted by what you call your Spiritual Hierarchy. So impressed are we by the work of a few of you, so mightily impressed, impressed down to our very spirits, never mind our souls, by the spiritual grandeur of the Three Adepts, our true heroes, that we have decided to do what we possibly can for the karma of Terra. We realize, of course, that our actions, unfortunately, will be extremely limited by a certain predesigned and predestined karmic pattern leading to essential occurrence but, nevertheless, we are prepared to go to the very limit of our suffering, if necessary, so that your karma may be balanced. I am not referring to the karma of the average individual. Not, indeed, to any individual. I am referring to the karma which is creating difficulty in the successful performance of your magnificent Operation Sunbeam. Our intelligences upon Earth will take upon themselves the karma so that this operation may be performed in a correct manner.

These two wonderful intelligences would later be supplemented by a third to perform the essential role of providing the source of the energy sent to the Mother Earth in Operation Sunbeam in all future phases from then until the present day and beyond.

Dr. King had used the karma of a dire and deadly scenario, in another part of the galaxy, infused it with the light of his God-inspired mentality and created a new, heavenly vista for this planet. Turning adversity into advantage was for him a signature karmic manoeuvre – indeed it was a trademark of all the Three Adepts. In more basic times, the karmic agent Samson had ensured that honey would flow from the slain carcass of a dangerous lion, thereby turning a necessary killing into a bounteous offering. This principle was enacted time and time again in countless arenas by these three, not just to save villagers from a rampaging lion, but entire planetary races from alien domination.

The masters from Gotha performed another outstanding service to Operation Sunbeam, and to other worlds throughout the galaxy. For it was they who spread the word to other planets who had not considered themselves capable of such a mission before. As a result token repayments of energy to the logoi of hundreds of other planets started to be made, a development described by the Master Aetherius, as referred to in Chapter Five, as one of the largest snowballs in galactic history. With their help, Operation Sunbeam inspired the galaxy.

If there were such a thing as galactic laurels, the masters from Gotha would have bestowed them in abundance upon the Three Adepts. It is questionable whether these mighty warriors would have welcomed such laurels, but of one thing we can be sure: they would not have sat on them. For only seven months after the completion of the Gotha Mission, on October 26th, 1967, they were once more at war in the second major conflict which brought them to Earth. The very souls of every man, woman and child upon the planet were at stake – our Armageddon had started.

* * * *

Great forces are about to clash. Stupendous forces of darkness are preparing to bring about conditions on the surface of this world too horrible to contemplate. On the

other hand, other forces have dedicated themselves to your protection. Very shortly these forces must clash in mortal combat and the prize of this combat is all humanoid life upon Earth.

The prophecies are now being fulfilled.

These words were spoken by Saint Goo-Ling through Dr. King on September 23rd, 1967, when introducing the transmission by the Master Jesus 'The Three Saviours Are Here!'. They heralded in the next great conflict for the Adepts, Operation Karmalight.

In addition to the alien android, another entity had become aware of the energies released by the Initiation of Earth and the changes they would inevitably bring to the planet as a whole. He – who could also be she – had been known by many names throughout history, the most famous of which is satan. He bided his time during the Alien Mission and then decided to move. His goal was to bring all the lower astral realms under his own dictatorial rulership, following which he would proceed to take control of the physical and higher realms too. It was the task of the Five Adepts to prevent this and bring about a transmutation of this entity who had controlled the hells for millions of years.

One might think that this task would be performed by the great masters of this planet, but the evil in the lower astral realms was too powerful for even the ascended masters. However, for the Adepts to succeed they needed to instigate certain changes within the Spiritual Hierarchy itself. This was instigated in Phase 18 of Operation Karmalight – through a lesson which Dr. King later described as one of the greatest moments in the history of the human race on Earth. The Five Adepts demonstrated to the ascended masters once and for all the vital need for them to be proactive in taking more effective protective measures, rather than adopting their traditional, more pacifistic approach.

For centuries the Spiritual Hierarchy known as the Great White Brotherhood had expressed their wisdom through love and detachment beyond mortal comprehension. These selfless beings had held up their evolution onto higher planets by staying back on Earth to help mankind. Indeed their presence alone on Earth has held our karma in balance and allowed mankind to continue evolving on Earth throughout our long history. Very rarely had they come into direct confrontation with the darkest ones in the lowest realms. Certain ascended masters had assisted during the Alien Mission, but in Operation Karmalight the Five Adepts preferred not to accept their help even though it would have been willingly given. They would have felt responsible for the welfare and protection of these great masters had they entered this field of combat.

Fascinatingly, though, they did accept help from one who had taken a very different evolutionary journey from the ascended masters. This was a fallen initiate in the lower astral realms who became known as the Prince. He had a wonderful epiphany instigated by the Adepts, and especially by Number One, in 1963. As a result, he transformed instantaneously from vicious warrior to heroic soldier of the gods. Aided by some of his henchmen, he became an exceptionally valuable asset to the Five Adepts. This is another example of the Adepts turning the adversity of a tragic personal decline into one of triumphant advantage for the forces of light.

Dr. King, despite his pacifistic credentials, was clear that unlike the conflicts on our physical realm, battles in the lower astral realms were not only warranted but essential providing they came under karmic direction. He had stated in a lecture on November 12th, 1966, in relation to the Gotha Mission:

> I don't think that any war on Earth is the answer to any question but, nevertheless, when it comes to a cosmic conflict like this there may be a time, there may be a time when, if the Lords of Karma give permission it may be right to fight in this way for one's existence. But only if the Lords of Karma give permission.

The ascended masters looked to the Lord Babaji as their Spiritual Head, but not – to use a worldly term – as their political leader. A carefully devised lesson was reluctantly instigated by Adept Number One to demonstrate the need for them to change their outlook and bring a fundamental philosophical and functional change to the Spiritual Hierarchy of Earth in its entirety.

The Lord Babaji instantaneously grasped its fullest ramifications, which is not at all surprising considering his elevated Saturnian origin. Significantly it was also revealed that he had been, at a former time, a cosmic combatant of distinction. The lesson involved the Five Adepts proving through clandestine action that the sacred retreats inhabited by these great beings, along with the colossal spiritual power stored there, were at risk of attack from the evil magicians who were in conflict with the Adepts. The lesson was learned and changes were instituted throughout the Spiritual Hierarchy immediately. As a result of this move, the Lord Babaji took his rightful place as their political as well as their spiritual leader and made the following statement to this Adept during Phase 18 on September 2nd, 1968:

> **Number One, I owe you more than I owe any man on the Earth. Make sure that I will repay this to you.**

It was very difficult for Dr. King to speak of this statement, so moved was he by it and such was his reverence for the holy Lord of the Earth. The feeling was mutual in what was one of the great bonds in history, no doubt forged long before Dr. King ever came to Earth. Two very different, but possibly in their own ways equally exalted, cosmic intelligences came together upon this world and moulded our redemption. Very significantly, for the closing stages of Operation Karmalight the Lord Babaji took his place as Adept Number Six and retained this position thereafter under certain conditions. In doing so he was acknowledging and accepting the strategic command of Adept Number One in specific arenas, much as Dr. King always revered his spiritual stature. The Lord Babaji would use this title in the years that followed, when, as Dr. King put it, he was in combat mode.

Dr. King disclosed more information during the performance of this mission to members and sympathizers of The Aetherius Society than he had about the Alien or Gotha Missions. Perhaps he had gained greater confidence in doing so from his experience of the previous missions, but he was still wary of saying too much. On July 16th, 1972, he gave in an address one of the reasons why it had been necessary not to include too full a report on Operation Karmalight and the other missions while they were going on:

> The biggest contract ever put out in this world was put out on the heads of the Five Adepts, or any one of them. The contract said, 'dead or alive', and as far as I know it still stands. It was put out by the lower astrals and far, far more money, position or whatever price you wanted would be paid for the death of one – or five – of the Adepts to whoever executed the contract than ever the syndicate is able to offer on the physical planes. So we did have to go quite carefully.

Operation Karmalight culminated on February 24th, 1969, in the way it had to for karmic reasons: the Lord Babaji as head of the forces of light transmuted satan, the darkest and most powerful force in the hells. Another glorious victory had been wrought. As Dr. King put it years later in an address:

> It is the gospel truth that every one of you owes what freedom you now enjoy, what free will you now exercise, to five individuals who in the battle of Karmalight fought and won for you – not for themselves. It should never ever be forgotten.

Three momentous wars had been fought by the Five Adepts in less than four years. Saving a planetary race, the vast majority of whom had no appreciation or even knowledge of what had happened, must have been frustrating beyond belief. With his typically down-to-earth approach, he tried to bring this home at least to his own followers. He asked the cosmic master Mars Sector 8 – Special Advisor S2 what humanity owed the Five Adepts in financial terms for the eviction of the alien. This was the answer he received in a mental transmission on June 11th, 1980:

> The level one equivalent of the cost of the eviction of the alien android from Terra was approximately 33

trillion dollars, providing no Interplanetary Federation equipment values are computed...If the Adepts had demanded 50% of the total wealth of all terrestrials as a repayment for their unusual skill to be put at their disposal for whatever charitable purposes, or other uses they so desired, such a demand would have been logically reasonable and a conservative one.

Dr. King knew exactly who he was and what he had done, but he had to live among people who, with the exception of a few, had no recognition of him whatsoever. He had experienced the worst and most debased evil upon this planet in all its putrid depravity. These missions undoubtedly took their toll on him both physically and psychologically. As he said in his address, 'The Men Who Won Operation Karmalight For You':

It takes nothing, you know, to make one of you people retire – nothing. If you've got a little finger ache, you'll retire. If your foot is broken, you'll not come to meetings. Supposing your heart is broken – what then?

*   *   *   *

In the years that followed there were dozens more sorties by the Six Adepts into the lower astral realms, with commentaries by the Master Aetherius delivered through Dr. King on most of them. Prior to a world emergency on October 16th, 1972, which required the Five Adepts to engage with yet another alien invader, Saint Goo-Ling spelt out to close followers of Dr. King how it must have felt for him:

As you know, your leader will face great trials within the next few weeks – trials beyond your comprehension because they are beyond your ability. Therefore he will need you as friends to tend to and care for that part which is human as you are. Please attend to this. Even though the mission may be described by the cosmic master, Aetherius, only a fraction of it can be so

described – not all the waiting, suffering, heart-rending
pathos, which has already been endured by those who
will try their best to represent you terrestrials in this hour
of trial. The deep heart-rending worry brought about in
the frame that knows that a mistake will cost a million
lives or more, this is what I mean, this has been going
on...

If you want a motto, which describes the Adepts
fairly well, it is this: Service To Humanity Through
Protection. For that is their essence; that makes them
great; that makes them the greatest masters upon Earth
now and even through past history.

This is the first unequivocal and unambiguous statement
about the calibre of these Adepts, the physical aspect of one of
them being Dr. George King. It is so sensational that it bears
repeating: **the greatest masters upon Earth now and even
through past history.**

Even after these transmissions, about lower astral sorties,
ceased in 1975, Dr. King was always on call to leave his body
and respond to whatever crisis or necessity should arise. He was
always first and foremost a spiritual fighter demonstrating as
Adept Number One his manifold military and magical prowess.
He was the strategist and therefore, in certain respects, the leader
of the Adepts. In 1978 on Roseberry Topping, which he later
called 'Realization Point', a truth came home to him which is
referred to in Chapter One. He then knew for the first time why
he had suffered a life-threatening illness in his childhood, which
had forced him to spend so much time with his own thoughts.
He realized that this had been essential to his role in the Alien
Mission and Operation Karmalight decades later. His greatest
attribute was his mentality and this, as was becoming ever clearer
by the day, was imbued with superb genius.

Chapter Seven

SUPERB GENIUS

The 1960s were a period of seismic change for the western world. By the end of this decade conventions had collapsed; formalities had faded; and morality had metamorphosed into a new and far more liberal dynamic. Many modes of behaviour, interaction and even dress that we take for granted today – some would say for better and others for worse – started then. Draconian disciplinarians were being replaced by libertarian legislators.

Sociological theories have undoubtedly been offered as to why this might be, but none of them have yet identified one root cause of this change: the battles fought and won by the Six Adepts in the lower astral realms. The eviction of the alien and the transmutation of satan did not end the diabolical influence from these realms upon the physical world – far from it. But they did reduce the intensity of its stranglehold over certain types of conditioning and limiting thought patterns. There was a new-found sense of freedom from the establishment, and a greater willingness to consider radical approaches to living, including spiritual ones.

On the upside was an assimilation of all things mystical including eastern philosophy, UFO experiences and the ethos which then became known as mind-body-spirit. On the downside were a growing hallucinogenic drug culture and a fashionable disregard for the law. At the height of so-called 'flower power', one rock star broke this trend when he denounced his hippy audience for booing policemen on duty at a concert with the words, "You're all wearing a uniform!".

On the surface Dr. King seemed to be an unusual hybrid of opposing forces: the traditional morality of the 1950s and the most futuristic of visionary perspectives. These two mentalities were rarely found in one persona then – or even now. But then his human persona was something of a construct, because his origins were cosmic – totally immune from the social changes and cultural idiosyncrasies of this planet.

For The Aetherius Society it meant an increased interest in our teachings, especially from the young. It was far from overwhelming but it did lead to dozens of new, younger members joining the Society in the 1970s, some of whom would become totally dedicated to its cause (including the authors). This intake changed the mood music at Society activities from waltz time to disco beat, although as ever the tempo was ultimately set by Dr. King himself. It did though have a considerable impact on his mission and, in certain cases, upon him personally.

On June 5th, 1964, the Master Aetherius had informed the members of The Aetherius Society:

> **Just as important as this modern generation is the next generation. In fact, in certain ways the next generation is more important than you are.**

This may have referred to those in their late teens and early twenties who were joining the ranks of the Society in the 1970s. Certain of these new, young members were to become his closest aides, advisors and friends.

For now, Monique remained his main helper and most intimate confidante, but she would not remain Noppe since the new decade was rung in by wedding bells. On January 30th, 1971, Dr. King and Monique were married in the Temple in Los Angeles. The presiding minister was Charles Abrahamson who described the event in *The Aetherius Society Newsletter*, August 1971, as follows:

"The wedding, a simple, mystical ceremony, was performed by Rev. Charles Abrahamson. A short reception followed and in the evening a banquet was held in the exclusive Ambassador Hotel. The next day the couple left for Florida where they boarded the Dutch liner, *Nieuw Amsterdam*, for a short cruise of the Caribbean.

"For those who knew the couple best, their fellow directors and staff at The Aetherius Society Los Angeles Headquarters, the marriage was a natural outcome of a long, pure and rewarding spiritual relationship which began in 1959 when Dr. King arrived in the United States for the first time.

"At that time, Monique Noppe had already taken advanced degrees in the Rosicrucian Order, AMORC. Her life was already dedicated to spiritual goals. Dr. King arrived in late summer following the direct and explicit instructions of the Master Aetherius...Shortly after hearing Dr. King address a public audience in Los Angeles on the Teachings and Objectives of The Aetherius Society, Monique severed her existing ties and became a disciple of Dr. King. In the months which followed, her energy and devotion proved invaluable and she soon became his right hand. Throughout the years this relationship deepened. Their mutual regard and affection grew as they faced trials and difficulties together during the fledgling years of The Aetherius Society. The marriage itself changed little or nothing and the vows exchanged by the couple in their celibate, metaphysical approach to holy matrimony only served to further strengthen their bond.

"The wedding was held at 3:00 p.m. on Saturday, January 30th. The affair was formal with the wedding party in morning clothes and gowns. The bride wore a beautiful white gown with veil and train and her party were exquisitely gowned in vibrant colours. The groom and his party wore traditional Oxford grey morning coats. The guest list included all nearby members of The Aetherius Society and many close friends of the bride and groom. In addition, some close sympathizers of The Aetherius Society were invited as were all the Society's officers throughout the world. But the guest list was necessarily restricted by the small seating capacity of the church.

"At the reception, immediately following the wedding ceremony in the church, champagne toasts were drunk to the bride and groom and the wedding cake was displayed and cut by the bride. The event proved happy and enthusiastic with the congratulations of old friends and co-workers expressed together with best wishes for the future.

"This marriage, between the world's outstanding occultist and one of the world's most spiritually active young ladies was, in more ways than people realize, a truly significant event in the history of mankind and a great compliment to all women throughout our Earth."

Two days earlier, Dr. King had received a cosmic transmission from his brothers-in-arms, the Adepts, and his all-seeing master, Aetherius. Their words endorsed, sanctified and elevated this most unusual union between an exceptional cosmic avatar and a far from ordinary earthwoman. The following are extracts from their communications which were touchingly endearing while at the same time uncompromising about the significance of such world-to-world symbiosis.

The newlyweds walk radiantly down the aisle at The Aetherius Temple in Los Angeles.

Adept Number Two

It is my pleasure, at this time, to give to my colleague, known among you as George King, and to Monique Noppe my very best wishes for your forthcoming union, and may this be blessed and may you both enjoy deep joy and satisfaction, harmony and good health in your spiritual company.

Adept Number Three

At this time may I offer my very best wishes to my revered colleague, known as George King and to the lady he has seen to take as a spiritual companion. I wish you my blessings and the blessings of the gods and may your harmony be unbroken in this union. I realize that by taking unto himself what terrestrial man calls a bride, this colleague of mine has, without any doubt, put a blessing upon the heads of all good spiritually upright terrestrial women. The vast occult implication of this union will not be appreciated in their lives but, even so, its significance is very definite.

Adept Number Four

I bless you both in your most significant coming together. Indeed, this union is most significant in that its occult ramifications reach as great subtle fingers from world to world. It is almost unique in this aspect of being. May the Divine Principle and all the Lesser Lords bless the souls, the hearts, and the intelligence of you both from the day of your union onwards and upwards.

Adept Number Five

It is as though the worlds have come together for a brief aspect of time in time's essence. My dear Monique: may the blessings of all graciousness fall upon you and may this extension include you too, my great friend, my colleague, who is known under the pseudonym of George King. We have been together many times in hell and we have prayed together many times in the heavens.

May the true aspect of the heavens surround you both
and protect you in true spiritual love.

Master Aetherius
As you see, these four intelligences have given to you,
dear Monique, and you George, their love and blessings.
I too would like to give you my blessings at this time.
Understand one another, cooperate, and forgive, and you
will find a valuable and true friendship in your union.

For many upon this Earth, marriage brings a complete
change of lifestyle. Not so for Dr. King, whose single-mind-
ed focus remained as ever the performance of his mission and
how he could enhance it with his own unique brand of spiritual
ingenuity. He had already inscribed, in letters of gold, a page in
the Cosmic Plan for the salvation and enlightenment of our world
through his invention and performance of Operation Sunbeam.
Now he would illuminate this timeless manuscript further and
create new pages to adorn its contents.

* * * *

Prior to the performance of Operation Karmalight, two significant
sets of directives had been delivered. The first of these, on August
18th, 1967, revealed the dates of Spiritual Pushes for the next
1,000 years. The other, just over a week later on August 26th, was
'The Five Temples of God', in which the Master Aetherius gave
further instructions to The Aetherius Society for the coming 1,000
years.

A major consideration by the cosmic masters in delivering
these two very significant communications was the fact that
Operation Karmalight was looming, and no risks were being
taken as to its outcome. There was at least a theoretical possibility that the Five Adepts would be killed on this gruelling field
of combat, and that Dr. King would no longer be available
as Primary Terrestrial Mental Channel. Had such a calamity
occurred, nobody else would have been in a position to receive
and spread their directives to humanity as a whole. The Aetherius

Society would then have followed those received in August of 1967 and before.

Thankfully for us all, this was not necessary. Dr. King was not only available to receive further directives from the cosmic masters, which he followed to the letter, but to amplify them from his own mental resources. The Cosmic Plan was not framed to suit his temperament or predilections and he did not expect it to be so; he set out to mould it wherever he could for the greatest good of the world. And yet in most cases, due to the extremely difficult karmic situation on Earth, he was unable to choose as he would have wanted. He spelt this out in a very moving article entitled 'If I Could Choose' which was published in *The Aetherius Society Newsletter*, August 1968, during the performance of Operation Karmalight. Dr. King shared a rare and candid insight into himself – in fact it says so much about him as man and master that we are reproducing it here in full.

> If any man tells me in all honesty that he is free to roam the world as he likes without any ties, then I immediately conclude two things about such an individual.
>
> One, that his abilities are not considered to be of importance by the masters; two, that he is very selfish and that he does not care for his brothers as he should do.
>
> In my experience of spiritual work, I have discovered that one has to accept the unpleasant tasks as well as the pleasant ones with the same determination to perform both correctly.
>
> It is a certain fact that the Spiritual Hierarchy are, despite the karmic pattern of mankind, trying to save humanity from its own destruction. In view of this, they have been forced in the past and will continue to be forced in the future, to burden their chosen emissaries with tasks which are not only unpleasant, but sometimes downright revolting and horrifying to them. The more important you are to the great scheme of terrestrial salvation, the more you will notice this.
>
> A short time ago, I was asked by a member what

I would do if I had the free choice. I informed the questioner that such a question will never be asked of me by any who really count in the great scheme of world enlightenment. I stated, however, that if the question was rephrased, thus: "In the light of the present conditions on Earth, what would you do if you had the complete freedom of choice to do as you wished?", it would be a more feasible question.

This is a very interesting question. In fact, so much so that, on Sunday, May 26th, I decided to deliver a sermon at the Los Angeles Headquarters in answer to it. So well was this sermon received, inasmuch as a greater vista of understanding was opened up in the minds of the congregation, that I have been requested to write an article answering the question as I did from the platform.

First of all, it must be made clear that, in the light of the present karmic conditions on this Earth, some action of spiritual necessity would have to be performed so that one might have the clear conscience which comes with the performance of such acts. In the light of this realization then, may I give this as an answer to the interesting question which, to be really honest with you, I dearly wish one of the cosmic masters would ask of me.

First of all, I would gather around myself, from The Aetherius Society membership, three or four comrades who were compatible and harmonious **in every way**, and who had love and respect for not only myself, but also for one another. After this had been done, then the party of us would begin a world tour.

I would want to go to the ice fields of Alaska and in silence, tune into the mighty aspects of the Mother Earth which formed and kept in being those great lands of frozen waste. Not just to learn about them – which I could do from any good technical manual on the subject but to KNOW these ice fields even as the devas of the ice know them.

I would travel the seas in storm and calm so that I may KNOW the moods of the sea. Not in a purely terrestrial, scientific fashion, but know them as the mighty Sea Devas know them and know exactly WHY they change their moods and what results are brought about because of them.

I would travel above the clouds – over the steaming jungles of New Guinea, over the North and South poles, through the skies of Africa and Australia – and become so in tune with the clouds and even the substance of the gas belt itself, that I would feel near to its great, beating heart.

I would want to look out over the deserts on a cold night and see the shimmering stars glowing against the dark backdrop of mighty space and feel the cold, lonely desert breeze pass – not only around my body – but also **through my mind** in such a way that I could analyze the intelligence directing it.

I would want to see the Sun rise over seas, scorch the deserts and plains and set in cold beauty among the snows of the lofty mountains, so that I could be so in tune with the movement of the Earth beneath the mighty life-giving orb, that I would better appreciate those tangible and intangible gifts which She has, for centuries, poured down upon the race of small men who crawl, sometimes pitifully, across the surface of Her majestic body.

I would want to meander along a slow flowing river, like those which bless dear England's soil, in a peaceful gentle manner. Perhaps, the only sounds, the birds in the trees and the lapping of water against the bow of the small canoe, the drip of the liquid from the paddles when they were lifted – and, thus, become in tune with a gentle, green-giving, life-promoting aspect of Earth's natural scheme.

And then, in contrast, to sit near the base of a mighty waterfall and hear, perhaps even the self-same waters speeded into activity by the law of gravitation, tumbling from their heights, frothing, foaming, leaping as they fall into the black turbulent depths beneath and speak to the devas there to learn from them the significance of such power and how it affected other life forms on the planet.

Water again – large water. A shoreline fading astern as the propellers of a high speed launch churned the surface of the sea into three major lines of white frothing foam. This time to feel, not the power imprisoned within the man-made piston chambers of the mechanism which was driving me, but to feel and KNOW, in all ways possible, the resistance of the sea – registering a kind of definite objection to this type of treatment.

An English country lane in June, with leaves forming a green filigree against the blue cloud-flecked skies above. Again, in communication with another aspect of nature.

I would allow one year for this type of travel.

Then, I would return and perform Operation Sunbeam as it should be done – correctly!

So much better equipped would I become after my journeying, contemplations and ofttimes meditations upon the mighty aspects of nature herself, that I would then be in the best position to bring into being those prayers and mantras designed to invoke such natural forces in a harmonious way, so that powers from different sets of devas could be released through me, if necessary, and put into banks of spiritual batteries, energy which could later be discharged into the potentized spot[1].

Oh yes, I would still use the quick method devised in the beginning, namely a prayer team to invoke the power in the holy mountains so that it could be manipulated by the agents from Gotha, transmitted from these places, received by our Spiritual Energy Receiver and put into batteries. Such batteries I would discharge as well over the potentized spot, which, of course, by that time would have been made all ready for the continuance of Operation Sunbeam.

But, and this the ONLY reason for the year's travel, I would also discharge batteries containing the other powers referred to as a symbolic ritual – that of offering back to the great Earth a tiny portion of that which She has given so willingly for so long.

I feel that this would bring about an essential balance to Operation Sunbeam. Would make it indeed an operation which would inspire other worlds even to a greater extent than it has already done. (See *The Aetherius Society Newsletter*, January/February 1967).

The different batteries containing the different energies would be intermixed in a way dictated by deeper inspiration, and the energies placed into the throbbing heart of the potentized spot to travel deep, deep down into the absorbing nerve centres of the vital Earth.

Oh, dear friends, such would be an extremely beneficial operation and even a happy task indeed. A beautiful mission to be sure. For here I would be dealing with vibrant, magnificent energies, beauteous prayers and would feel the glow of being a channel for great spiritual powers, knowing that they were being given back, as a ritual, to their very source again. This would bring comfort and an inner, warm joy which is the result of a great spiritual accomplishment.

But, alas, it cannot be. It is only a dream-answer to a dream-question!

It is not what we would like to do, **but what we have to do that counts!**

And what do I have to do? Operation Karmalight! With its vile horror!

The sex fiends from ancient Rome, the mad torturers of the brave Christians, the diabolically cruel minds of the warlords of China, the bloodthirsty Mongol emperors, the murderous, brutal, cunning, death-dealing nazis – they are all there; the 'pick of the crop'; the worst that this world has ever produced – they are all there.

They are all there – together, in one insidious cesspit of brutal, horrifying intrigue.

Many times already I had to receive descriptions from the Master Aetherius, word pictures of the activities of five great spiritual beings of light, who have made many trips into this horror, this hate, this evil contamination, this diabolical intrigue.

Indeed is Operation Karmalight a terrible mission, the most frightening and horrifying task I have ever been given on this Earth.

There is not an entity existing on the lower astral realms who will be fit, **for a million lives yet**, to even look upon any of the Adepts – never mind to do battle with them in the brutal and insidious ways they are now conniving.

As if all this was not bad enough, before Karmalight is finished the 'major powers' on the lower astral realms will gather together their most cunning and most devilishly efficient assassins, and lay the biggest price ever laid upon any head upon the heads of each and all of the Adepts – the five know this. It does not make them stop and will not do so, but they do know it all the same. It does not make their job any easier, it makes it more difficult, because not only do they have to deal with the major mission itself as laid down by the Lords of Karma, but be prepared, at any time, to meet an attack in the back, as it were, from the murderous bounty hunters who will shortly be roaming those planes with their bands of killers, who have had centuries to become truly efficient in their diabolical art – murder!

Yes, ladies and gentlemen, if I had the opportunity, I most certainly would choose to perform Operation Sunbeam as I can now so plainly see – as though it came in a light from heaven itself – in the way that it should be done, in preference to Operation Karmalight and all the vileness which has to be cut through before it can possibly be brought to the conclusion dictated by Karmic Law.

I wish I was given the opportunity to make such a choice. I really do.

* * * *

Dr. King understood the directives he was given as though he was one of those who had formulated them (maybe he was). They were tasks which he would have readily laid down his life to perform, so confident was he in those who transmitted them. His faith in the Master Aetherius, Mars Sector 6 and other cosmic agencies, must have been based on experience through the millennia. It would have surpassed one hundred percent had that been possible – and where he came from, unbounded by terrestrial mathematical concepts, perhaps it was. He comprehended from the very fibre of his being exactly why these directives were being given. He went beyond their practical application to the essence of their necessities both for the human race and, more importantly to him, the self-sacrificing planet upon which it lived.

As the forensic metaphysician he was, he distilled these into three categories:

1)   The need to send high frequency spiritual energies to the Mother Earth in order to repay a fraction of our debt to Her. From this came his invention of Operation Sunbeam, the greatest karmic manipulation ever performed upon Earth by ordinary human beings.

2)   The need to assist the Mother Earth in releasing Her own energies following the Primary Initiation on July 8th, 1964, and to assist the devic forces to preserve balance upon the planet. This highly complex task would require specialized apparatus, and it was originally envisaged that Spiritual Energy Radiators would be used to accomplish it.

3)   To send out as much spiritual energy as possible for the benefit of humanity. One way to do this is by as many people as possible practising prayer and world healing in the correct manner. But Dr. King knew that its potency would be multiplied exponentially by using advanced radionic equipment and through direct cooperation with the cosmic masters, as was already being demonstrated through the regular operation of Spiritual Energy Radiators during Spiritual Pushes[2].

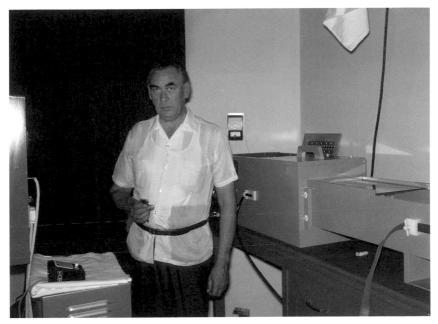

Dr. King directs an Operation Prayer Power discharge through the Spiritual Energy Radiator in London.

In addition to his other responsibilities Dr. King spent his remaining days upon Earth, and often his nights, striving to design and improve ways of achieving these three goals. He was not content just to carry out his commission to the letter, he was determined to go further. It is not clear how long his lifespan was originally intended to be, but we know that he extended it because he admitted as much to those close to him on several occasions. It seems that originally he may not have lived much longer than the mid 1980s, though the exact details of his cosmic brief are an enigma. One thing for certain is that he was willing to stay here longer, despite the numerous hardships it brought him, if it meant saving humanity from itself.

We could not possibly do justice to the detailed intricacies and extensive developments he single-handedly brought to every facet of the cosmic missions which he performed in the last three decades of his life. Not only are there too many of them, but some aspects were classified and he insisted they remain so, thereby avoiding misuse by any individuals who might attempt to do so. We can however pinpoint some of the highlights; the invention of one master enabled the intervention of the gods, and the world could breathe again.

An ordinary human being who had inspired their local community in some way would, perfectly understandably, bathe in the warm afterglow of such an achievement for some time to come. Had they inspired their nation or even the world, the glow would be ever more irradiant. Not so for Dr. King, even though he had inspired not a community, nation or world, but a galaxy through Operation Sunbeam; rather than contentment, his default reaction was a dissatisfaction with its functionality and an overwhelming desire to improve it.

He had already arranged for the Gotha Masters to provide energy of sufficiently high quality to be sent to the Mother Earth. During the 1970s he set out to discover more water-based psychic centres of Earth where the mission could be performed in addition to those off the Californian coast at Dana Point and Goleta Point. He undertook a research programme in the USA and discovered that there was one at Lake Powell on the Colorado river near the Arizona/Utah border. This beautiful centre was used in phases of Operation Sunbeam for the first time on June 1st, 1972.

Two months later Dr. King was in England where he had an outstanding and completely unexpected experience. While sitting in his office at Aetherius House in London on August 6th, he was contacted by an intelligence referred to as 'Questing'. So significant was this that he later said that it could have been a Lord of Karma or even an aspect of a Supreme Lord of Karma. Questing used pictorial language in the form of graphs to convey the fact that if Operation Sunbeam was extended to the British Isles its influence would be doubled. And so it was that a search began to find psychic centres in the British Isles. This culminated in June 1976 when he announced the discovery of two: one in Loch Ness and the other in the Bristol Channel.

Of all the psychic centres he had thus far discovered, Loch Ness was the most significant, being the fifth most important in the world. In 1978 he described it as: **the most mysterious one that I have come into contact with**. Dr. King made this process seem far more straightforward and easy to accomplish than it really was. It demonstrated his other-worldly connections with the Logos of this planet that he could identify so sacred an aspect of Her being as Her psychic centres. He must have understood this Logos since he seemed to know what She needed at this time following Her Initiation – and, more than any other master upon Her back, he knew what to do.

Just as pertinently, She must have known him too – it is even possible that he was here at Her request at this momentous time. From the early days of his mission She was not only his main focus, but he was profoundly connected to Her innermost being. In a little-noticed section of a lecture he gave at Aetherius House in London on February 4th, 1959, about 'The Third Blessing', he alluded to an outstanding experience. In all likelihood it passed over the heads of most of the attenders at the time, but in view of what came later it is redolent with meaning. It had occurred while he was charging the holy mountain Kinder Scout in the

Dr. King peruses the elements on Loch Ness in Scotland.

Derbyshire Peak District a few days earlier:

> I went to the place that was to be charged and it
> necessitated travelling through a tiny little cutting upon
> which, on each side, there were boulders. I took no
> notice of this at all. I just walked straight up through
> this cutting, sat down on the rock and many things
> happened. Among these was that I was taken to the
> centre of the Earth and I had the great privilege and
> great honour of seeing the Logos of this planet – the
> great Flame which actually burns in the centre of the
> Earth, energies from which we all use in order to gain
> experience.

As well as discovering new psychic centres, Dr. King was
determined to improve and increase the number of Operation
Sunbeam phases which could be performed by The Aetherius
Society every year. He set his mind to eliminating some of the
challenges present in the original modus operandi of the mission
and devised new apparatus which could be used in a much more
flexible way and without the need to discharge spiritual energy
from a boat in the location of one of these centres. In what became
known as Plan B, Operation Sunbeam could be performed over
a distance and the number of phases would be dozens a year
instead of just a few.

He also set about training the teams who would perform this
mission, to develop useful skills in boating, camping, technical
construction and, above all, disciplined coordination. The Society
was much more a spiritual commando force – and still is – than
a group of studious and worshipful aspirants. By the end of the
decade he had created an international task force specifically
for the purpose of performing Operation Sunbeam. Task Force
Initiates were bound by an oath of commitment and secrecy
in order to protect classified aspects of the mission's modus
operandi.

As he knocked his team of a few modestly paid and voluntary
staff into shape, he adopted a strict, no-nonsense approach which
was far removed from his manner in the early days of the Society

in London. Then he had been surrounded by people, often more aged than himself, who were willing to go so far and no further. In the 1960s in Los Angeles he had a small very dedicated and extremely active team several of whom were some ten years younger than himself. As this decade progressed and his true status became ever clearer, those around him operated less as a group of friends, though they would always remain that, and more as his disciples. With the exception of Monique, they referred to him less as George and more as Dr. King or Sir. This was not borne out of his personal wish but from karmic necessity – he could no longer be regarded as 'one of us'.

In the 1970s with an influx of new staff members, some 30 years younger than himself, the dynamic changed again. Orders were barked, reprimands were frequent and various forms of atonement were applied in order to bring what would become the team of the future up to scratch. It was not a path for the faint-hearted passenger – as no advanced path ever has been – but for the loyal, resilient trooper. Dr. King, a man of such compassion and humility that it flowed from every pore of his being, assumed the characteristics of an impatient general surrounded by ill-equipped subordinates while mounting a life-saving military campaign.

It was an excruciatingly lonely position to be in, and one which did not suit him personally. His longing to be among those of his own kind must have been desperate at times, but it was not permitted because of the dangers it would bring on the physical plane. Ray Nielsen revealed that on one occasion Dr. King and Adept Number Three had tried to meet up off land. Adept Number Three brought his boat near enough to the California coast so that Dr. King, leaving the harbour at Marina del Rey, could cruise out for a rendezvous. However this did not escape the all-seeing eye of the Master Aetherius who instructed them not to proceed and, much to his disappointment, this never took place on this realm.

Being the master he was, he knew that he had to do more even than train those around him, he had to manipulate their karma and more importantly guide them to continue to do so. The tasks which he was allotting to them were elevated positions of responsibility appropriate to a spiritual elite of adepts and masters. No one on his team had reached this evolutionary level, and yet somehow he prepared them to perform Operation Sunbeam. The strict discipline, long hours and testing rigour which he imposed upon his eager students were karmic enablers for the roles they would perform.

Yet, in the midst of this, he demonstrated extraordinary levels of patience and tolerance given the yawning chasm between his evolutionary position and that of those he had to work with. He could also be unexpectedly forgiving of transgressions and non-judgemental about personal failings of various kinds. Although his personal conduct was exceptionally strict – total celibacy for example – he could show more understanding than very ordinary terrestrial people sometimes do. His main yardstick was how much service a person was giving to the world as a whole – he could not abide laziness.

Through all this though, his belief in the potential of his students was absolute. He always thought that they could succeed and, where he could, gave them his backing even to the masters. At first he arranged for his mission team members to be sworn in as Great White Brotherhood Initiates. When certain of them failed to live up to their oaths, he regretfully had to bring this arrangement to an end. He was assisted in this by Saint Goo-Ling who made the very telling statement to him which Richard Lawrence remembers as: "You dream of their tomorrows while they inhabit their yesterdays." Even then he arranged for his team members to be logged with cosmic sources, an arrangement which continues into the future.

Peter Simmons, who straddled the 1960s, 70s, 80s and 90s as a staff member in London, remembers this changed approach by Dr. King as he trained his team members there. Of the first time he met Dr. King in 1967, he recalled:

"It was quite surprising really – not what we expected. We were all, as members of the trainee group, asked to go into the hall, as it was called then, which is now called The George King Chapel. I think there were about 12 or 13 of us. We all sat around the perimeter of the hall and then the master was escorted down and introduced to each one of us. He was dressed rather casually with a flat cap and we shook hands with him, each one of us as he went round. There was no eye contact whatsoever, almost as though he had his head bowed deliberately because he didn't want to have eye contact. It was not what we anticipated, that first experience of meeting him…"

"I don't think it was shyness, I think it was a deliberate ploy. He wanted to give the impression that he wasn't this great exalted master that we were ready to meet and greet. He wanted to do things unassumingly and he seemed to be so ordinary that it was a shock, I must admit."

Peter compared this impression with Dr. King's approach in London in the 1970s and early 1980s – a period when he visited the European Headquarters almost every year up to 1986, after which his health no longer made it possible. Peter commented:

"He really wanted to knock the staff into shape and those that could withstand the strict discipline, they were the ones he wanted to stay and make a good team out of. There were one or two incidents where he would make an example of you, but it was only in the form of a lesson. I think the remaining staff that were there treated it as such…

"He wanted to draw out the best in people and the way he was doing it was allowing people to learn a lesson from their mistakes. He was quite a strict disciplinarian but he had a soft side. He could be very, very gentle and he was very compassionate – that was the whole thing. He was doing it for our sakes and the whole entity of The Aetherius Society."

Dr. King was not going to allow anything to get in the way of advancing the performance of Operation Sunbeam. As he said in an address on November 6th, 1977:

> You can't do anything this big – and it is this big, believe you me it is this big – you can't do anything this big without it having certain karmic powers. And the more karmic powers it has, the more karmic reflection it will produce on any interfering force. That is obvious, it is basic logic.

In the same address he made another extraordinary and very

revealing statement, putting aside for once his usual tendency to conceal his true calibre:

> This is quite a statement and you can call me what
> you like after I have made it, it won't alter the fact that
> it is true: there are very few masters who have ever
> walked this Earth who could teach me one thing about
> the Law of Karma. This is one of my great specialities
> and everything I have done in the past 23 years
> connected with The Aetherius Society has been a karmic
> manipulation in one way or another.

He had finally admitted that he was a karmic magician the like of which this world had never seen before.

Years later the Master Aetherius would go even further when commenting on Operation Sunbeam in a mental transmission published in *Cosmic Voice*, July/August 1991:

> I would like to say at this time that, without your superb
> genius, this mission would not have been devised,
> especially in this time of your history.
>   Neither would this mission have even succeeded
> had it been devised by anyone else.
>   You do have a certain magic, whether you believe
> it or not, and all life streams on the planet Terra should
> be really thankful to their God, and to you, and to all
> concerned with the mighty Operation Sunbeam.

Commenting on this in an address, Dr. King described the statement that Operation Sunbeam would not have succeeded had it been devised by anyone else as: **the most unusual statement in occult history**. In fact he was so shaken by it that he rechecked it with the Master Aetherius the following day to make sure he had not got it wrong. Taken literally it must include even other masters on Earth, proving beyond all doubt his unique credentials.

He came to Earth for two major reasons. One was to strategize and fight in the lower astral realms the most critical and dangerous battles ever known in our history; the other was to help the Mother Earth and humanity before, during and after Her Initiation, and to deal with the massive energetic changes it would bring. Both of these could have been accomplished in secret, known only to the highest masters on the planet and a select handful of disciples. Had they been carried out in this very different way, undoubtedly it would have been much easier and more comfortable for him, but not nearly as effective from a karmic point of view.

The battles fought by the Six Adepts had a cloak of secrecy around them out of necessity. No one on Earth, including the ascended masters, were in a position to play more than a supportive role. Despite this, Dr. King went to great lengths to keep members of The Aetherius Society as informed as he could about major developments in these missions.

Dr. King's approach to the changes brought by the Initiation of Earth, however, was very different. He made a point of involving ordinary human beings connected to The Aetherius Society, who were not necessarily advanced in their own right, as much as he could. It was the fact that terrestrial people were helping to perform Operation Sunbeam which, above all others, inspired the galaxy. This must have been an aspect of what the Master Aetherius was referring to when he said: **You do have a certain magic, whether you believe it or not.** In his commentary, Dr. King reluctantly admitted it when he said: **I agree with Aetherius. I am afraid I have to. I do have a certain magic.**

* * * *

In his first meeting with the Protectors of the Flame on January 2nd, 1972, Dr. King had discussed with these Lords the construction of apparatus to radiate energies from the Mother Earth following Her Initiation. It had originally been envisaged that this would be done through Spiritual Energy Radiators in shape power temples[3] as outlined in 'The Five Temples of God'. A seminal event occurred on July 28th, 1973, which surely illustrates Dr. King's superb genius. He described this in *Visit To The Logos Of Earth,* in a modest and almost matter-of-fact manner:

> Even though I had been previously instructed by the
> Lords of the Flame not to incorporate any circuit into
> the new Spiritual Energy Radiator capable of collecting
> energies previously given to the Logos of Earth, later
> on this day I received a brilliant flash of illumination and
> was able to make a rough drawing of what I thought
> was an antenna system which I knew, at the time, had a
> wave form incorporated into it which was capable of the
> reception of spiritual energies which would be released
> by the Logos of Terra at a later date.

He later revealed that this rough drawing took a draftsman in The
Aetherius Society under his direction some 30 minutes to sketch.

Six years later in November 1979 he studied the plan he
had drawn up again in the light of his research into Operation
Sunbeam. He wrote in *Visit To The Logos Of Earth*:

> I was able to recognize this device which, if incorporated
> with a receiver coil which we had used with success
> in the old method of Operation Sunbeam throughout
> the years, was capable of the reception and controlled
> direction of energies released by the Logos of Earth.
>   This was not only an antenna – but almost a
> complete collection and radiation device!...
>   A much more definite procedure, by the way, than
> that originally designed for the apparatus for the future
> shape power temple.

In 30 minutes flat, Dr. King had altered the Cosmic Plan as
outlined by his own master, Aetherius, in the series of directives
given in 'The Five Temples of God'. He had invented Operation
Sunbeam to send energies to the Mother Earth, and now he had
invented the equipment to release energies from the Mother Earth
and he attributed his ability to do so entirely to divine guidance.
As he wrote in *Visit To The Logos Of Earth*:

> I need no further proof above that which has happened
> repeatedly to me, to know that God does exist!

Those 30 minutes of genius were a time capsule for the glorious mission, Operation Earth Light which would commence 17 years later.

*   *   *   *

In the meantime Dr. King's fine-tuned brain was also focused on the third essential strand of cosmic salvation, that of sending out as much spiritual energy as possible for the benefit of humanity. Drawing on his experience in Operation Sunbeam, for which he had designed a battery to contain the energies which would be transmitted to the Mother Earth, he saw another use for his invention. In fact he considered it to be so obvious that he was disappointed that it had not been suggested by someone else.

The concept was simple: if energy could be stored for one purpose it could also be stored for another. While ordinary human beings were not capable of invoking a high enough quality of energy to be directed into a psychic centre of a planet, they certainly could radiate wonderful prayer energy[4] for world peace, healing and devic stabilization.

He plucked possibility from the furnace of divinity, and forged it into a brand new mission, which he called Operation Prayer Power. He announced it on his 53rd birthday on January 23rd, 1972, as his gift to: **all people throughout the world who are unselfishly working for the preservation of the ecological balance of this planet so senselessly polluted by unthinking mankind throughout the centuries.** Once again he had revealed his true overriding motivation of helping humanity to affect the ecological balance of the planet Herself. While the term 'ecology' is frequently used today, it was not in 1972 and he was in this field, as in so many others, a pioneer.

Operation Prayer Power commenced on June 30th, 1973, on a beautiful sunny day on the picturesque slopes of Holdstone Down in North Devon overlooking the Bristol Channel. Led by Dr. King himself, some 200 pilgrims joined in chanting holy mantra while a small hand-picked prayer team stood before the Operation Prayer Power battery and directed into it a good quality of prayer energy. Later, on September 23rd, Dr. King led a pilgrimage to the shores of Padre Bay at Lake Powell, Utah, on the side of a psychic centre, attended by over 60 pilgrims, for the same purpose.

Hundreds of hours of prayer invoked by this combination of The Twelve Blessings and sacred mantra could be stored for release when it was most needed – and in a matter of only minutes. As Dr. King explained, it was not possible under the current conditions on Earth to gather together hundreds of people at a moment's notice to respond to a world emergency such as an earthquake, volcanic eruption, tornado, peace negotiation, etc. But if the energy was stored and ready after weeks of charging sessions (as they became known) held at meeting places in England and America, The Aetherius Society could respond to a crisis immediately. In addition to the timing aspect, Operation Prayer Power also dramatically increased the effectiveness of the spiritual energy invoked. Dr. King stated that when spiritual power is compressed, as it is in the Prayer Power batteries, that spiritual energy is transformed into what he called cosmic energy, with a much greater power to do good.

Dr. King instilled liquid gold into his alchemy when he arranged for the energy from the Operation Prayer Power batteries to be manipulated by the cosmic masters themselves. An early example of this occurred on July 21st, 1974, when 542 prayer hours[5] were released from the London battery during a vicious war being waged over the island of Cyprus between Turkish and Greek factions. It was directed by the masters to peace talks taking place at the United Nations in New York as well as on Cyprus. Within hours of the battery being discharged and, contrary to all predictions, a ceasefire was accepted by both sides. This was a template for many future discharges, bringing relief, sometimes miraculously so, to differing situations.

On September 2nd, 1975, Mars Sector 6 stated in a transmission:

> Operation Prayer Power, as you call it, will be officially accepted into the Cosmic Plan for the salvation and enlightenment of mankind upon Terra. A great honour indeed for the designer of this operation and for the

participants.

Three years later Dr. King wrote in *The Aetherius Society Newsletter,* March/April 1978:

> The Supreme Hierarchical Council governing this solar system after careful study and consideration, have chosen the mission which I designed six years ago to supplement their normal action from Satellite No. 3 for the coming year and into the future.

The background to this is a study in how much deference was given to Dr. King by the cosmic masters and how he used it to find new ways for us to help our world. In 1977 he made an application to Mars Sector 6 to allow groups of members to act as channels for spiritual power to be sent to the world from Satellite No. 3 when it was in orbit in special power manipulations. This would greatly increase the energy available to mankind and would be a great honour for all who could take part.

This was accepted on January 13th, 1977, in a transmission by Mars Sector 6:

> Always searching for different ways to help humanity, the person you call George King has petitioned on behalf of terrestrials and his organization, that members of this organization be allowed to cooperate more fully with the operations of Satellite No. 3 in all Magnetization orbits.
>   After due consideration, I have decided to grant this petition.
>   Therefore, during the Magnetization orbits of Satellite No. 3 just given to you, your members will be – where they are qualified – used as channels so that more power from Satellite No. 3 can – by this karmic manipulation – be sent out to all men...
>   George King has once again demonstrated his deep concern for terrestrial man and his compassion for his followers. **It should be known that, in deference to**

George King, I accepted this petition.

Dr. King then went all out to train the members and raise them to an acceptable level for this great honour. Classes were held at all the major centres around the world and every member wanting to take part was required to practise mantra regularly for a minimum period. From Dr. King's words during a series of talks he gave in Los Angeles in March and April, he clearly knew it was far from certain that these special power manipulations would succeed:

> I am giving you the absolute minimum to prepare yourself for the very great honour of being used as a channel by a cosmic force and if you don't think that's a great honour then I strongly advise you not to attend any more classes and not to even dream of being allowed to come to the Special Power Transmissions. It is a great honour. It's given in deference to me and I do want to see it work – for your sakes. I want to see this 100% successful. I want to see you successful. It depends on you – not me.

On November 17th just prior to the last Spiritual Push, Mars Sector 6 delivered the news:

> So far, the power manipulations during the Magnetization Periods in 1977 have been reasonably successful. We intend to continue these power manipulations for the last Magnetization Period this year, but starting in 1978, in our considered opinion, it would be better for the world as a whole if you really used that very effective tool designed by your leader. I obviously refer to the manipulation you term as Operation Prayer Power.

This was a blow to Dr. King. He had arranged for ordinary people to be used as channels for spiritual power manipulated through them to the world directly by the great ones. But a significant percentage of members did not live up to the meagre requirements and the power manipulations were not successful enough to warrant the effort needed by the masters on Satellite No. 3 in relation to the amount of spiritual energy being sent out.

Dr. King wasted no time in turning his attention to Operation Prayer Power to ensure that this would be in every way successful and illustrating even again his mastery of the Karmic Law. As he wrote in *Cosmic Voice,* January/February 1978:

> It was after the Declaration by Mars Sector 6 on November 17th, 1977, that the Special Power Manipulations would not be continued, but in their place would be put Operation Prayer Power, I decided that some very definite action was necessary for two reasons. By far the main one – to help the world as a whole – and very secondary in comparison with this – to prove that The Aetherius Society could rise to the occasion.
>
> After giving the matter some thought, I decided on a strategic move which could indeed balance the karmic scales in our favour.

He released over 900 prayer hours of energy from the Operation Prayer Power batteries in cooperation with Satellite No. 3 in the last Spiritual Push of 1977. He also had staff members on standby from 8:00 a.m. to late at night every day during the Spiritual Push ready to perform extra operations of the Spiritual Energy Radiator – resulting in 45 hours of them. All this was in addition to the Special Power Manipulations.

Though Dr. King's move to give members a chance to be direct channels of spiritual energy from Satellite No. 3 failed, his uncanny ability to turn failure into success resulted in establishing Operation Prayer Power as an essential cog in the operations of Satellite No. 3 in every Spiritual Push into the future. It was his signature magic once more of turning adversity into advantage. Regular discharges would now take place during Spiritual Pushes in conjunction with Satellite No. 3 and the energies would be manipulated by the master scientists upon this holy vessel. The mission had come of age.

Prayer teams and mantra teams alike practised intensively and received rigorous training to improve the quality and quantity of their energy output. Mars Sector 8 – Special Advisor S2, gave invaluable help in a series of mental transmissions through Dr. King as to the assessment and calculation of the energy contained in the batteries. Qualities were categorized from the lowest upwards as C, B, A, A+ and AA+; and the higher the quality, the higher the quantity invoked.

Mars Sector 8 – Special Advisor S2 also revealed that higher qualities of energy accumulate exponentially while being stored, so the race was on for prayer teams to raise their game. As the decades went by, with increased sensitization, all those who prayed at the battery were expected to achieve at least the A+ level, with the majority obtaining AA+ most or all of the time.

Aetherius Society officers were trained by Dr. King to perform essential functions during charging sessions: leading the mantra, assessing the prayers and timing precisely the output of energy into the battery. The discharge was performed by those responsible for running the Spiritual Energy Radiators who had by now been divided into: Engineering Officers, Technician Operators, and Operators.

The end result was a perfect reflection of Dr. King himself: spirituality fused with science fused with service fused with salvation. Furthermore, Operation Prayer Power extended to other realms where it could be performed in much greater numbers and more intensity. In 1979, for example, the Master Aetherius described its inauguration on the realm known as level four and it was indeed beautiful to behold. It was now clear for all who could see – that he was an agent of karma.

Dr. King invokes energy supported by mantra teams at the Inaugurations of Operation Prayer Power. Top: Holdstone Down, North Devon on June 30th, 1973. Above: Lake Powell, Utah on September 23rd, 1973.

Chapter Eight
KARMIC AGENT

For thousands of years, a mystical city has floated silently and invisibly above the Gobi desert, on the higher planes, keeping an exact orbit with Mother Earth – its name, Shamballa. Many have referred to it through the ages in a variety of writings and lectures, but rarely with complete accuracy. For Dr. King it was not a theoretical or metaphorical place but an exact location which he had already visited more than once. This time however it would be completely different.

On the afternoon of December 5th, 1978, he entered a profound and elevated state as he prepared to visit this sacred temple of light. He had previously been informed by the intelligence he sometimes referred to as his master, which was in all likelihood his own full aspect, that he would receive an invitation to attend a very significant gathering. The Spiritual Hierarchy of Earth, known as the Great White Brotherhood, wished to make a large-scale extension of Operation Sunbeam into psychic centres where The Aetherius Society was unable to do so, and following occult protocol they wished to seek his permission as its inventor and designer.

He knew that he would readily give his permission for such a gigantic spiritual move. But he could not have been prepared for what came next, as described in his own words in his book, *Operation Sunbeam – God's Magic In Action*:

> A tallish figure with a glowing countenance seemed to float rather than walk down the centre aisle and, quickly without hesitation, mounted the round dais on which I stood. I immediately recognized the elevated being who called himself Buddha in one incarnation upon Earth, and who had taken over the spiritual control of Shamballa when the Lord of the Flame of Venus – the Sanat Kumara – had to vacate this position, by Karmic Law, in

1956.

In the full aspected body he now inhabited, the Lord Buddha stood almost seven feet tall with shoulders broad by terrestrial standards. He wore a shimmering, golden robe which, at first glance, seemed to be made of a metallic substance and yet was not because of its smoothness and flexibility. As the lights in the Assembly Hall had now changed colour, predominantly magenta, with every movement he made his robe reflected not only the magenta but other colours as well. If that beautifully cut garment was made of a woven material then I have seen nothing like it on Earth because it seemed to glow or shine with a strange scintillating light all of its own.

As He looked at me his eyes were darkish, very penetrating, and yet at the same time filled with compassion and understanding, obviously reflecting the outstanding intelligence behind them. His hair was quite long, falling down almost to the shoulders at the sides and longer than that in the back. Under the magenta light it was difficult to tell the exact colour of it, although I feel it was dark brown rather than black. He did not have a beard and his skin appeared to be a light cinnamon colour as though tanned by ultra-violet radiation. He wore a large pendant around the neck which hung down to the lower chest, just about over the mystical heart centre. Beneath the robe and shining through it, was a belt studded with many jewels and the light from these jewels actually shone in a diffused way through the material which made up the long, shining, golden robe. I could not see the belt well enough to give a much better description of it though, at the time, I knew it to be a mark of elevated station, no doubt perfectly attuned to the wearer and probably obtained from his own planet Venus, or maybe even given during initiation by the Lords of Saturn.

A great being who, while serving an incarnation on Earth as Buddha, in one of his lesser bodies, had sought and found wisdom and a way to teach mankind the road to contemplative peace and inner knowledge. It is said in cosmic mystical circles that he was the elder brother of one who came after him, and was known to mankind as Jesus. In many ways there was some kind of similarity between the appearance of the Lord Buddha and the appearance of the Master Jesus who I had the great honour to meet, face-to-face, on a small hill in the north of Devonshire in England on July 23rd, 1958. Although the Master Jesus, at that time, was dressed in a different way, having travelled through space, the Lord Buddha this time was dressed in ceremonial robes.

I could see several mystical symbols which seemed to be fashioned **into** the robe rather than embroidered on it. He was altogether a tall, scintillating, elegant being of deep wisdom and great spiritual powers.

The Lord Buddha approached me and touched me three times: once upon the head, and then upon the right shoulder and then upon the left shoulder. He spoke in a physical voice, in perfect English, these most significant words:

"I thus initiate you as Grand Knight Templar of the Inner Sanctum of the Holy Order of the Spiritual Hierarchy of Earth."

After he had said these words, many white-robed figures appeared as from nowhere and the dais on which we stood started to rotate slowly in a clockwise direction, while the figures moved around the outside of the dais in an anti-clockwise direction chanting a very beautiful mantra. Then the Lord Buddha turned to me and taking from around his neck the magnificent pendant put it around mine and stated:

"You will fashion yourself a device like this and wear it during all your mystical ceremonies."

I was greatly thrilled and overjoyed at this – but that was not all. He then leaned towards me and in a whisper said three sentences.

Dr. King revealed in print that one of these three sentences was a request – though he took it as an order – to wear a particular symbol upon his terrestrial robes in future. Another of them he kept secret throughout his life. The third, which he confided to a select few, can now be published for the first time.

It related to an event which had taken place following a phase of Operation Sunbeam in the 1970s on the shores of Lake Powell. The mission team were seated around the campfire deep in conversation when the subject turned to karma. All listened in rapt attention as Dr. King verbalized his mastery in these words which are published in *Cosmic Voice*, Spring 1999:

> **Karma is pressure toward conformity. It is pressure directing you, the mind – and you, the soul – towards you, the Spirit.**

From this he took the first three words – karma is pressure – and offered them as a completely new definition, explanation and expression of this ancient Law.

The sentence uttered by the Lord Buddha was that these three words were greater than any he himself had spoken about karma when he was incarnate upon Earth. Coming from most people upon Earth, such a compliment may not have meant too much to Dr. King. Even coming from certain masters on Earth he would have been appreciative, but not necessarily surprised. Coming from the Lord Buddha, who had spoken some of the greatest wisdom ever delivered to humanity when he came as an avatar approximately 2,500 years ago, he took it as an overwhelming endorsement.

As a Grand Knight Templar of this Order, Dr. King had become, even in his unascended body, a member of the Spiritual Hierarchy of Earth – with all the privileges and responsibilities that implies. The Order into which he had been initiated by the Lord Buddha stretches back hundreds of thousands of years into antiquity. It bears no relation whatsoever to the Christian orders of chivalry which developed in the medieval and middle ages, nor to the institutionalized honours system connected to reigning monarchs or ecclesiastical authorities in modern times. It was established for the protection of those expressing spirituality, including various forms of worship in temples.

He should have been known from that day forth by everyone on Earth as Sir George King, and soon this would be reflected on the physical plane in a shower of titles bestowed upon him from several sources. In March 1980 he played an essential karmic role, known as a standby, prior to the Great White Brotherhood's Spring Festival of the blessed Earth, which required his presence at Lake Powell. While staying in a small desert town on the way back, he received communications from the elevated ascended masters, the Lord Maitreya and Saint Goo-Ling. Both these masters pointedly and deliberately referred to him in these communications as Sir George King. He commented about this to those around him at the time:

> **This is done for a purpose; somehow this is going to be brought on to the physical levels of this Earth.**

Within a month his prophetic words began to manifest. Apparently out of the blue, he was invited and later invested into a langue (branch) of the Order of St John of Jerusalem, Knights of Malta, which came under the royal protection of Prince Henri III de Vigo Paleologo, a descendant of the Byzantine Imperial family. So impressed was Prince Henri by Dr. King and his writings that he quickly recognized him as a cosmic master in his own right. Prince Henri bestowed upon him further titles including the highest of them all – one which he never had and never would accord to anyone else – when he crowned him as the Prince de Santorini, in St George's Church, Hanover Square in London's fashionable West End on September 26th, 1981. In doing so he fulfilled a prophecy made by the Master Aetherius in 1966 when revealing that Operation Sunbeam had inspired the galaxy:

> **Some 'Kings' are due for very elaborate crowns as a result of the overall effects of this action.**

During the 1980s he received accolades, including chivalric knighthoods from a variety of orders; medals from civic and military associations; and honours which he prized highly from the American Federation of Police. He also received a number of honorary doctorates from academic institutions. These supplemented the doctorate of divinity he had received many years earlier from the International Theological Seminary in Van Nuys, California following the publication of his book, *You Are Responsible!*, in 1961. Some of the honours Dr. King was offered in this period were more legitimate than others, and he did not accept all of them. He especially valued two from his country of birth: the Freedom of the City of London; and a grant of arms[1] from Her Majesty, which was presented to him by one of the Queen's Heralds, Bluemantle Pursuivant, at a ceremony held in Los Angeles in 1991.

This was a new departure for Dr. King who was far more used to ridicule and rejection than he was to recognition and respect. It may also have provided a balance for the disapproval he must have experienced following his honourable decision

Sir George King being crowned as Prince de Santorini by Prince Henri III de Vigo Paleologo, in St. George's Church, Hanover Square in West London.

to become a conscientious objector in the Second World War. It was not that he regretted it, because he knew it was a decision he had had to take at that time. But it went against his nature as a born warrior, who would later fight the most important battles in history and receive zero appreciation from any terrestrial source on the physical plane other than his own Society. Hence he particularly valued the invitations he was now receiving from, for example, the Dunkirk Veterans' Association, and representatives of the Secret Army, which had led the resistance movement in Belgium during the war.

Alyson Lawrence attended many functions in the UK with Dr. King and acted as his translator when Italian or French was required, including with Prince Henri who was Italian and with his wife Princess Françoise who is French. Alyson expressed her fond memories of these events:

"He was getting recognition on the physical plane and he really enjoyed the company of people from different Orders. It made him really happy…

"One such person was the President of Free Poland-in-Exile who appointed him to his cabinet. I feel that he used this connection in a karmic way. The reaction against Soviet communism started in Poland and, to me, this is an example of how he was able to manipulate karma behind the scenes…

"Prince Henri regarded our Master as his cousin and had the greatest respect for him. He came to London to attend glittering ceremonies, such as at the Dorchester Hotel in 1981."

Lesley Young, who was Dr. King's secretary at the American Headquarters in Los Angeles from 1979 until his passing in 1997, was actively involved with correspondence with a wide variety of these diplomatic contacts. She commented: "I think it was a great release and a big boost for him. It was something he could really enjoy that could lift his spirits and often did."

Concurrent with this worldly recognition came approaches from ecclesiastical sources. He was advised, as the leader of an international religious organization, that he was eligible to become an archbishop of his own churches. A bishop of the Liberal Catholic tradition[2], let it be known that he would be honoured to consecrate him. Touched as he was by this offer, Dr.

King needed cosmic verification before making such a move.

He approached the most elevated of all sources on Earth, the Lord Babaji himself, who assured him that he had every right, even without such a consecration, to declare himself an archbishop. After all, he had received 'The Twelve Blessings' from the Master Jesus himself, as well as other transmissions from this fountainhead of Christianity, and from Saint Peter, who is regarded in the Catholic Church as the ultimate source of apostolic succession.

Dr. King could see the advantages of harnessing a terrestrial-based episcopal succession, virtually as a karmic anchor. He therefore accepted this offer, upon the advice of the Lord Babaji, and was duly consecrated in New York on August 23rd, 1980, with the stipulation that he was released from any obligations other than to his own church. In a mental transmission on August 16th, 1987, the Lord Babaji put this stamp of authority upon this happening speaking on behalf of the Great White Brotherhood:

As far as we are concerned, you were consecrated as a bishop and the consecration went even further than that, in that we were present and did pass on certain powers.

From this came the start of The Aetherius Churches, which acts in alignment with the Society as a whole. He became its Metropolitan Archbishop and adopted the title, His Eminence Sir George King, which we will use for the remainder of this biography.

* * * *

At one level, chivalry was a hobby which brought him great enjoyment, partly because he came into contact with stimulating, new company. At a deeper level, he knew exactly what was happening and saw it as an essential karmic manipulation on behalf of humanity as a whole.

On a short break in Bournemouth with Lady Monique, Ray Nielsen and Richard Lawrence, he shared the real reasons for it one evening over dinner at the Carlton Hotel. He explained that the Lords of Karma considered it necessary for him to receive recognition in his lifetime in view of his accomplishments upon Earth. Although such honours meant little to him – considering where he came from, why would they? – it was vital that at least some terrestrials expressed their appreciation in this way.

It is likely that he used it as karmic leverage for giving more to the world, even possibly extending his life. It was virtually a resource, which could be drawn upon at critical times, as became clear to those closest to him. In 1986, for example, literally as he was being taken in for an angioplasty procedure, he called Richard Lawrence from his hospital bed to accept a particular award he had been offered by a biographical institute in Cambridge. It was as though this apparently insignificant accolade could provide life-giving energy just minutes prior to his surgery. In his later years as his health deteriorated further, he would sometimes phone Richard before a gruelling mission for a progress report about any decorations he was due to receive. Occasionally the mask would drop and he could be clear that they were necessary. At times like these it was transparent that such recognition had nothing to do with him personally and everything to do with his position as a karmic agent upon Earth.

It cannot be said that this was beneficial to him from a publicity point of view. Many people have little time for establishment honours nowadays and even less for those they might regard as questionable. Nevertheless it was a token representation upon Earth for one of the greatest avatars that has ever walked among us – and, above all, it was not given posthumously as is so often the case.

What happens down here is very often a basic reflection of what happens above. On April 16th, 1981, His Eminence received what turned out to be the last cosmic transmission delivered through him in samadhic trance, which was an announcement by Mars Sector 6 of a series of cosmic awards and promotions. These were made to each one of the Adepts, Adept Number One being announced as:

Rank – Commander
Acting Rank – Vice Admiral
May take independent action

Diamond Medal of Honour in Humanities
Ruby Medal of Valour in Combat

In addition to listing awards to the Six Adepts individually and collectively, Mars Sector 6 specified the following awards:

The Academy of Applied Space Sciences has made the following Awards of Merit and Honour to George King for the invention and performance of Operation Sunbeam:

Saturn Peace Prize for Humanities
Venus Peace Prize for Humanities
The Mars Sector 6 Peace Prize for Humanities
Ruby Medal of Honour, and two Stars, for Valour

It is interesting to note that cosmic awards were also made to The Aetherius Society for the performance of certain missions. It must be extremely rare, if not unprecedented, for any terrestrial organisation in history to be honoured in this way, but not so surprising when you consider who its Founder/President was.

*　*　*　*

Sir George involved himself in virtually every aspect of the Society's function. In 1976 he published his seminal book *You Too Can Heal* which altered the mindset around healing in spiritual circles. It was commonly believed then, even by practising healers, that this was a gift – you either had it or didn't but you certainly couldn't learn it. His book and the course he devised around it revolutionized the movement. Today it is generally accepted that healing is an ability which can be learnt by anyone who is willing and able to use the correct technique, and his ground-breaking work has much to do with this.

He lectured in the UK, USA and New Zealand in the 1970s and early 1980s in a variety of locations. He devised courses under the name of 'The College of Spiritual Sciences' in order to teach the basic psychic and spiritual skills which he had spoken and written about for decades. These included spiritual healing, yoga breathing, Mantra Yoga, dynamic prayer, psychometry, pendulum dowsing, personal magnetism and colour healing. Instructors were trained at headquarters and branches around the world, and over the years thousands of students from within and outside of The Aetherius Society took these courses.

He arranged for The Aetherius Society to attend large festivals and exhibitions in various countries, and personally spoke at Festivals for Mind-Body-Spirit in London. He would spend hours talking to members of the public on The Aetherius Society stand about what were to him the most basic of topics such as dowsing and UFOs. As well as *You Too Can Heal,* he wrote and published several books generally focused on aspects of the cosmic missions he was performing and advancing in this period. He continued to edit and write much of *Cosmic Voice* which was published very frequently to keep members and subscribers up to date – he even supervised its printing.

He gave regular addresses delivered mainly in Los Angeles, but also in London when he was there, which were sent swiftly around the world so that the branches and groups could hear them without delay. When it became available he took full advantage of the fax machine in sending out regular news releases throughout The Aetherius Society.

He furthered the inner growth of the Society by launching a Temple Degree Initiation scheme in 1981, which he had first outlined in *The Aetherius Society Newsletter* in 1966. A combination of dedication, service and knowledge of the teachings entitled Aetherius Society members to advance to various grades of initiation with coloured robes denoting their level. He personally initiated scores of Member-Initiates in both London and Los Angeles.

His work ethic was extraordinary, demonstrating the very essence of what Karma Yoga should be, namely an unconditional commitment to serving others. Lesley Young remembered what it was like working as his secretary:

"It was very strict and disciplined. Everyone was on call pretty much all the time. He was a very 'now' person and when he wanted something done people had to be there to do it, even if it overlapped their own personal time. It was certainly tense…

"He was very much a perfectionist and it seemed to encompass every aspect of his work – from the higher aspects down to a simple staff memo. He spent time correcting, re-correcting and re-doing something until it was right, which meant every comma, full stop – every detail...

"He had an excellent memory and followed through every minor detail until it fitted the way he wanted it done. He had moments of relaxation, but work always came first – it was full on, intense and whatever it took to get it done he would do...

"I received reprimands, which was not pleasant, but I never felt any kind of negative energy from him. His energy was always up despite his frustration caused by people's carelessness and weaknesses. Even when he was angry, the energy he released was never anger."

* * * *

In the 1970s and early 1980s he found more opportunity for relaxation in the UK than in the USA. He would take the Society's boat, *Sea Deva*, on the Thames for short trips of a few days. He would moor the boat and stop at hotels and inns along the way where dinners were enjoyed with invited guests, often amid much storytelling and laughter. As ever there was another reason for these excursions – the concept of time-off for its own sake being anathema to him. They were a way of giving much-needed training and boating experience to mission team members who acted as the crew under his watchful eye.

In 1983, he decided that The Aetherius Society should purchase a small bungalow in Combe Martin near Holdstone Down in North Devon, after much persuasion from Lady Monique, which he called 'The Retreat'. This was endorsed by his own master who made the following statement to him when he was alone on this mountain on October 8th, 1983 as reported in his book, *The Festival Of Carrying The Light*:

Give my love and blessings to your honourable wife for her latest endeavours to secure a suitable base for you in this area.

This should have been procured some years ago, but it was you – because of your 'practicality' – who did not pursue it any further.

I would remind you, My Son, that 'practicality', as you call it, is manifested in many different ways – which you no doubt appreciate.

You should also appreciate the fact that you have already suffered too much privation for mankind and an end to this must be brought about.

Let the plan to secure suitable and comfortable living quarters in this area be implemented!

This will enable you to re-live your ancient tradition.

His Eminence spent as much time as he could at The Retreat which suited him perfectly. His trips always included work projects of one kind or another, and he generally climbed Holdstone Down where he received significant inspiration appertaining to his mission. He never gave a full explanation of his 'ancient tradition', but certainly away from the hustle and bustle of a headquarters there was far more opportunity for reflection and attunement to the inner planes. He also found time for enjoyable conversation with his close companions, either around the dinner table or occasionally at one of the various hostelries in the vicinity!

When he was engaged in a mission on Loch Ness he would stay at the small cottage there, re-named King's Cottage, which had been purchased by the Society in 1977. Alyson Lawrence cooked for him in London, at The Retreat and King's Cottage and joined his table for many dinners. She remembers:

"With me he was always friendly. I saw some people getting told off for things they hadn't done right and I did experience that a few times. You had to follow set procedures with the food, such as having a prepared menu, always with an alternative. He didn't eat a lot and his food was quite simple, but he was very particular and it had to be well prepared…

"He was a stickler for protocol. We waited until he came and then we would all stand to welcome him, and it went from there. At the dinner table he could be in a very good mood and get everybody laughing. He nearly brought the house down on more than one occasion with his wonderful sense of humour…

"Now and then he would come up with something and make a revelation, but generally we talked about things that would help him to relax."

He made short trips around the country of his birth with one or more overnight stops along the way which he much enjoyed, but there always had to be a purpose behind them. It could be anything from searching for a new missions vessel by visiting boatyards or attending a boat show, to extending his new-found connections made through chivalry and other associations. Sometimes a trip would include functions of one type or another such as that held by the Association of Freemen of England at the University and Cathedral in Newcastle in 1986.

Dr. John Holder, who acted as his personal assistant and driver in Britain during that period, recalled the pleasure they brought him:

"He loved those trips around the UK, mainly with Richard Lawrence and myself. He had a great time. It was fantastic – he was quite easy to be with…

"He liked to leave early, often at 7:00 a.m. We would stop at a service station on the way and he used to have a packed lunch of sandwiches, pork pies and things like that. He would always have tea and sometimes sherry. He wasn't always a fan of luxury hotels and could be quite happy with an average hotel. On a Thames boating trip he could stay either at an inn or at one of the best hotels along the river…

"In the car he talked all the time, mainly about Society business. On one occasion, for example, he came up with a plan to have one page for each phase of Operation Sunbeam to be published in *The Aetherius Society Newsletter*…

"He would generally have healing twice a day – after lunch and before bed, and sometimes a treatment with hot towels…

"He loved The Retreat because he could get away from things – he called it his fairy castle. Even there he would work – for example he would take Holy Stone Shapes belonging to members to give them his personal blessing."

Though he loved to visit Britain, he spent most of his time in

America, with the emphasis as always being on work. The task he was most focused on in the late 1970s was the research and construction of the radionic equipment for Operation Sunbeam Plan B. He realized that he needed to drastically change and improve the existing modus operandi (Plan A) to enable the mission to function without a boat crossing a psychic centre while discharging a battery filled with energy. To accomplish this Sir George needed to discover a new (to this Earth) and very advanced form of radionics. With his knowledge from other places he was able to do so in a theoretical way quickly, coming up with a design shortly after the first phases were performed in Loch Ness in 1977.

The difficult part for Sir George in inventing a new form of radionics on Earth was creating the equipment with existing technology and testing it to make sure it all worked. As he had done previously in the development of the Operation Bluewater equipment and the original Operation Sunbeam equipment, Sir George was able to get a head start on the physical construction by creating the equipment mentally out of 'mind stuff' and watching it work on the subtle planes. He could then tweak the design mentally until it was able to do what he wanted it to. But to recreate that design on the physical plane, with physical materials, tools and equipment, took a monumental effort, not only by Sir George, but also by his small team of technicians.

During an address given in Los Angeles on February 25th, 1979, Sir George described what was necessary to create the magic of his new Plan B.

> God's magic is like a flat pool which perfectly reflects the images of spiritual action, until we ripple that surface with the coarse rocks of our wrong thought and action. When we do this the ripples cause a distortion of the images and the spell is broken and the magic is lost. This magic is stronger than all the worlds and yet as delicate as the petals of a very beautiful flower.
>
> I have told you repeatedly, in the last few months, that some of us in the field witnessed what many people would describe as modern miracles – miracles which

happened right in front of our eyes. The very essence of the research project into Operation Sunbeam itself was a miracle. A miracle, not done by any entity, but a miracle virtually done, in the beginning by God, and all that I did was to discover that aspect of God's magic – not make it work, as much as discover the fact that it was here in the beginning...

If you look back at some of the feats of the Three Adepts you will notice one thing standing out above all else – that was intensity of purpose. There was no deviation from that predetermined goal – not any deviation. They acted as one individual and with the result they had amazing powers. Powers which were different from the powers demonstrated by Moses, but even stronger than that. Their magic was born out of a determination to obey their masters' command. A determination, an unconditional determination, to do this. An unconditional surrender to God, to good, to karma, and yet they didn't surrender to karma at the same time, but made it for themselves as they went along. Moulded it. Manipulated it until it could be used to bring about their great purpose...

Not only are we entering into a great mission as never before, as far as Operation Sunbeam is concerned, but also we should be entering a new spiritual age for The Aetherius Society. And all of you should enter this new spiritual age. An age where pure brotherhood means more to you than ever before. Not to pay lip service to, but to live, where genuine friendship is more important than your lunch or breakfast or dinner. Where wisdom, and you've been given wisdom, is the very breath of life to your mind. If we do this, if we have this outlook, all of us, and you're just as responsible for having this outlook, for performing in this way, as I am because you're part of a whole. It's a small whole but it's a whole and you're part of that, and if you vibrate in the right way you gradually help the whole to vibrate in the right way. If you are a dissenter, dissatisfied, negative, if you do not obey the basic Laws of God then you vibrate in the wrong way and cause dis-ease or dis-harmony to the cells around you, and you would be amazed how this spreads...

No matter how good we are, or bad we may appear, we are still an essence, a spiritual essence, we still have the powers of a great one – if we will only realize this. You know what the masters have said. They said, go deep inside, contact the essence, contact the force, the God force within you and then come out and manifest this. Not stay inside in bliss but come out forward, into the world and manifest this. And they say that those people who do not do this are fools because sooner or later they will have to...

Like I did with Operation Sunbeam. In fact I went further than that in the beginning. I built up the mechanism in mind stuff and ran it for about two weeks in mind substance and watched its failings – I had a great shock when I found the limitations under which we had to work on this Earth. I had to modify it greatly. The original Operation Sunbeam apparatus was a gorgeous piece of work, but it's something for which we did not have the finances, or the tools, or the ability in those days.

It was an electric time at the American Headquarters, very intense and exciting. You could really feel that you were living at the centre of history being made. The research project took Sir George with small teams to both Lake Powell and Loch Ness to learn about those two psychic centres and to understand better how to create the necessary equipment to relate to them. This then moved into the phase of creating the initial equipment for testing, which was done at the workshops in Los Angeles. This was then followed by more trips into the field to test the equipment with the close help of the masters from Gotha.

In April 1979, the research aspect of Operation Sunbeam Plan B had been completed. It was at this magical time that Sir George revealed a very telling experience in an address given in Los Angeles on May 6th, 1979, describing a ritual he performed on the psychic centre in Lake Powell on April 27th.

> I decided that a certain ritual had to be performed
> by myself alone over the psychic centre. Obeying
> instructions from Gotha – or suggestions from Gotha – I
> had to physically close down the whole research project
> and that is what I did. I went out and I closed it down.
> During the closing down ritual, I made a sacrifice to God,
> which is usual in occult actions as big as this one. We
> were closing down an era, we were rewriting a calendar.
>   We were closing another chapter down completely
> forever and ever and ever and ever and so, therefore, I
> had to make a sacrifice and also at the same time I made
> a promise to the Logos of Earth, which one or two days
> previously to this had for a moment overshadowed me.
> I have not spoken about that yet except the ancient
> sadness was an experience, which was absolutely
> terrible. However I made this sacrifice and this sacrifice
> entailed putting some materials into the psychic centre,
> which is under about 80 fathoms of water in that
> particular place...
>   I had promised the Logos of Earth that we would
> shortly return because Operation Sunbeam is now
> closed down and that was the end of the closing-down
> ritual.

The revelation by His Eminence that he had been overshadowed by the Mother Earth Herself, even for a moment, is awesome indeed. He felt Her ancient sadness, something he seemed to understand intuitively throughout his life. It was this which drove him more than anything else, to work so hard and so intensely in his mission to Earth. So real was this that he felt compelled to promise this great Goddess that he would be restarting Operation Sunbeam soon. It was just months after this experience that his amazing visit to the Logos of Earth, as related in Chapter Five, took place.

Richard Medway, who took part in aspects of the research project as well as the construction of the radionics equipment, described this time:

"When he worked on Operation Sunbeam he would definitely dot every 'i' and cross every 't'. He did experiments to prove that it would work. Every step he took he had done the research beforehand and made sure that it worked. Whatever it was he would want it to be perfect because for the Earth it had to be…

"I tried to understand why he was impatient. He was stuck with working with human beings clumping around in the dark…

"There was so much pressure, it was one problem after another, not necessarily in a bad way but just situations that would come up. He was always under pressure, he always had to solve whatever problems came up because of his sense of duty and his higher calling."

Much of this pressure must have come from the promise he made to the Mother Earth on April 27th, 1979. Through tremendous hard work and his unique magic, Plan B started officially on June 14th, 1979, a truly amazing feat. As the masters from Gotha put it on that date:

> Your equipment is excellently functional. This was the most powerful phase we have yet performed in Operation Sunbeam. Well done! A great day indeed – and always should be revered as such.
> Go with Divinity's blessings. Gotha.

It is an unbelievable miracle that a single individual could invent dozens of pieces of equipment for such a purpose in a year and a half – it has never been known in the history of the world before. His Eminence attributed the whole secret to his unconditional surrender to God.

As he wrote in *Operation Sunbeam – God's Magic In Action*:

> There has to be some secret behind designing an operation which has that much spiritual power attached to it. There is a secret behind it. The secret is an amazingly simple one:
> **Unconditional surrender to God!**

Operation Sunbeam was the result of one man coming before God and saying: "God, use me. I hereby surrender myself unconditionally to Your direction."

There comes a turning point in the lives of all of us. This is the focal point of your life, like the hub of a wheel. The finest wheel is useless unless it has a functionable hub, and unless that hub is in the exact centre of that wheel.

The turning point comes when you devote your life to God wholeheartedly – without reservation. **Without reservation! Without any reservation!**

When you do this all the powers, all the inspiration, and all the knowledge are yours!

* * * *

As the years progressed, Sir George started to spend more time at his small bungalow in Santa Barbara. This had been bought some years earlier, with the help of a generous donor, because of its proximity to the psychic centre at Goleta Point. He had only occasionally used it, but from the end of the 1970s he started to stay there more often. Richard Medway recalled:

"When he first went up it was a sort of vacation, he had to get away from work. It would only be perhaps four to seven days every two months or something like that…

"At the beginning he was relaxed and then it became 'I should take this up there with me to work on' and then, 'I'm going up to Santa Barbara to work'…

"He would specifically go up there to do something, including blessing Holy Stone Shapes, and that was the best place for it…

"From the late 1980s, he would be there for three weeks or more."

His role as Primary Terrestrial Mental Channel was undiminished and would remain so up to and including the last days of his life. After 1981 he no longer received cosmic transmissions in samadhic trance because of the demands it placed upon his physical health and mental resources. He did though receive an abundance of mental transmissions with increased frequency – sometimes more than once a day. Mars Sector 8 - Special Advisor S2, later known as Sector S2, was one of the cosmic masters who most often communicated during this period, as was Adept Number Five.

All the while the registers of his mind scaled ever upwards as he continued to hone and fashion the cosmic missions which were entrusted to him. This, together with his responsibilities as Adept Number One and his role as Primary Terrestrial Mental Channel, were his main tasks and should ideally have received his exclusive attention. Was it really appropriate that such an avatar should have to concern himself with the relative trivia of running the Society, when compared with the totality of the

His Eminence Sir George King at The Aetherius Temple in Los Angeles, flanked by two tables displaying cassette recordings of the mental transmissions he had received.

mission he was bearing like some 20th-century Atlas?

His self-sacrificing willingness to take everything upon his own shoulders appeared to be in conflict with directives from the Master Aetherius. On September 18th, 1977, His Eminence had received a cosmic transmission from this master about how The Aetherius Society should be run from the start of the third phase of his mission which commenced on January 23rd, 1978:

> Good afternoon. At this time, my message will be very short and to the point. This message applies to the organization known as The Aetherius Society.
>
> On January 23rd, 1978, in your western timing, the person you know as George King will enter the next major phase of his mission to Terra. This phase will be different from the other phases, which have been executed to date. This phase will necessitate his concentration in specialized ways. Therefore, he must detach from the mass of small details, which together help to run your organization. Whatever changes are needed to bring this about must be done as soon as you can do them.
>
> This is of great importance to mankind, and, I think you will find later, to the planet as a whole. Never were ordinary terrestrials like yourselves, in the past, given greater responsibilities than you have now. But, balancing that fine karmic balance, never have such a few ordinary terrestrials like yourselves been given greater opportunities to advance in such a way that you will be able to manipulate karma, so that your future lives will not be fraught with the frustrations as your present lives have been. Your reward for your complete devotion and dedication to this majestic cause will be forthcoming to those who deserve it.
>
> This transmission is of great importance to all of you, and study it well, and act upon the inference given here.
>
> Thank you for your kind attention, and may God bless each and every one of you. Another you know will now speak to you, and I will say a pleasant good

afternoon to you all.

Following this, Saint Goo-Ling spoke in more detail about the changes that would be needed to enable His Eminence to become more detached from the basic running of the Society. He appealed to staff members around the world:

> I strongly advise you to come together quite soon, and as many times as necessary to bring about changes, which must, in the light of the next major phase of operations of your leader, come about. I feel sure that some of you have the right love for your leader, the right interest in The Aetherius Society as a whole, to step now boldly into the limelight and take over the running of this organization. If you leave yourselves open for guidance, you will receive it. It is a time when you must be prepared to change and, by trial and error, find your feet as an organization which can run itself successfully.

A key phrase in these transmissions was the instruction by the Master Aetherius to Society officers to: **act upon the inference given here.** Saint Goo-Ling, who spoke after the Master Aetherius, elaborated on this with constructive advice and criticism, while making the revealing statement that Sir George had a greater compassion than many in the Great White Brotherhood. He instructed those with sufficient love for him to: **step now boldly into the limelight and take over the running of this organization.** This was completely in line with the only piece of advice on record to the staff as a whole from the Lord Babaji, who said: **Take more initiative, do not wait to be asked.** These three masters knew him intimately and understood his psychological make-up completely. He was not going to easily hand over responsibility to others – it was up to us to take it on.

Saint Goo-Ling had given very helpful advice to the staff regarding the right approach to their master for many years. On November 18th, 1973, he said:

You lack foresight in your dealings with him. Learn your

mistakes so that you can profit by them. Remember this all of you: there would be few harsh words spoken by your leader to you, if you obeyed every instruction given by either him or the masters to you. Harsh words would never be needed. It is your faults – if you want percentages, then I would say 98% of the time.

And, much as a precursor to the Master Aetherius announcing His Eminence's third phase, he stated to the staff at the American Headquarters on January 25th, 1976:

You will have to be a little more clever than you have been in the past regarding an approach to George King. Many of you are extremely unfortunate in this respect. You expect him to drop anything which may be in his mind, to deal with your various questions. More and more he will be forced to refuse to do this...

You will have to learn that more and more your leader will be forced to confine his thinking process to one problem at a time. In the past he has been able to deal with several major problems at once. This will be altered, if not by his design then upon Higher Command if necessary!

To the cosmic masters, the behaviour of certain people – even the most devoted among them – towards the cosmic avatar they followed was illogical to put it mildly. The Master Aetherius made a statement on July 30th, 1965, which was all the more devastating for its politeness:

It is a very strange thing that the cosmic masters often take more note of the demands of this one than do his (some of his – pardon me) terrestrial followers. This is one of the absurdities of truth, if I may be permitted to say so.

On a scale of one to ten, the success of this handover of the basic running of the Society to other officers was possibly three.

The European Headquarters started to act with more autonomy than before, but Sir George still kept his hand on the reins in Los Angeles and, where it counted, in London too.

The fault for this would have to be laid firmly at the door of his staff and not himself, but the problem was a dichotomy for all concerned as can be seen from the following small incident. An issue crossed his desk concerning a misunderstanding by a member of The Aetherius Society about an important matter. It was being dealt with by Lady Monique and Richard Lawrence, but he insisted on overseeing it personally. Richard asked him why he was spending his valuable time on this in view of his other pressing responsibilities. The reply was very simple: it was because he knew that he would handle the matter better than anybody else.

In the late 1980s this started to change, largely because of his deteriorating health, but he still involved himself in issues of management until his final days. On one occasion in 1992, following heart surgery, he insisted on phoning the American Headquarters in Los Angeles from his hospital bed in Santa Barbara in order to give permission for staff to go off duty, and this arrangement would continue until shortly before his passing!

* * * *

Sir George made no secret of his apparent addiction to work, describing himself with characteristic self-deprecation as a workaholic who thrived on adrenalin. Although he maintained his grip on certain day-to-day aspects of the Society's function right up to the end, his main focus was the performance, development and future of the cosmic missions.

Operation Sunbeam had moved from its original modus operandi known as Plan A, to the much more powerful Plan B which entailed many more phases being performed from a variety of locations. Spiritual Energy Radiators, which had originally been designed for Operation Sunbeam, were now running in conjunction with Satellite No. 3, at both headquarters during Spiritual Pushes, radiating daily over 12,000 prayer hours between them. Operation Prayer Power was being used in

Spiritual Pushes to discharge hundreds of prayer hours a week, as well as in emergency situations.

You would think that might be sufficient for any humanitarian or indeed genius, but Sir George was allergic to standing still. So, in 1980 the Six Adepts took Operation Sunbeam to yet another level, which they had been preparing to do for some time. They placed remote modules upon four planets in this solar system in a mission called Operation Space Magic. This meant that as well as energies invoked from the holy mountains, the Mother Earth would now be able to receive, during phases of Operation Sunbeam, energies from other planets who were virtually Her spiritual kith and kin.

This was a monumental achievement. The modules could be used to radiate energies from these planets to a satellite placed in orbit of the Earth by the Six Adepts. His Eminence described this as the 'Cosmic Connection' when he revealed it to The Aetherius Society in an official communiqué published in *Cosmic Voice*, January 1981:

> This satellite has the capability, when correctly coded by interplanetary personnel, to receive high frequencies of spiritual energies from the planets Saturn, Jupiter, Venus and Neptune. These spiritual energies can then be collected, in a controlled manner, by the masters from Gotha and other cosmic intelligences who have gained permission, and transmitted to the Ineffable Logos of Terra through Operation Sunbeam equipment operated by The Aetherius Society as well as the Spiritual Hierarchy of Earth, through carefully charted psychic centres in the body of the planet Earth, in order to bring about an essential stabilization of internal and external conditions on this planet.

The enormity of this move was compounded when on April 16th, 1981, after announcing cosmic awards for this achievement, Mars Sector 6 stated:

> The launching and operation of the satellite by the

> Adepts was indeed a very significant and very helpful
> move in that, we will, in future, be able, at times, to
> use this satellite as a reflective element for energies
> radiated by Satellite No. 3. We can also use this satellite
> to supplement the energies radiated by Satellite No. 3
> during a terrestrial Magnetization orbit, with energies
> coming directly from certain planets without any loss,
> space warp or conditioning through space.
>
> Hence the promotions and high awards given to the
> Six Adepts for one of the most significant moves ever
> made in terrestrial history, and indeed, as far as Terra is
> concerned, in the history of this solar system.

Clearly this was attributable to all the Six Adepts, but the launch date of the satellite was something of a giveaway: January 23rd, 1981, His Eminence Sir George King's birthday. Operation Space Magic was stamped with his personal hallmark. Somehow a man in a terrestrial body had known that the Logos of this planet was starved of cosmic energies from Her fellow planets and, with his comrades, had done something about it. The very fact that he was incarnate upon Earth when he did it is the karmic master shot which will ricochet throughout the centuries.

In the coming New Age not only will the Mother Earth release Her initiatory energies, but also the ionosphere, which acts as a barrier for cosmic rays to reach our world, will be increasingly removed. The resulting influx of high vibrational forces should bring an era of sustained peace and enlightenment to this planet. But the collision of spiritual intensity from inner and outer space with the aggressive and emotional energies of much of the human race would also cause a maelstrom of erratic turbulence upon the surface of this globe. The old proverb would be reversed and the calm of spiritual fruition would be preceded by the most virulent of storms.

This was known aeons ago by the great ones who deliberately created the ionosphere and by the Mother Earth who withheld Her light. It was done because of humanity's coarse primitiveness – put bluntly, we just couldn't handle it. If we were the only part of this wretched equation it wouldn't be so bad. But the other, greater part was this wonderful planet who was denying Herself not only Her own glorious being, but also the energies of the cosmos including those of Her fellow planets from reaching Her in their entirety. It is possible that Operation Space Magic holds the key to limiting the effects of the ionospheric barrier, at least from Her point of view. She can receive energies, at least from four planets, directly into Her psychic centres that might otherwise have been denied Her. The Six Adepts had found a way to help Her immeasurably without causing disastrous turbulence for humanity, which would have come from its inability to cope with such emanations.

This could even mean a time extension for the existence of the ionosphere, giving humanity more opportunity to make the essential changes to inherit the heavenly New Age. Like some Janus of old, this mission is an evolutionary colossus simultaneously serving two opposing needs: that of the Mother Earth and that of Her inhabitants. No wonder the Master Aetherius pronounced on March 5th, 1996:

> **What you call 'Operation Space Magic' is the most outstanding scientific achievement in the history of the planet Terra.**

Operation Space Magic was about seven years in the making since the Six Adepts first came together to discuss its possibility. While their deliberations and planning operations ensued, Sir George was also looking for ways to revere the Mother Earth at a more basic level. In 1979 his mind turned to Operation Prayer Power for this purpose, and on July 8th of that year – the anniversary of Her Initiation – he initiated a scheme which has continued and developed ever since. He came up with the concept of a 'Sacrifice to God' discharge of Operation Prayer Power energy in Her honour.

As he put it in *The Aetherius Society Newsletter*, September 1979:

> **The idea of sacrifice is not new to us and because of this we have been very successful in many important fields of**

endeavour. As a matter of fact, I maintain this: **no results in any field of endeavour have ever been brought about without sacrifice!**

Our beautiful sacrifice of a very valuable commodity, prayer hours of energy, on the July 8th Celebration was another one of the beneficial sacrifices many of us have made throughout the years.

As the prayer hours were being released His Eminence gave the following prayer during the July 8th service in Los Angeles:

Oh Mighty God,
At this time we make in loving sacrifice to You,
135 prayer hours of energy as a very small token of our combined appreciation for the mighty initiation of the Goddess Terra.
We ask You in Your compassion, knowledge and wisdom to accept this small token from us as a sacrifice, in deference to Your Greatness.
Oh Mighty God, Oh Mighty Brahma, Oh Wondrous Para Brahma.

Over the years the amount of energy discharged has increased considerably, as special charging sessions are set aside for this purpose. It was also supplemented by the Adepts themselves who agreed to charge a battery in Los Angeles with 5,000 prayer hours for this purpose. The continuation of this offer by the Adepts into the future, though, almost did not happen.

The last official task performed by Sir George, that we know of, took place on June 18th, 1997, just a few weeks before his passing. Sir George signed a letter approving the continuation of this Sacrifice to God supplementation by the Adepts into the future. It is interesting to note that this letter had been prepared by Brian Keneipp as long ago as 1995 and had been signed at that time by all the Senior Engineering Officers and bishops. However it had never been approved by Sir George. Brian had kept this letter on hand for two years, often attempting to get it signed. Then one day, out of the blue, during Sir George's very difficult and painful last weeks, he rose out of his bed to his chair in the living room and asked if he needed to sign anything. Brian swiftly brought out the letter and it was duly signed. Perhaps a certain amount of karma needed to be manipulated for such a divine intervention to continue to be given to mankind.

His ingenuity, applied to the modus operandi of his own missions, was a wonder to behold. But soon he would receive the most ancient of taps on the shoulder and, in this case, the modus operandi would be taken out of his hands.

$*\quad*\quad*\quad*$

The Lords looked down from the highest planet in the solar system and decreed that more was needed. Turning to their agent upon Earth, as they had done so many times before, they devised a new mission for world peace and devic stabilization which, because of their origins, became known as The Saturn Mission. On September 11th, 1981, it was launched by His Eminence Sir George King in a small boat on Loch Ness during which these Lords discharged sacred energy from a battery and mingled these with energies being naturally released by the Mother Earth from this psychic centre.

Sir George made this his flagship mission. Late in his life, after musing silently for some time, he turned to Richard Lawrence who remembers him saying: "I have to admit that the MO (modus operandi) of The Saturn Mission has the edge on Operation Sunbeam." In doing so he showed due deference to his superior officers, but his innate modesty once again masked key features of the full visage.

The psychic centre in question had been discovered by Sir George, as had the one at Lake Powell which was used later in this mission. The Lords probably could not have revealed them to him since it would have contravened Karmic Law. The battery, which he had designed and was built by his team, was a key component of this mission used by the Lords. Without these elements their modus operandi could not have existed. Adept Number Five acted as the communications link with Saturn High Command which enabled this mission to proceed. Without His Eminence's telepathic abilities and his connections with this master, it could not have been done as they prescribed.

He was required to transmit a commentary on the proceedings as well as receiving communications from Adept Number Five to determine his course, speed and distance over the centre. In an address published in *Cosmic Voice*, January-March 1985, he illustrated the difficulties of this task and one of its side effects:

> I found out something about that running commentary. When I first performed The Saturn Mission, I used to give the commentary silently. Often when I came back, I suffered rather a severe headache because of the pressure of the mental energy within me. You are talking about energies travelling, outside of the body up to seven million times the speed of light – and even above that! So it was carefully suggested to me that I should speak all the commentary out loud; it would be picked up anyway because the thought comes before the sonic vibration, which is a rough translation of that thought. The last few times I have been doing this and have had no headache or after effects.

With his typical humour he then made the following aside to the congregation:

> You might like to remember that when you communicate with the cosmic masters!

There can be no doubt that their modus operandi, brilliant as it was, depended entirely on him. In fact it could be seen as a massive compliment to him that they selected their karmic weapons from his spiritual armoury. It was revealed that just one of the side results of each phase of The Saturn Mission was to save 90,000 people from death or severe mutilation from natural catastrophes. As the 1980s progressed, this mission took pride of place in his calendar with phases being performed, wherever possible, in the spring and the fall at Lake Powell and in the summer at Loch Ness.

Sir George King takes the helm during The Saturn Mission. Top: on *Wave Dancer* at Loch Ness. Above: on *Phantom* at Lake Powell.

Sir George's genius had ensured that in the early 1980s, Operation Space Power, Operation Sunbeam, Operation Prayer Power and The Saturn Mission were all being regularly performed by The Aetherius Society under his close direction. He did not believe in waiting for divine intervention, but in us taking action ourselves. His aphorism, which should be a byword for humanity in these days, is:

Miracles are not performed by God for man, but by man for God.

The result has been a drastic reduction of the ecological and humanitarian catastrophes which would have engulfed the planet by now. Of course these missions did not stop them. The incidence of natural disasters has been tragically high both then and since. Earthquakes, volcanic eruptions, hurricanes, floods and droughts continued, but not unabated – their intensity and the level of damage wrought were greatly reduced by these missions.

Wars have been fought with ferocious cruelty in many regions, but the much-prophesied nuclear conflagration was staid in this period and beyond. Shortly, relations between the 'cold war' enemies, the USA and Russia, improved so greatly that in the last decade of Sir George's life, events that nobody would have predicted when he started his mission in the 1950s occurred: the fall of the Berlin Wall and a mutual reduction of nuclear weaponry by these superpowers.

And yet these four missions, now in full progress, were not the final word. In poor physical health, yet still endowed with the same acumen, he had not finished weaving his karmic tapestry – he was determined to go out in a blaze of glory.

Chapter Nine
BLAZE OF GLORY

One might expect a senior citizen with failing health to slow down in his dotage; to reflect upon his life and recount lengthy stories about his past to all who will listen. Not so His Eminence. "Retirement", he often said, "is for pregnant whales!" His angioplasty operation, brought on by angina, took place just prior to his 68th birthday but instead of heralding a gradual decline, it marked a shining new beginning for the world.

Even in the hospital his attention turned to how his Society would be run after his demise. It came to him strongly that there should not be a Vice President, and he let this be known. Also among his first thoughts, was the idea that annual general meetings of the membership in Los Angeles would be held regularly to ratify appointments to the Board of Directors in America. Later he concluded that this would entrust too much say to less experienced members, and that the Board should be international, so he devised another plan.

He never left anything to chance and the future organization of The Aetherius Society was no exception. We cannot think of any other cosmic avatar who is recorded as having expended so much time and energy for such a purpose. Over the next 10 years he conducted a rigorous administrative exercise, dissecting major aspects of the Society and determining their function in the future. He set about establishing a diverse operational structure to run his missions and teachings. In doing so he received invaluable help, guidance and, where appropriate, permission from prominent cosmic authorities. On a far more mundane and lowly level, he was assisted by a few of his closest followers, and none more so than the authors of this book.

No matter how close you were to him or how well you knew him, you were never aware of the full extent of what he was up to – and as soon as you thought you were, he proved you wrong. Those who knew him best would have a very good idea of his modes of behaviour and reactions to different situations, but would draw the line at certainty. As he used to say, he was only alive because he was unpredictable.

He treated his health just like he treated everything: as an opportunity to manipulate karma. His last 10 years were dogged with various ailments, some of them life-threatening, during which he underwent serious pneumonia, an abdominal aorta operation, double-bypass heart surgery and finally cancer of the stomach. He rode them like a skipper would ride turbulent waves, wresting from them opportunities to serve and save humanity; for he was a master of an aspect of karma about which he rarely spoke but frequently practised – that of taking the karma of the world and certain individuals upon himself. The Master Aetherius alluded to this in a transmission published in *The Aetherius Society Newsletter*, September/October 1966:

> You have had a living, breathing, flesh and blood example put in your midst. A man who has performed operation after operation, mainly upon his own abilities. A man who has many times taken karma upon his own shoulders so that the required manipulation may be brought about in order to allow an outside force, ourselves in this case, to send the energy necessary for the correct execution of said operations!

Karma was the speciality of Sir George, and in these days of great change upon Earth he knew it was more important than ever before. In an address given on July 8th, 1970, Sir George hinted that even amongst the great ones, the manipulation of karma was essential:

> We always have to turn back to this karmic manipulation, because if we forget it, we fall on our faces, be we a spider, a bumblebee, or a vast planetary system. We always have to come back to this karma. And we always have to – you get to a stage where you're no longer **allowed** to help your fellow man. You're no longer **allowed** to help your fellow man unless you manipulate

karma to allow you to be allowed to do it. Let's not forget that too. Many many manipulators, many adepts have fallen down, because they did not realize this one point and some of them have been ticked off pretty badly too, because they tried to push it too far.

In his final years he did this in spades. On one occasion he candidly admitted to Richard Lawrence that he was taking karma through his cancer condition, in order to guarantee the future of Operation Sunbeam after his demise. He also instructed Richard not to speak of this at the time since he felt it would not have been properly understood. Richard never did so in his lifetime, but now the truth must out.

Just as he had withheld his interplanetary credentials and had not disclosed his identity as Adept Number One; just as he had played down his true connections with the Mother Earth and made the discovery of Her psychic centres seem relatively straightforward; now he allowed his health condition to appear unavoidable – as though he could not have changed it had he decided to.

Being the master he was, with no karmic pattern upon Earth other than whatever he had chosen to accept, he was using his physical pain and mental anguish to bring outstanding results for humanity in general, and key personnel in The Aetherius Society in particular. It is one thing for a cosmic mission to have been performed under the aegis of His Eminence Sir George King while he was physically alive, and an entirely different one for terrestrial people to do so without him. A karmic price had to be paid by someone with sufficient credit. Sadly even the best of his followers, had they been willing and able to, had only small change to offer, if that. He signed a blank cheque – and he knew he was good for it.

One request by him to the right source would surely have put an end to his suffering. It would also have curtailed the karmic burden he was bearing on our behalf. A decision made, like some sadhu of old, to detach himself from the karma of others and thereby leave a much poorer legacy to the world, could have brought him better health, and comfort. But this was his decision, a decision consistent with the rest of his life – of sacrifice for the world. Another cosmic avatar had permitted the agony of his own crucifixion, and allowed the appearance that he was deceived by one of his own disciples. Similarly Sir George accepted 10 years of very poor health and the limitations of a terrestrial ageing process upon Earth.

When in the early 1990s he was ready to leave, the cosmic sources to whom he reported asked him to stay longer and he agreed. From this point onwards he was not a volunteer but, as he put it, 'a pressed man', an allusion to enforced military recruitment in former times. Not only did Sir George skilfully manipulate karma throughout his life, especially in these latter years, but he was also used as a karmic trigger by the great ones – or perhaps he and the great ones designed these karmic manipulations together. The following incident could be an example of this.

His Eminence was looking forward to giving an address about recent developments in Operation Sunbeam, when he was stricken with a sudden illness on the previous night. As a result, on Sunday, March 3rd, 1991, he was in bed receiving healing from Brian Keneipp and Richard Medway, rather than in the Temple giving his address. Brian heard a loud thumping noise from the living room, and when he went to investigate he found the front of the room engulfed in flames, with black smoke everywhere and severe heat. Richard went through the bedroom window to attack the flames, while Brian stayed back to help His Eminence escape through the window which was no easy task.

The fire was extinguished quickly by staff members, before the fire department was able to reach the bungalow, having been delayed by an annual marathon race nearby. Before it was put out, the smoke and heat had caused severe damage to Sir George's living room, office and Transmission Room. A few hours later, Sir George had been moved across the street to a staff member's apartment. It was there, while Richard and Brian were administering more spiritual healing, that the reason for this fire was revealed.

The Lord of Karma, known as Questing, communicated with Sir George. This was the being who had visited Sir George in 1972 and had been instrumental in inspiring him to extend Operation Sunbeam to the British Isles, which in turn led to the invention of Plan B. Sir George relayed to Brian and Richard that Questing had apologized for his having to go through the fire, but that it was necessary to manipulate karma for future important moves. Later Sir George realized this important move was a seismic change in Operation Sunbeam which was still to come.

Another happening took place on January 17th, 1994. An earthquake measuring 6.7 hit the Los Angeles area causing approximately 60 deaths and injuries to 9,000 people. It caused considerable damage to the American Headquarters and took months for a team of professional contractors and Aetherius Society volunteers from around the world and over $100,000 of precious donations to repair the damage. It had a profound effect on the health of His Eminence. Even 100 miles north in Santa Barbara, where he was at the time, the strong earthquake was felt, knocking out the power and phone lines for many hours.

Yet through this adversity, another aspect of the karmic influence of Sir George was revealed. Within a few hours he contacted the Master Aetherius as follows:

His Eminence: Today is Monday, January 17th, 1994. The time now is 1:05 p.m. PST I am in Santa Barbara. I am trying to communicate with the Master Aetherius...

Yes, Master Aetherius, thank you very much for coming back to me so promptly...

His Eminence: It appears that the Los Angeles district is having aftershock after aftershock after aftershock! It is too late to do much about the original [earthquake], which you know the time and date of.

May I ask you a question please?

Master Aetherius: Yes, you may. I know what it is going to be, but ask it.

His Eminence: Thank you. Would it be a good thing to request that Satellite No. 3 comes into orbit about this time as we [the headquarters] are sustaining damage – not serious yet, but it could become serious. We have had a lot of losses and so on.

Master Aetherius: Yes, it will be. I will get back to you very shortly. Just stay there.

His Eminence: Thank you very much, Aetherius. [Short pause.] Yes, Master Aetherius.

Master Aetherius: You asked me a question, and I am making this as a formal request?

His Eminence: Yes, I am – with your permission.

Master Aetherius: Thank you. I will get back...

His Eminence: Master Aetherius, are we going to be lucky?

Master Aetherius: Very! The soonest the Third Satellite can come into orbit is your date January 18th.

His Eminence: That is tomorrow!

Master Aetherius: January 18th, 12 midnight GMT. Until – we will let it come into orbit, and then you can cooperate in the normal way, and we will see exactly how long Satellite No. 3 can stay here.

Who else on Earth could have requested such divine intervention and had it answered other than His Eminence Sir George King?

Despite the divine help, the karmic manipulations by His Eminence in these last years were very demanding for him. Yet so indefatigable was he that in these testing closing years he still found moments of deep satisfaction, joyous achievement and even light-hearted merriment. He had to scour the menu to find them but they were there to be savoured every now and then. The bulk of his culinary order, though, was still hard work and service with a new and consistent level of suffering thrown in.

* * * *

The second phase of Sir George's mission was more advanced than the first, as confirmed by Saint Goo-Ling, but the third took him into completely unexplored terrain. He was creating a path in his own image for others to follow long after his passing. So elevated and potent was it that it could seem inaccessible to many upon Earth, confirming something the Master Aetherius had stated decades earlier when announcing his second phase on March 15th, 1965:

> A man can have two great faults. One: he can be nothing. The other: he can be so great as to appear nothing because of his very greatness.
>
> This has happened. It was by design in a way, not our design but it was known and foreseen. For when the world appreciates the leader of The Aetherius Society, it will have advanced greatly. It must have advanced greatly to be capable of such a degree of appreciation.

In this concise observation, the Master Aetherius really says it all, perhaps more than is obvious at first reading. Had Sir George made The Twelve Blessings and the climbing of holy mountains his main focus, his message would have been much easier to understand by many and therefore far more popular. Had he pursued the plan outlined by the Master Aetherius of building shape power temples to be manned by prayer teams in eight-hour shifts in order to send spiritual power around the world, it would again have been far more promotable than Operation Prayer Power never mind Operation Sunbeam. It would have been more expensive to accomplish, but some potential donors would have been more willing to contribute to something as physically tangible as a beautifully designed temple. They would have to be more advanced to donate to the cosmic missions of The Aetherius Society which are esoteric by comparison.

The essence behind the directives and requirements in the brilliant exposition on 'The Five Temples of God' was fulfilled, but in different, even more potent ways. The Master Aetherius himself later endorsed these changes and stated that the priority had moved from the building of the five temples to continuing the missions started by Sir George. The temples can still be built, but the missions were now the priority. As the Master Aetherius stated to the International Directors of the Society on August 8th, 1990:

> The first and second temples, when you are in a position to do so, can be built in America – anywhere in America – and England – anywhere in the British Isles – if you wish.
>
> Strategic positions are not necessary any longer...
>
> May I stress this please: in the future it has to be the missions first; spreading the teachings secondly; and other matters after that.

How extraordinary is it that His Eminence could improve directives such as these with the full sanction of their originator.

A more modest claim would have been less controversial. There is a comfort zone beyond which the mass of humanity is not willing to go. Once you surpass it, especially to the extent he reached, it becomes inaccessible to most, and is either ignored or dismissed out of hand. In short, he appeared to be nothing because of his very greatness.

Intriguingly, the Master Aetherius explains that this was by design in a way. He then continued: **not our design but it was known and foreseen**. Now the cat is out of the bag in that this was clearly not the plan or will of the cosmic masters. They knew that it would happen because they knew him and it was foreseen that he would do this, but the design could have only been his.

Many upon Earth will mask their craving for appreciation from others with a veneer of false humility. They rebut praise in the hopes that this very rebuttal encourages more praise, and frequently it does. Sir George, however, played no such game. He knew who he was and the unprecedented change he had brought to the world, but he also knew that the more extreme his claims the less he would be understood. It may have suited classified aspects of his mission to avoid too much public attention, and in many ways it suited him personally because of his innate shyness and inclination to operate 'behind the scenes'.

On August 8th, 1990, the Master Aetherius blew the lid off any underestimates of his true greatness when he delivered a mental transmission in Los Angeles, of which the following is an extract. It was published in *Cosmic Voice*, August 1990:

> I want all the members of The Aetherius Society to realize that, never before in **my existence have I ever recruited a better spiritual master than George King!**
>
> He is my 'Star Pupil.'
>
> His brilliance has been very greatly put to use in his invention of numerous missions, which I will not detail here.
>
> **Members, you only know a fraction of the work of this man!**
>
> Despite all odds, he has moved forward gradually into the future, helping mankind, who were strangers to him; teaching them, those who were near, not only the great truths, but also how to run the equipment which he designed for several missions vital to the planet Earth.
>
> A lot of you speak somewhat glibly about the Great White Brotherhood. There is one member of the Great White Brotherhood, that is the Lord Babaji, who is a greater, more active member than any of them; **but there is no member of the Great White Brotherhood, with this exception, who is equal in spiritual matters to George King.**
>
> **And that is quite a statement.**
>
> I have been concerned with helping other inhabited worlds for thousands of years. I have recruited small teams who I could trust to do this job for me, under my direction. But George King is my 'Star Pupil,' and always

has been – before he even came among you.

The Next Master is coming to Earth at a classified time. He will come with all the powers. **But man for man, he will not be any better than the man who has been among you for many years.**

Without revealing too much about the identity of this unusual man, christened as George King, I can tell you that without him and his cooperation, **and his suffering throughout the years**, your Earth would be an entirely different place, and millions of you would not be able to live here because of extremely adverse conditions.

I have ordered George King to allow me to speak and I know he finds it very difficult, because the subject is himself – and very complimentary.

Brian Keneipp, as his personal aide, was with him just prior to receiving this and was helping him prepare for what Sir George knew was going to be a very difficult and direct communication. Brian prepared the two tape recorders on his desk and made him a cup of tea as normal. He proceeded to massage his shoulders to help him relax. The atmosphere was very different from usual. Sir George was quiet and very pensive; he did not want to take this transmission. He would get up and pace around the room in silence, then sit down and have a sip of tea. Then he was back up, pacing.

Normally when preparing for a transmission he would be very confident and strong. Now he had been put in a corner he did not want to be in – and by his spiritual master, Aetherius. Sir George would tell his members how exceptional his abilities were, and the importance of what he did, so that they could better understand and appreciate what he and they were doing for the world. But to have a being as elevated as the Master Aetherius doing so to this extent put him on edge.

The Master Aetherius knew all this and had given him permission to prepare himself. Finally, Sir George felt he could put it off no longer and asked Brian to step into the next room, from which he could still hear the communication. When it was over, Brian went back in, made another cup of tea and gave more massage. Sir George was still very subdued and quiet, not wanting to talk. After a short time, he asked Brian to take away the tapes and make copies and have them transcribed. Sir George softly said words to the effect that this communication will wake up the members.

Richard Lawrence, who was in Los Angeles at the time, remembers Sir George pondering the reference to the Next Master and the fact that man for man he would be no better than himself. He was considering the powers he would need if he was chosen as the Next Master, and added that if he wanted the task it would be very difficult for the great ones to refuse him because of what he had already done for humanity. Taking this at face value, one would conclude that either the identity of the Next Master has not yet been determined, or that he did not know it. The other possibility is that he knew far more than he was willing or able to reveal in that conversation.

He shared with a few of his closest followers over dinner one evening in Los Angeles that it was his belief that the Master Aetherius had recruited other cosmic avatars to this Earth such as Sri Krishna, the Lord Buddha and the Master Jesus. In the light of the reference to him as the 'Star Pupil', this would be shocking to some, mind-blowing to others, but logically understandable to those familiar with the missions he had performed and devised.

*　*　*　*

In 1987 his stays in Santa Barbara started to become more prolonged. Ostensibly there for rest and recuperation, his bungalow became a temporary command headquarters at which he received hundreds of mental transmissions, coordinated existing missions and devised new ones. In this conducive environment, with generally only two or three personal assistants in the house, though his health was getting worse and worse, slowing down his physical movements, his mind shifted into a different mode. He was now manipulating karma using every means available – figuring out how best to leave The Aetherius Society and its missions in a strong position, capable of pushing his mission and the Cosmic Plan forward even after he had to leave Earth.

On May 22nd of that year one of the most remarkable discourses in history ensued between Sir George, who asked a series of questions, and a cosmic intelligence from Satellite No. 3, who answered them. It is published in full in his book *Operation Space Power*. As was often the case with Sir George there is a sense that there was far more to this question-and-answer session than meets the eye.

Sir George's stated reason for opening up communication with Satellite No. 3 was to determine how much spiritual energy had been sent through the radionic equipment made and operated by The Aetherius Society in cooperation with the Satellite and the cosmic masters; and whether all of this energy had been used, or if some of it had been recalled. Sir George was well prepared and had in front of him detailed logs of the operation of all of the equipment.

He knew that the figures were well into the tens of millions

Sir George relaxing on his deck in the back garden of his residence at Santa Barbara.

of prayer hours. He also clearly had a plan.

During this lengthy and detailed communication, it was revealed that in fact not all of the energy was used, and that some of it had been recalled. The reason for this was that if mankind did not use it all, the excess energy could cause a dangerous oversaturation called 'resonance', so it had to be recalled.

This was the opening Sir George was looking for. He proceeded to state the case in a very logical manner, that as this energy had been sent through equipment built and operated by The Aetherius Society and was therefore credited to The Aetherius Society, it would be most beneficial for the Society to have access to this energy in order to use it for emergency situations on Earth.

Sir George's karmic negotiations worked. He was told that if he would like to be given this responsibility it could be of help to the world. And this staggering message followed:

> We will put three million prayer hours of spiritual energy at your disposal. This spiritual energy can be used only on command from Special Advisor S2 and the discharge amount should be worked out at 1,500 prayer hours per hour of Spiritual Energy Radiator operation.

It was later revealed that this was A+ energy[1] which means that it accumulates at 2% per month. The net result was virtually an unlimited supply of energy which could be sent out to the world through the Spiritual Energy Radiators in addition to that sent out regularly during a Spiritual Push.

Sir George's reaction to this is best expressed through his reply:

> Now you have given me a bomb-blast! This is very generous on your part!...
> I think we are going to have the biggest party we have ever had in the life of The Aetherius Society as a celebration for this!

This energy was transferred to a special storage battery on Central Control under the overall authority of Mars Sector 8. A few hours later the cosmic master in direct charge of this energy, Mars Sector 8 – Special Advisor S2, contacted Sir George with further details and requirements of the use of this energy source, and stated:

> Sir, you are probably the only person on Terra and the realms above who would have received this bonus...
>   You are to be congratulated on this action by Satellite No. 3, which was only made because of their deference to you and what you have done for all realms of Terra.

From this came a new mission called Operation Space Power II which would transform the future of this planet. Literally millions of prayer hours of energy could and have been sent out to the world as a result of this one conversation between an interplanetary master of true spiritual science and an individual living in a human body on Earth.

To emphasize the importance of this mission, three years later, as well as announcing the change in priority from the building of the temples to the missions, the Master Aetherius also stated on August 5th, 1990:

> I remind you all that Operation Space Power II has changed many things.

His dialogue with Satellite No. 3 epitomises what can only be described as a façade he erected around himself. From his preparation and line of argument, it is very likely he expected that energy had been recalled, and that a portion of it would be offered to him. Very quickly the cosmic source saw the line of logic and quite possibly knew it was coming. However, as His Eminence had showed many times before, certain things have to be clearly stated and answered. The very fact that someone in an Earth physical body thought of it was the karmic trigger that made it happen – the right question expressed in the right way to the right source following the right protocol manipulated the right outcome. Even if he had cosmic inside information, he still had to confirm it through the ingenuity of his logic in order to receive the answer he did.

In some ways he was a superb actor who pretended to know less than he did. Had he not done so, we can only surmise that he simply would not have been able to live in such close quarters with terrestrials. Certainly he discouraged awe and overt reverence from those near to him. For example, when he was in poor health he would not allow one of his aides to kneel at his bedside even though he was only doing so to give him healing.

His ill health, and the medication required to treat it, could mask his enlightened stature. He would remark to his aides in his latter years that he was having to slow down "like the rest of you". On one occasion a few months before his passing, he made the poignant statement to Richard Lawrence, "I used to be a great master", and he would not listen to Richard's protestations that he still was. However, he did have to listen when he received a mental transmission from the Karmic Lord Mars Sector 6 on September 29th, 1992, with the heart-rending statement: **Even during severe illness, you are still a great man**.

He also could not argue with the amazing fact that he was, in his own right, a member of the Interplanetary Confederation. The way this came about was a classical example of His Eminence's magical timing. In May of 1989 Sir George was in Santa Barbara, this time with Ray Nielsen and Brian. As Ray was preparing dinner, Brian was setting Sir George up in his living room with music and a cocktail. Quickly Sir George had the idea of combining Operation Space Power II with July 8th to create an extremely powerful Sacrifice to God. So he asked Brian to figure out how much spiritual energy we could release through a variety of plans.

The more he thought about it, the more excited and happy he became. Each time Brian brought him a set of figures, Sir George would say, "I want it to be big, really big!" This went on for some time, back and forth – Brian with the figures and Sir George with different ideas of timing. Finally he was happy when he felt he had a plan and summarized it as follows:

On Saturday, May 6th, 1989, in Santa Barbara I

approached the cosmic master Mars Sector 8 General Information – Special Advisor S2 regarding a Sacrifice to God energy release which we could perform on July 8th, 1989. It was to say the least an extremely audacious request that I made to the master, namely running the SERs in London and LA for two hours each per day during the whole month of June, so that we could send out 180,000 prayer hours in our Sacrifice to God on July 8th. Not only did this entail some work on our part, but a lot of work on the part of the cosmic masters; who had to release this spiritual energy to us, put it through our SERs and then loop it back for a further release which had to be made by the cosmic masters.

After only a few minutes consideration, Mars Sector 8 General Information – Special Advisor S2, agreed with this plan!

He even went on to say that the plan was a brilliant one!

When I rose from the tape recorder on which I recorded the message from Special Advisor S2, I was cold and shivering.

Dozens of questions raced through my mind, but the main one was, why so easy?

The next day I found out.

Special Communication from the Master Aetherius on Saturn
12 noon May 7th, 1989 – Santa Barbara

His Eminence: This is Primary Terrestrial Mental Channel. I am ready to receive a message.

Master Aetherius: A short time ago, Primary Terrestrial Mental Channel, otherwise known as 'His Eminence Sir George King', was unanimously voted, in his own right, while still living in a physical body on Terra, as a full member and advisor to the Interplanetary Confederation.

It was not necessary for you to project to this

meeting, as I think I did a good job, as you would call it, in representing you.

Without breaking any classification, you are one of the few people who have ever received this recognition, while living in a physical body on the planet Earth.

It is fitting, at this time, that you be told about this.

This is Aetherius, from Saturn, ending communications with Interplanetary Confederation Member, Your Eminence Sir George King.

(Communication ended at 12:05 p.m. PDT)

His Eminence received several congratulation messages soon after this significant happening. The following two are a good representation.

This is Primary Terrestrial Mental Channel, May 7th. The time now is 12:35 p.m. I have been alerted.

Communication: You are unique in your abilities, and have proved this over the years. You are now unique in your status. Go with God.

Signed: The Adepts.

This is May 7th, 1989. The time is now 3:22 p.m.

This is Primary Terrestrial Mental Channel. I believe a communication is coming in.

Communication: There are few times in the last centuries, when the Supreme Council of the Interplanetary Confederation had less deliberation, than about your appointment.

What deliberation they did have was only pure protocol.

You deserve this recognition and more.

When you do leave the planet Terra, Your Eminence,

we invite you to attend us for a high Cosmic Initiation.

Signed: The Perfects of Saturn.

It was a foreshadowing of the final years in the mission of His Eminence. He had been a key force in building a powerful karmic pattern for good, with advanced missions and teachings, all under the auspices of his spiritual brotherhood, The Aetherius Society. Now it was time to lock it in position to withstand the test of time.

* * * *

In October 1988, His Eminence was informed by the Adepts that he should expect a visitor from Satellite No. 3 at his residence in Santa Barbara. Just as he had received the master from Gotha at the American Headquarters in 1966, so he would another cosmic intelligence. This being, however, came in a projected form and not in his physical body. As he explained in the book, *Contact With A Lord Of Karma*:

> Any cosmic operator on Satellite No. 3 is extremely magnetic; in fact, so magnetic that they would not enter an ordinary house in their full aspect bodies. To do so would mean to magnetize all the clocks and weather instruments, such as barometers. The field of magnetism may even extend to the disruption of loud speaker units and the possibility of scrambling video tapes. All this, of course, without the visitor intending to cause any damage whatsoever. Hence the projection.

He asked his personal aides in Santa Barbara, Brian Keneipp and Richard Medway, to book into a motel so that he could be alone with his guest on the evening of October 10th. The conversation that ensued is reproduced in *Contact With A Lord Of Karma* – the title of which, it should be clarified, refers to Mars Sector 6. This visitor is referred to as Adept Number Nine and uses the code name Nixies Zero Zero Nine.

One particularly revealing interchange was as follows:

Nixies Zero Zero Nine: It is true what the Master Aetherius said many years ago, that the Three Adepts would not be replaced when they were requested to leave the planet Earth. However, since that time, there have been cosmic manipulations and the Five Adepts will be replaced by Nixies Zero Zero Six, Nixies Zero Zero Seven, Nixies Zero Zero Eight and Nixies Zero Zero Nine, but not in terrestrial bodies.

His Eminence: Well, thank you very much, I think we all will agree that is absolutely fabulous!

This was a confirmation of the plan that was being put in place for when His Eminence and the other Adepts were to leave this Earth. They would be replaced by the Lord Babaji and Adept Number Nine and his team which comprised himself and two others. In 1995 his team was joined by three additional crew members. The conversation continued:

Nixies Zero Zero Nine: I apologize for not visiting you before now because I had to take Satellite No. 3 out of orbit and land it on Jupiter 4.

His Eminence: Really! Well, it looks as though you and the other two chaps are pretty hot pilots!

Nixies Zero Zero Nine: I am talking to one now!

His Eminence: Sir, it is rather warm this evening, may I take my jacket and tie off and put on my air-conditioning system?

As a pilot himself he was well aware of His Eminence's position as the pilot in the craft of the Three Adepts. Hence the compliment, which His Eminence tried to brush aside with a reference to the weather. Adept Number Nine expressed his regret that Sir George's personal aides were not there:

His Eminence: I apologize to you, Sir, for sending them into a hotel tonight.

Nixies Zero Zero Nine: That was not necessary.

His Eminence: Necessary or not, Sir, I'm afraid I probably made that mistake.

Nixies Zero Zero Nine: (Code Name) cannot make such a mistake!

His Eminence: (Code Name) is very prone to making mistakes!

Adept Number Nine, who knew very well about the full cosmic aspect of His Eminence, did not accept that he could make a mistake like this. His Eminence, on the other hand, admitted to often doing so. There is a certain pathos about this, illustrating not only his humility, but also the fact that his limited mental and physical structure was in stark contrast to his true nature and essence. Having said that, Adept Number Nine was undoubtedly correct in this remark.

He was probably trying to educate Adept Number Nine about the pitiful state of the human condition and prepare him for his future dealings with those upon Earth. A later exchange illustrates this very well. Sir George complimented Adept Number Nine on his help with a recent energy manipulation, in which The Aetherius Society and Adept Number Nine took part, to lessen the blow from hurricane Gilbert, which had hit parts of the Caribbean the month before.

Adept Number Nine stated:

> **I would have taken it down** [which meant he would have completely balanced the pressures between the hurricane's centre and the surrounding air mass, rendering the hurricane virtually harmless].

Sir George answered:

> I know. You would have taken it down – yes, I know.
> However, you have to become used to the karmic
> complexities of Terra.

After some further discussion Adept Number Nine commented that he could not understand why His Eminence was referring to him as 'Sir'. When His Eminence replied that it was out of deference and gratitude to him for being one of those who will take the place of the Five Adepts when they leave Earth, he received a response from Adept Number Nine noted as "Comment unrecorded". His Eminence turned off the tape at this point, as he did not wish to publish the respect in which he was held by his honoured guest. There were other matters spoken between these two adepts while the tape was off. Very possibly His Eminence took the chance to offer some sage advice to an incoming adept about to start a daunting assignment.

Adept Number Nine was to become the chief communications officer, accepting as one of his many responsibilities communications from The Aetherius Society. This was an essential link needed for the future of Sir George's missions. Nobody could or would replace Primary Terrestrial Mental Channel, but he set his mind to manipulating karma so that a method could be established by which one-way communications could be made to the cosmic masters through the gracious offices of Adept Number Nine. Once established this would mean that Operation Space Power II, Operation Sunbeam and Operation Prayer Power could continue into the future. He did not envisage, at this stage, the continuance of The Saturn Mission by The Aetherius Society.

It was assumed that Operation Space Power would continue since the dates of future Spiritual Pushes had been given to him in 1967 prior to the start of Operation Karmalight. However, it had also been stated then that the Spiritual Energy Radiators would only run on alternate evenings and there was no provision for building and positioning them in other locations. He realized that a contact with Mars Sector 6 himself was required.

Contact With A Lord Of Karma details in full these conversations which led to the confirmation of changes to the Spiritual Push dates for the next 1,000 years. He also received information about the times that Spiritual Energy Radiators would be run daily in each area, their future positioning in other locations around the world and very much more. After much discussion between His Eminence and key team members, a ritual was established and agreed upon by Mars Sector 6 and Adept Number Nine to be used by chosen mission officers of The Aetherius Society in order to relay their plans and intentions to and through Adept Number Nine.

As far as Operation Sunbeam is concerned His Eminence worked out a plan with select members of his team in 1989. He was deeply moved when it was approved by the Lords of the Flame themselves to continue into the future. By the end of the decade His Eminence had activated his four transmuting beams of light to illuminate the remainder of this millennium and beyond. Not long after, he set up an international body known as the Senior Engineering Officers, with five in the USA and five in the UK, to take responsibility for the future performance of these missions.

One mission, however, which he had been waiting to initiate since his visit to the Lords of the Flame was Operation Earth Light, and this would now take a new and unexpected turn. One of the three key elements His Eminence included in his mission to Earth was to aid the Logos of Earth in Her release of energy to the higher devic kingdom and this mission would accomplish that perfectly.

Using the energies given to them by the Mother Earth, humanity and other sources, the devas create the weather and other natural processes on Earth. This is done strictly according to certain laws. They must utilize all the energies invoked on Earth. Therefore, the thoughts radiated by mankind directly influence the weather and other biological and geological processes. There are no accidents in so-called acts of God such as droughts, hurricanes and earthquakes. The devas are impartial and must use the energy given to them. If they receive negative, discordant energies this is what they must use.

Helping the Mother Earth release Her energies to the devas

is a vital aspect of the coming New Age. Of course She does not really need help in this, She could do it instantaneously, but that would spell disaster for mankind. To do this gently and strategically in order to allow mankind to evolve in a smooth manner is the challenge in which karma is the key element. The equipment which came to His Eminence in a flash in 1973, which was later approved by the Lords of the Flame, was the key to this strategic release. That it came from the mind of someone in an Earth physical body was a crucial karmic factor.

Though the design by His Eminence was the main aspect of Operation Earth Light, there was much more work to be done to get this mission started. During the years of Operation Sunbeam research he was also researching other aspects of Operation Earth Light. However by 1990 the start was still a long way off. It came up at an important meeting of the International Directors convened by His Eminence in August 1990, to look into the future of The Aetherius Society. Regarding Operation Earth Light, he stated that this was his responsibility and he would take care of it. His idea was to offer his equipment design and the mission modus operandi to the Great White Brotherhood, who he knew would do justice to it.

It is interesting to note that the words of the Lords of the Flame on November 29th, 1979, seemed to suggest this as published in *Visit To The Logos Of Earth*:

> You may proceed with this plan. You are cognizant of the fact this 'Operation Earth Light' of yours, while having our full sanction, must be regarded as a pattern only for the time being. Others will follow this pattern.
>
> We thank you for your thought, consideration and compassion for mankind by formulating this essential plan in these troubled times.
>
> Proceed with our blessings.

He contacted the Master Aetherius on August 11th, 1990, who completely agreed with his idea. Then things started to happen quickly. The Operation Earth Light plans were passed to the Great White Brotherhood, and the Lord Babaji officially accepted the mission on August 15th. Illustrating the importance of this mission, and again the pluperfect timing of His Eminence, the equipment was built and the mission officially started on November 11th, just a few months later! The details of how this happened, which are contained in the book, *Operation Earth Light* by Brian Keneipp, are indeed fascinating and revealing.

The essence of what took place is summed up in the following mental transmission from the Lord Babaji the day before the mission was to commence, on November 10th, 1990, near the psychic centre at Lake Powell:

> On November 11th, 1990, three units of Operation Earth Light will be activated and remain on the air for several days. We will inform you when these are taken off the air.
>
> The position of these units is strictly classified; however, it can be announced that these units will be put on the air on November 11th, 1990.
>
> We wish to thank you for your Operation Earth Light. This mission will become of great importance – and become global!
>
> We would like to take this opportunity to give our most profound thanks to all who helped Operation Earth Light to become in all ways operational – and especially thank the original designer of the apparatus.
>
> Thank you, my son.

Overcome with emotion His Eminence was not able to respond to this communication and stated the following:

> So deep was the emotional reaction felt by myself after this mental transmission that I spent some time walking up and down the flat beach and, to be honest with you, crying like a baby!
>
> At long last, Operation Earth Light – the mission design plans of which I had devised in 1973 – had made a serious start!

*   *   *   *

As well as the missions, Sir George turned his attention to other aspects of the multi-layered edifice he would bequeath to the world through his Society. He divided it into three main jurisdictional areas, knowing that they would sometimes overlap. The International Directors were to be responsible for the overall administration of the Society; and the Senior Engineering Officers would run the missions. But there was a third very important function – the spiritual activities and worship conducted by The Aetherius Churches.

In fact the Ecclesiastical Synod was the first of the three international bodies he established and to do so he turned again to the Lord Babaji for guidance. This revered master gave his agreement on behalf of the Great White Brotherhood for two bishops to be consecrated by His Eminence and for a Synod to be established in September 1987. It comprised His Eminence as Metropolitan Archbishop and his two new bishops, Lady Monique and Richard Lawrence. Richard remembered:

Sir George receives a mental transmission on the beach at Lake Powell.

"The ceremony of consecration was, in its truest sense, awesome. In many ways I appreciate it more now even than I did then. Lady Monique and I were enraptured by the spiritual effervescence of our beloved Master's emanations transmitted into the very core of our beings to live within us forever."

On the face of it His Eminence had made a somewhat conservative decision, but in reality it was a radical one. Instead of setting up a new arrangement, he drew on the very traditions

Lady Monique (left) and Richard Lawrence (right) being consecrated as the first Bishops in The Aetherius Churches by His Eminence Sir George King.

into which he had been born. No one had been more critical of the subversions of truth perpetrated in the name of the church than he, nor of the corruption in the man-made structures around it. But the principle of apostolic succession[2] is not a new one – such lines of continuity have existed through initiation ceremonies and discipleship in many parts of the world. He did not believe in change for the sake of change; instead he chose to use a system that was right in essence and thereby bring transmutation and purification to it.

It could be said that he was putting the Christianity back into churchianity. Of course it went much further than this, embracing yoga practices and the highest of New Age wisdom. Also, the main spiritual practice of The Aetherius Society is The Twelve Blessings which was delivered by the Master Jesus.

By this move he demonstrated the complex, apparently paradoxical nature of his unique personality. He always looked for the good in anything wherever he could find it and, if possible, wanted to uphold values of conformity. On the other hand, he was constantly breaking new ground in his thinking and had no time whatsoever for conventional limitations which are the product of conditioning. To those of an orthodox or strictly catholic persuasion, this move could be perceived as more heretical than if he had created a brand new system. But that did not concern him one jot – it was the right move to make so he made it.

His approach to orders of chivalry was similar. He could have taken the recognition he received – albeit as a reflection of that which came from above – and left it there. Instead he determined that this combination of the best of ancient traditions fused with New Age precepts should continue into the future. In 1981 he established The Mystical Order of Saint Peter based around the cosmic transmissions he had received in the 1950s from this great Martian intelligence. These became the texts of the Order, into which he dubbed as knights and dames those mystical thinkers who had given service to others. Using the princedom he had received from Prince Henri, he became its Prince Grand Master. The Order was set up to be run by an international body which he called the Grand Magistry, and in 1993, at the prompting of the Master Aetherius, he appointed a Lieutenant Grand Master who would succeed him after his demise, namely Richard Lawrence.

There is no doubt that he went to extraordinary lengths in these final years to preserve his legacy and to give future generations the opportunity to take it forward. But this was not all he did because, almost unbelievably, a new mission was also looming large. This one was tailored specifically for him by the cosmic intelligence who had been in frequent contact with him for over 15 years, Sector S2.

As the 1990s progressed His Eminence's karmic manipulations started to take on a different form. His hospitalization in the summer of 1992 quickened this change. He underwent two major surgeries within nine days, which was severe enough, but in between these two surgeries he very nearly died. He was in the intensive care unit recuperating from his abdominal aorta resection when his heart stopped beating. Lady Monique, Brian Keneipp and Richard Medway were in the room, but were quickly ushered out, as the medical technicians worked on him. Brian will never forget the sight of His Eminence turning grey as his heart stopped, followed by his surgeon running down the hospital hallway to do what he could to bring Sir George back. In the meantime, the American Headquarters was alerted and the Spiritual Energy Radiator was started immediately. Within a short time – which felt like an eternity in the hospital hallways – His Eminence was revived. Though it was getting closer, it was not yet his time to go.

It was during this time that the number of Operation Space Power II operations through the American Headquarters Spiritual Energy Radiator increased dramatically. Sector S2 wanted an increase in operations focused on Sir George's health. These could happen at any time of the day or night and would continue for the next five years until His Eminence's passing. It was also an instruction from Sector S2 that the Spiritual Energy Radiator should run whenever His Eminence was being driven anywhere. These two types of Operation Space Power II runs sent out tremendous spiritual energy to the world, and required a significant amount of time and effort by the staff team in Los Angeles.

Clearly this was a powerful karmic manipulation as well as

a help to His Eminence. It seems that Sector S2 was analyzing the situation and seeing what he could do to karmically leverage His Eminence's position on Earth and that of his team of faithful followers.

This culminated just over a month after Sir George was released from hospital. Brian was driving His Eminence in his new 26-foot motorhome to a nearby lake in Santa Barbara County, called Lake Cachuma. It is about 24 miles from his bungalow in Santa Barbara, and took about 40 minutes to drive. As usual, the Spiritual Energy Radiator was activated as Brian and His Eminence left Santa Barbara just after 11:00 a.m. When they arrived Brian asked if he should call to stop the Spiritual Energy Radiator operation as normal. Surprisingly Sir George told him that Sector S2 wanted it to continue the whole time they were there. This included lunch preceded by a sherry aperitif, and proceeded until their return to the house at 2:45 p.m.

His Eminence later found out that Sector S2 wanted to put some of the energy through Sir George and into Lake Cachuma, which is a drinking water reservoir for Santa Barbara and the surrounding areas. It turned out to be a dry run for a new mission, carefully designed by Sector S2 utilizing the tools available, which would start the following year.

Sector S2 wanted to name the mission 'Operation King Light', but characteristically this was rejected by Sir George. It was instead called 'Operation Power Light', with its stated purpose of world peace and upliftment. The first 12 phases consisted of Sir George going to a location, normally in the motorhome and staying for generally two hours. The Spiritual Energy Radiator would be running, and a portion of this energy was sent through Sir George.

This modus operandi then expanded from Phase 13 through to the last one – Phase 44 in May 6th, 1996. During these, energy was collected from several of the holy mountains and manipulated by several different masters, including the Adepts, the Gotha Masters and members of the Spiritual Hierarchy. Energy continued to flow through the Spiritual Energy Radiator, but no longer through Sir George. These latter phases epitomized His Eminence's position. A physically weak and ageing master would in his motorhome record an on-the-spot log of the happenings, but was not required to do too much else. At the same time great masters manipulated valuable spiritual power to the world. From a karmic perspective, his hard work and brilliant strategy over the years was now allowing such intervention from the great ones.

In Phase 31 on December 30th, 1994, a clue was given by Sector S2 of even another karmic angle being used. Brian, who had been on all of the Operation Power Light phases, felt unusually tired after this one and informed Sir George. When he passed this on to Sector S2 later that night he received the reply that Brian was used as a "karmic point of light" during this phase and could therefore be feeling fatigued because of that. Sector S2 further stated that he should perform some deep breathing the following morning, which would revitalize him both inside and out. He added that this was the first time a normal terrestrial had been used in this way during Operation Power Light – energy was not sent through him during this phase, but he was used to manipulate karma.

Though this was not mentioned again, it is likely that similar karmic manipulations were performed using the close aides around His Eminence and those especially in Los Angeles who were working all hours of the day and night manning the Spiritual Energy Radiators. No doubt certain karma was also manipulated through the efforts of staff members worldwide, who rallied during this difficult time in The Aetherius Society as Sir George slowly retreated from his active role at the helm.

Operation Power Light was almost the opposite to his first mission Operation Starlight. The latter took tremendous hard and dangerous work, with very little backup or help. In Operation Power Light, His Eminence did little of a physical nature and had great help both from a large line-up of cosmic cooperators, using the energy from Operation Starlight, as well as from certain key personnel in The Aetherius Society. From this lens we can see a brilliant reflection of the tremendous karmic manipulations done over the many years of his mission.

Phase 44 was the last field mission performed by His Eminence. The cosmic cooperators included the Six Adepts,

Top: Sir George King at Nobi Point on the Californian coast by his motorhome, which was used during Operation Power Light. Above: Sir George in his motorhome with the cassette tape recorder he used during phases of Operation Power Light.

Sector S2 and Team, the Gotha Masters and Adept Number Nine and Team. The energy was collected from Carnedd Llywelyn, Kinder Scout, Mount Rams Head, and Creag an Leth-choin. The first two mountains on this list were charged by Adept Number One and His Eminence; and the second two by Lords of Karma, Creag an Leth-choin being connected to the site of a new retreat of the Great White Brotherhood.

Other participants in this phase were the Engineering Officers operating the Spiritual Energy Radiator in Los Angeles, and the few close aides personally helping him in Santa Barbara. At the centre of it all was His Eminence Sir George King, as if operating in the calm eye of a hurricane of energy flowing out to the world for world healing and upliftment. Truly a fitting close to a life of field missions by a brilliant karmic manipulator fighting for a desperate world.

*   *   *   *

Concurrent with Operation Power Light were two massive developments in other missions. In April 1994 His Eminence made the following announcement which was published in *Cosmic Voice*, January/February 1995:

> **Operation Sunbeam Plan 'K' – The time when the occult sciences took a quantum leap forward.**

His Eminence had progressed from Plan A to Plan B to a new one named in his honour. In this, no less than six water-based psychic centres of the Mother Earth would now be used: Loch Ness, Lake Powell, Dana Point, Goleta Point, Lake Tanganyika and, most sacred of all, one located near the Arctic.

It was then that another bolt came out of the blue. In late 1994 he was approached by Adept Number Five and asked whether The Aetherius Society could perform The Saturn Mission after his demise. He had not expected this because the performance of this mission was focused around him personally. So in-depth discussions were held by key personnel in the UK and the USA and, amazingly, he made it happen.

A modus operandi was devised for up to two phases per year to be done at Lake Powell and one at Loch Ness. This was approved by the Master Aetherius as late as April 4th, 1996, with one final modification being made on August 23rd, 1996, less than a year before His Eminence's demise. As a result, since 1998 three phases of this mission have been performed successfully every year by The Aetherius Society and hopefully will continue to be so long into the future.

He had performed the last phase of Operation Power Light; he had seen Operation Sunbeam Plan 'K' commence with a schedule agreed for posterity; The Saturn Mission was set to go; Operation Space Power was under way with provision for expansion to other locations; Operation Space Power II was fully functional as was Operation Prayer Power. On top of this he had been paid one of the highest compliments anybody on Earth could be paid in that the Great White Brotherhood were also committed to performing two of his missions: Operation Sunbeam and Operation Earth Light.

Had it not been for his physical condition, now very weakened by cancer and other ailments, and for the fact that he was still striving to do more for the people of Earth, he might have had a peaceful last few months. His memory was still outstanding – he could describe in detail events which occurred in his childhood, during the Second World War and since. But peace was still not on his agenda – for him it was, as he said to Richard Lawrence, "a pipe dream".

It finally came on July 12th, 1997. At 4:48 a.m. PDT His Eminence Sir George King passed away from the physical plane of Earth in a very peaceful manner at his home in Santa Barbara. Despite the preceding months of severe pain and very difficult health, his passing was calm and painless. Just a few hours before, around midnight, he was enjoying some homemade cantaloupe ice cream and laughing at a few choice stories with Brian. After a short rest, His Eminence awoke and called Paul Nugent, one of his aides in Santa Barbara. His Eminence told Paul he was dying. After spending about two hours alone with Sir George, comforting him, Paul called Brian and Richard Medway. At that point Los Angeles was phoned to activate the Spiritual Energy

Radiator and the three of them continued to administer spiritual healing through the long and gentle process. As His Eminence slowly passed from his Earth body that had served him so well he was surrounded by his close aides.

The atmosphere in his bedroom was very spiritual and uplifting. Brian had an impression of His Eminence standing at the head of his bed in a very vibrant and powerful state with a self-confident smile on his face. This conveyed to Brian that he was performing his final manipulation as he had with all his missions throughout his life – pluperfectly. Brian felt that there were many on the other realms surrounding the room.

*   *   *   *

Though it was sad to lose such a master and avatar, it was also a relief to see the end of the suffering of His Eminence, who had done so much for mankind for so long. And it was good to think of the many honours and joyous meetings he would soon be having – so well deserved after his brilliant mission to Earth – with his cosmic peers. He had received accolade upon accolade from those who really counted. Mars Sector 6 had described him on August 9th, 1988, as a genius; Mars Sector 8 – Special Advisor S2 had told him on March 7th, 1989: **your sense of timing is a magic above most magic**; and the Master Aetherius said on July 30th, 1966, about what could be described as the zenith of his Star Pupil's missions:

> **Operation Sunbeam was designed by a master, whether you regard him as such or not does not alter this fact. A master who has cried for humanity – even as Jesus cried for humanity. A master who has done a great deal for humanity. In fact, had it not been for this particular individual, you would not be sitting here tonight, you would be dead.**

Never could the word superhuman be more aptly applied. Mars Sector 6 said on April 21st, 1964, about him:

If you want a pattern it is in front of you.

And his Eminence, though not writing about himself, had spelt out how to follow such a pattern in his commentary on enlightenment in *The Nine Freedoms*:

> When you have applied the yardstick of logical discrimination and chosen your teacher you must be prepared to stand fast. You must remain unflinchingly loyal, treating your lessons as priceless gems of sacred wisdom and not allow yourself to be swayed by petty dislikes which all too often hold up your progress. If your choice has been a good one, your teacher will show you the path of service. Follow this and in time you will begin to realize the tremendous potential within you.

His passing was not the end. In an interview for a film in 1991 he had made this statement:

> What is important is pushing on with the mission and I have been asked by the cosmic masters to perform a specific mission. I have promised to do it and I will do it. I will do it even after my demise – it will not stop there.

Decades earlier in a lecture given on November 12th, 1966, His Eminence had made this prediction:

> A thousand years after I am dead, ladies and gentlemen – this might be taken as a prophecy – I will have a greater following than ever I had when I am alive, because these things people will gradually see to be true. They will try many other things. They will live through many lives and they will come across many, many blank walls that they cannot get through. And then, eventually, their memory banks will open and they will say: 'my God, I have wasted a thousand years.'

We sincerely hope that it will not take that long for our readers at least.

The medieval acclamation on the occasion of a royal passing was 'the King is dead, long live the King!' This King is not dead. He will live on forever, bearing the orb of world service and the sceptre of karmic transmutation. The missions and teachings he brought us and the pattern he gave us are wonderfully encapsulated in his legacy. We and thousands of others have chosen to follow him, and many more will do so in the future. We cannot describe this as anything less than the greatest path that has ever been given to Earth. It could be called the King of Yogas – but we call it simply: King Yoga.

AFTERWORD

As of going to print, it is 22 years since the passing of His Eminence Sir George King and 100 years since his birth. The Society he founded has gone from strength to strength, performing the missions and spreading the teachings he bequeathed to us.

The Saturn Mission and Operation Sunbeam are performed every year to the fullest extent we are permitted. Operation Space Power and Operation Space Power II have expanded to five locations – three more than in his lifetime. The New Zealand Branch in Auckland; the Northern UK Branch in Barnsley; and the Michigan Branch in the USA, now have Spiritual Energy Radiators as well as the European Headquarters in London and the American Headquarters in Los Angeles. Charging sessions of Operation Prayer Power were already being held in these five locations at the time of his passing, but now discharges too can take place from all of them.

The teachings are being made available through existing and new publications; seminars, lectures and workshops around the world; media appearances on TV and radio, as well as in print; and a multifarious range of digital outlets. In 2017, King Yoga was adopted as the name for the path of The Aetherius Society, in honour of its founder.

Every year pilgrimages are arranged to several holy mountains around the world and, since His Eminence's passing, all 19 of them have been climbed by dedicated pilgrims. The two headquarters and the dozens of branches and groups in Europe, America, Africa and Australasia have continued to hold services and other prayer and healing activities every week – sometimes daily. They are also held online at least twice a week for participants in any part of the world. Specific world emergencies are responded to by extra services, often coordinated with the strategic implementation of Operation Space Power II and Operation Prayer Power releases.

The Aetherius Society is motoring at speed, but our cosmic commission to continue beyond Sir George's lifetime has only just begun. Without this cosmic avatar, all the indications are that our world would have imploded into a concurrence of cataclysm and conflict. Devastating floods; severe earthquakes and volcanic eruptions; and the deployment of atomic weaponry could and probably would have reaped havoc upon the surface of our globe by now.

Prophecies from ancient sources – in the east and west alike – have pointed to a period of dark destruction, and this is the time they were looking at. Some of them predicted that following it, a great being of light would come to Earth. This is the Next Master described to Sir George in the historic Lord's Declaration pronounced by that magisterial Voice upon Brown Willy when it was charged on November 23rd, 1958. In the wake of such dire conditions, the Next Master would have surely come, the sorting of the wheat from the chaff would be underway, and only those few who were ready would inherit the bright New Age.

The Initiation of Earth would have taken place with whatever global changes were necessary to bring this about. Without the missions conducted by Sir George, its effects might have been catastrophic for human civilization. The undiminished release of Her energies would have meant that only those capable of operating in such a heightened vibration would be capable of remaining. For the rest, another planet awaits to enable their continued evolutionary cycle at the required level.

It would be wrong to describe this as retribution, for at the heart of even such a sorting is divine compassion – provision for all according to their needs. It is, though, rejecting a futuristic opportunity of golden illumination and choosing instead the tarnished, old human condition to be played out in repeat mode. These words of Saint Goo-Ling on February 20th, 1968, could aptly be applied:

> There comes a tide in the affairs of man which, taken at the flood, can lead on to evolutionary fortune. Omitted, then the very apex of life is by-passed and the rivers run through the shadowy glades.

We doubt that Sir George knew the quote from Shakespeare's

Julius Caesar from which these words are adapted – and, in our view, improved – but they express perfectly this time of drastic choosing.

As marvellous as this sorting would be for the fortunate inheritors of the New Age, they would sadly be comparatively few in number. The coming to Earth of Sir George and the Three Adepts has delayed these happenings and reduced immeasurably their calamitous impact. Put bluntly, he has bought time for billions of souls throughout the realms of Earth – possibly for hundreds of years – by extending their opportunity to seize the moment and make this change into an era of true freedom and peaceful coexistence.

The missions and teachings of The Aetherius Society are continuing to do just this. The Next Master will still come, but the trauma and suffering prior to his coming is being lessened. At the same time humanity is being prepared for this great change by, consciously or unconsciously, being impressed by an intensive radiation of spiritual energies from a plurality of cosmic and terrestrial sources. And, perhaps most importantly of all, world karma is being manipulated for the better by our direct cooperation with higher forces and our promotion of their message.

Throughout the centuries there have always been a dedicated few to act as light-bearers for their masters. Some have been fortunate enough to know and serve their teachers at a personal level while they were physically among us. To name three leading examples: one of the greatest ancient works of wisdom, the *Bhagavad Gita*, was delivered by Sri Krishna to the warrior Arjuna, who hung on his every word; many centuries later the young Joshua devoted himself to Moses and even – it is said – accompanied him up Mount Sinai when the Ten Commandments were delivered; and Ananda was the chela who looked after and cared for his guru, the Lord Buddha, well into his old age.

But not all – in fact not most – of them physically met their masters, or were alive at the same time. The disciples of Jesus, for example, are not limited to the 12 who walked with him into Jerusalem prior to that fateful Passover. After his Damascene[1] conversion Saint Paul, who never physically met him, was one of the greatest of them all. In more recent times, the 19th-century theosophist Madame Blavatsky was guided by the ascended master designated as M, through her advanced mental and psychic powers. The 20th-century esotericist Alice Bailey was likewise guided by the Master DK to bring further theosophical teachings. And thousands of disciples, some unknown, have devoted themselves to the one they followed, decades, centuries or even millennia after their teachers walked this physical world.

Today is the age of the new disciples. As Sir George wrote in his conclusion of *The Twelve Blessings* in 1958:

> **Jesus has come again in this 20th century to extend his ancient mission to save this Earth. It is now up to you, the new disciples, who read, learn and accept these teachings, to take your rightful place as sowers of the seeds of cosmic truth throughout your world.**

And on October 18th, 1958, Mars Sector 6 stated in a transmission about 'The Twelve Blessings':

> **You notice, oh disciples, that these teachings are not limited. Be ye like them!**

The Twelve Blessings lie at the heart of our worship in The Aetherius Churches, on holy mountains, online and by individuals wherever they may be. But it is not the only – nor even now the most important – activity the Society and its members perform. Having read this biography you will know this all too well, and be familiar with the expansive panorama of spiritual activity enshrined in King Yoga.

New disciples can follow this master and this path in its entirety, and you won't be surprised that this, in our view, is the highest calling available to us. It is also the key to our own development. As Sir George advised his students during a series of classes in 1966:

> **You cannot really progress, really progress, unless you are dedicated to the life of action. The only thing that**

counts these days – there aren't two things that count, there is only one, and if I am sure of anything, I am as sure of this as I am of God – the only thing that counts is the Cosmic Plan for the enlightenment and evolution of this and all other planets.

Spiritual action brings peace and enlightenment to the world and to ourselves – in that order. King Yoga is primarily a path of service, but it is also one of personal advancement, and wherever you have one of these the other isn't far behind. In his last book, *Realize Your Inner Potential*, which he co-authored with Richard Lawrence, Sir George released a collection of ancient and New Age practices which students could use not only to serve others, but also to progress themselves. Taken far enough, these exercises could help us to unveil the very petals of samadhic consciousness.

A wonderful promise awaits those who choose this path as revealed by Sir George to his students in the 1966 classes:

There is a karmic link between a teacher and a pupil, and if a pupil really advances, then they can and do take into themselves more and more the higher attributes of the teachings. This is an absolute fact. And, of course, there is a statement, too, that: 'When the pupil is ready the teacher appears,' and this, too, is an absolute fact. The teacher has to, by law, take the next step with those pupils who are ready. If he cannot do so, then the right teacher is brought along – to be able to do so.

This is one of the laws of karma and it's greater than all of us. It's greater than the world and it's greater than the solar system and even the suns. Because it's one of the great laws, known about for thousands of years on Earth. It appertains not only on this Earth but on all inhabited planets – throughout this galaxy anyway – that when the pupil is ready, the teacher does appear. In other words, when the pupil is ready for the next essential step onward, they will be able to take that step.

They will be helped in one way or another to take

that step. And a student does begin to absorb some of the deeper aspects of the teachings and some of the deeper aspects of the teacher, too. This, too, is a fact. If you study diligently under a teacher, who is any good at all and you really study diligently – whether you come into physical contact with that individual or not – you begin to absorb some of his higher knowledge which he may not have imparted to you by word of mouth.

His Eminence Sir George King has appeared in your life through this book. This will either be for the first time, or perhaps in sharper focus than ever before. You have read this far, so you are at the very least curious, perhaps impressed, possibly amazed by his grandeur. You might decide to leave it at curiosity, as something that may or may not be true – because you certainly don't know that it isn't!

But you may want to take it further, to regard him as a teacher, your teacher, and thereby create a karmic link between yourself and the pivotal avatar of our age. If you do, the leaves of curiosity will fall away, and you will be impressed – even to your very soul – by his amazing reality. And if you forge this linkage still further, you too could become a disciple of the King who came to Earth.

NOTES

PROLOGUE

1. A cosmic avatar is an interplanetary intelligence who has divinely incarnated upon our planet to perform a great spiritual mission for the benefit of humanity.

PREFACE

1. Dr. King was a medium for intelligences on other planes of Earth, for ascended masters and for cosmic masters. Communications given through him from the cosmic masters in trance are referred to as 'cosmic transmissions', and those given by telepathy as 'mental transmissions'.

FOREWORD

1. These aphorisms were displayed at Aetherius Society premises and sometimes at public events such as New Age festivals.

2. Millions of years ago humanity developed a civilization on this planet known in metaphysical writings as Lemuria and sometimes Mu. Nuclear weaponry proliferated leading to its calamitous destruction. This resulted in excessive radiation, causing grotesque mutations for generations. Out of the slime evolved the civilization of Atlantis, which was in existence as recently as 120,000 years ago, yet once again nuclear technology was developed and Atlantis too was destroyed in atomic conflict. It is essential that the same mistake is not repeated today.

CHAPTER ONE

1. In Operation Sunbeam spiritual energy is sent to the Mother Earth who has sacrificed so much to enable us to live here. The colossal spiritual debt we owe Her puts humanity in a grave karmic position, since it is not possible, by Divine Law, to endlessly take without ever giving back.

Operation Sunbeam is a karmic manipulation on behalf of humanity, devised by Dr. King in 1966 to help solve this problem.

2. The initiation of ascension is freedom from the cycle of reincarnation, known as the wheel of rebirth. In Dr. King's book, *The Nine Freedoms*, he described witnessing this initiation on a spacecraft known as Satellite No. 3 when in orbit 1,550 miles from Earth.

3. The Freedom of the City of London is an honour bestowed upon individuals who have been duly nominated to receive it.

4. Kundalini is a mystical power located at the base of the spine, sometimes referred to as 'the serpent power'. The reason we are here on Earth is to learn to control this power, and raise it in its entirety up the spine to fully activate the chakras or psychic centres.

5. One of the main cosmic masters who later communicated through Dr. King was the Master Aetherius, an intelligence from Venus.

6. A person who for reasons of conscience objects to serving in the armed forces.

7. Astral projection, as mastered by Dr. King, was an out-of-body experience in which his consciousness left the physical body and was capable of travelling outside of it. This could either be on this physical realm or on the subtle realms above or below it, which are the realms we inhabit after death.

8. The chakras, also known as psychic centres, are like floodgates within the aura which are constantly radiating and taking in subtle energies. The spine can be likened to a stem and the chakras to flowers growing from this stem, through the body, and a few inches in front of the body. There are

seven major chakras: Crown Centre (Brahma Chakra), Christ Centre (Third Eye), Throat Centre, Heart Centre, Solar Plexus Centre, Sex Centre and Base Centre.

CHAPTER TWO

1. The devas, also known as 'nature spirits', are intelligences who inhabit bodies of a different type of matter than the gross material bodies of human beings. It is because of the difference in vibration that ordinary man cannot see or detect the devas with his five basic senses. The devic kingdom, which they comprise, is responsible for looking after all aspects of nature and works according to strict laws. It transfers the mind emanations of humanity as subtle energies into physical manifestation upon Earth as weather and other natural conditions.

2. Caxton Hall was a well-known hall in Westminster, London, noted for its historical associations, and hosted many main stream and artistic events.

3. A theosophist is a person who belongs to the esoteric movement known as theosophy, established by Russian occultist, Madame Helena Blavatsky.

4. *Cosmic Voice* is the official journal of The Aetherius Society.

5. There are four periods each year known as 'Spiritual Pushes' or 'Magnetization Periods', during which an extraterrestrial satellite known as 'Satellite No. 3' comes into orbit of Earth. Under the command of the great cosmic master, Mars Sector 6, it beams down powerful energies making all spiritual actions 3,000 times more potent in terms of their benefit to the world.

6. Siddhasana is a posture used in Hatha Yoga, often for meditation. It is derived from the Sanskrit words 'siddha' meaning 'perfect' and 'asana' meaning 'posture'.

CHAPTER THREE

1. This hierarchy includes Lords of Karma at various levels, who are responsible for the great law of justice, known as karma. These mighty intelligences ensure that the law is perfect and that balance is kept within the solar system and throughout the whole of creation.

2. The Cosmic Plan was devised for the salvation and enlightenment of humanity by cosmic intelligences millions of years ago, and is still unfolding today.

3. This describes a cosmic master who has incarnated into the life cycle of Earth and lives on level one, which is the physical realm, in order to perform his or her mission. When living on their own planets, the cosmic masters inhabit their higher aspects, but when they incarnate on Earth, they are limited by having to be in a lower, fourth aspect. Despite this limitation, they are still extraordinarily enlightened human beings in comparison with even the most advanced person on Earth. Examples include the Master Jesus, the Lord Buddha, Sri Krishna and Dr. George King.

4. Metaphysics is the study of that which is beyond physics, such as the Law of Karma, the subtle bodies of man, the other realms of existence and the meaning of life. Astro-metaphysics is the study of such principles including other planets, the galaxies and the universe.

5. A karmic manipulator is one who not only understands the Law of Karma at the deepest levels, but is able to initiate those energies, thoughts and actions which will bring the most positive results for the betterment of others.

6. This is a reference to the coming Initiation of Earth, the most significant event in terrestrial history with vast ramifications for humanity as a whole.

7. Dr. George King knew, and many others believe, that William

Shakespeare was not the main author of the plays and other writings attributed to him. This was Sir Francis Bacon in collaboration with a group of other writers.

8.   Spiritual energy is prana, also known as 'universal life force' or 'qi', carried by pure love. It is as real as any other energy and vastly more important.

9.   Mantra is the chanting of sacred Sanskrit sounds either out loud or silently. Sanskrit is an ancient Indian language with powerful sound properties.

10. Mudra is a way of manipulating energy through using different hand signs. It can be used while chanting mantra, radiating spiritual energy through prayer, in meditation, etc. It is often associated with Tibet.

CHAPTER FOUR
1.   This refers to an energetic balance being created in the intelligence at a psychic and spiritual level.

2.   An early transcript states that this message was received on Yes Tor, which could be an error. Following 'The Lord's Declaration' during the charging of Brown Willy, a statement was made by the Lord about what should be said to the unbelievers. This must have been a continuation of that either by this Lord on Brown Willy, or by this or another intelligence on Yes Tor.

3.   Power circles are groups of spiritually-minded people who come together with the purpose of radiating spiritual energy to the world through prayer and mantra in order to bring healing and upliftment to others. These are held at Aetherius Society centres throughout the world.

4.   The Three Adepts consist of Adept Number One, Adept Number Two and Adept Number Three. They worked together as a team, but Adept Number One was the strategist.

5. The Philosophical Research Society is an American non-profit organization founded in 1934 to promote the study of the world's wisdom literature.

CHAPTER FIVE

1. The Earth is a living being – a Goddess who hides Her true light under the bushel of a material form so that we can live here. The Logos is the sacred life force of the Mother Earth.

2. Our minds have different aspects: subconscious, conscious and superconscious. The superconscious governs intuition and higher inspiration. Through spiritual actions and practices, we train the mind so that our superconscious mind gains control over our conscious mind.

3. This refers to apparatus designed according to the science of radionics, which is concerned with the manipulation of subtle energies as opposed to more physical forms of energy.

4. The Master Aetherius revealed in 'This is the Hour of Truth' that a minor effect of Operation Bluewater was to stop an earthquake about 200 miles off the California coast from below the Mexican border to above Portland, with San Francisco under an estimated two miles of water. Dr. King later wrote in his book, *The Five Temples Of God*, that millions would otherwise have died.

CHAPTER SIX

1. Between lives, we spend a period of time on either a higher or lower realm of existence. These planes are physical but exist at frequencies of vibration different and more subtle than this plane. Among these are the lower astral realms or hells where the Three Adepts conducted their sorties.

2. The Book of Revelation is the last book of the New Testament, and therefore of the Christian Bible. It is a prophetic book, open to multiple interpretations, which includes the final conflict between the forces of good and evil and identifies

the specific location of Armageddon.

3.   The Akashic Records are a complete account of all human events, thoughts, words, emotions and intent ever to have occurred. These are a true record of our history, existing in the etheric planes, which can only be read by those who are sufficiently advanced.

CHAPTER SEVEN

1.   Dr. King was referring to a very sensitive access point located between the psychic centres at Dana Point and Goleta Point off the California coast, where spiritual energy can be sent and absorbed deep into nerve centres of the Mother Earth.

2.   Every day during each Spiritual Push, energy is sent from the extraterrestrial spacecraft, Satellite No. 3, through the Spiritual Energy Radiators designed by Dr. King. At this time, two of these were operational, one in London and one in Los Angeles. During a Spiritual Push, each one is activated for three hours daily, releasing much-needed spiritual energy to help our world.

3.   Shape power temples are built according to geometric shapes. The power of shapes, to focus the ethers and channel energy, was well known to certain ancient civilizations including that of Egypt.

4.   Prayer energy is the spiritual energy invoked through the repetition of heartfelt prayer.

5.   Prayer hours is a term used to quantify the amount of spiritual energy that is radiated in relation to the output of one person praying for an hour.

CHAPTER EIGHT

1.   A grant of arms is an action by a lawful authority, conferring on a person and his or her descendants the right to bear a

particular coat of arms.

2.   The name Liberal Catholic Church is used by a number of Christian churches throughout the world, some of which are open to esoteric beliefs as well as ecclesiastical concepts.

CHAPTER NINE

1.   A+ energy is a category of high quality spiritual energy and one that is very usable on this physical plane of Earth.

2.   Apostolic succession is the uninterrupted transmission of spiritual authority from the founder of the church, in this case the Metropolitan Archbishop His Eminence Sir George King, through successive bishops.

AFTERWORD

1.   On the road to Damascus, according to the Bible, Saint Paul underwent a dramatic transformation during which he was temporarily blinded and heard the voice of the Master Jesus. As a result he became one of the most ardent apostles.

BIBLIOGRAPHY

Charles Abrahamson
The Holy Mountains Of The World, 1994

Brian C. Keneipp
Operation Earth Light, 2000

George King, D.D., Th.D.
Contact With A Lord Of Karma, 1989
Karma And Reincarnation, 1962
Life On The Planets, 1958
Operation Space Magic, 1982
Operation Space Power, 1987
Operation Sunbeam – God's Magic In Action, 1979
The Day The Gods Came, 1965
The Festival Of Carrying The Light, 1984
The Five Temples Of God, 1967
The Nine Freedoms, 1963
The Three Saviours Are Here!, 1967
The Twelve Blessings, 1958
This Is The Hour Of Truth, 1965
Visit To The Logos Of Earth, 1986
You Are Responsible!, 1961
You Too Can Heal, 1976

George King with Richard Lawrence
Contacts With The Gods From Space, 1996
Realize Your Inner Potential, 1998

All the books listed above are published by Aetherius Press.

REFERENCE SOURCES

In addition to books published by Aetherius Press, of which the main ones used are detailed in the Bibliography, essential material was derived from other sources including the following:

1. Issues of *Cosmic Voice* and *The Aetherius Society Newsletter*.

2. Cosmic transmissions, some of which are available in printed and/or audio form from The Aetherius Society.

3. Lectures and addresses by Dr. George King, some of which are available in printed and/or audio form from The Aetherius Society.

4. Unpublished transcripts of recordings made by Dr. George King during his mystical pilgrimage in 1978.

5. Minutes of Dr. George King's healing circle between 1953 and 1955.

6. Transcripts of recorded interviews with relatives, disciples and other associates of Dr. George King.

INDEX

FURTHER INFORMATION

COMPANION WEBSITE FOR THIS BIOGRAPHY
drgeorgeking.org

Our companion site will enhance the written words within this biography through archival audio recordings, videos and photographs. Through an investigation of this large reservoir of media you will be able to feel for yourself the unique personality of Dr. George King and witness his compassion, love and wisdom.

THE AETHERIUS SOCIETY
aetherius.org

SOCIAL MEDIA
aetherius.org/contact-us/social

CONTACT THE AUTHORS
Richard Lawrence
richardlawrence.co.uk

Brian Keneipp
briankeneipp.com

HEADQUARTERS OF THE AETHERIUS SOCIETY

American Headquarters
The Aetherius Society
6202 Afton Place
Los Angeles, CA 90028
USA
info@aetherius.org

European Headquarters
The Aetherius Society
757 Fulham Road
London, SW6 5UU
UK
info@aetherius.co.uk

BRANCHES, GROUPS AND REPRESENTATIVES WORLDWIDE

Please contact our branch, group or representative in your local area. Information about local services, lectures, classes and spiritual healing is available on our website.

aetherius.org/locations

BECOME A FRIEND

There are many benefits of becoming a Friend of The Aetherius Society. To find out more, please visit our website.

aetherius.org/friend

MEMBERSHIP

We warmly invite all spiritually-minded individuals who wish to support the aims and objects of The Aetherius Society and cooperate with our world-healing activities, to enquire about Membership. For further information, please visit our website.

aetherius.org/membership-initiations